CREATING MELODIES

A Songwriter's Guide to Understanding, Writing and Polishing Melodies

Dick Weissman

WRITER'S DIGEST BOOKS
CINCINNATI, OHIO

97   96   95   94   5   4   3   2   1

Library of Congress Cataloging in Publication Data

Weissman, Dick.
   Creating melodies : a songwriter's guide to understanding, writing and polishing melodies / by Dick Weissman. — 1st ed.
     p.   cm.
  Includes index.
  ISBN 0-89879-602-4
  1. Popular music—Writing and publishing. 2. Melody. I. Title.
MT67.W36 1994
782.42164'13—dc20   93-41943
                                                   CIP
                                                   MN

Edited by Julie Whaley and Mark Garvey

Cover design by Laura Kuhlman

ABOUT THE AUTHOR

Dick Weissman is a songwriter, musician and record producer. Over his twenty-five year career in the music business, he has written two feature film scores, songs for three theatrical productions that have been performed in New York, Denver and Detroit, and over fifty recorded songs and instrumental pieces. *New Traditions*, an album of his instrumental music and songs, was recently issued on the Folk Era label, and he is currently performing with a jazz-folk-classical trio called the Uncommon Thread.

He is an assistant professor in the music management program at the University of Colorado at Denver, and plays banjo, guitar and piano. This is his sixth published book about music and the music business.

ACKNOWLEDGMENTS

This book evolved over a two-year period, largely through conversations with Mark Garvey of Writer's Digest Books. I want to thank Mark for his encouragement and suggestions. Julie Whaley, my editor, did a great job of organizing the ideas and asking the right questions about the manuscript. Composer-arranger Dennis Dreith helped enormously; he writes and arranges music for films and television and is the International President of the Recording Musicians Association, an organization of union musicians who are most active in recording commercials, films, records and television music. He provided much of the information on new music technologies and insight into musical structure.

Many of the ideas in this book evolved through contact with a variety of songwriters and with my students at the University of Colorado at Denver, especially songwriter Brenda Matson, who served as a guinea pig for many of these chapters. Paul Musso was also a big help in printing out the music, and Dan Fox, as always, provided musical examples from his encyclopedic knowledge of musical form and style.

During the last two years I have written a number of commissioned songs for the Oil, Coke, Chemical and Atomic Workers Union, and this work helped me to clarify my ideas about where melodies come from, and what they do. Thanks to Tony Mazzochi, Phyllis Olmacher and Bob Wages for making that possible. Working with playwright Larry Bograd also assisted me in processing these concepts.

INTRODUCTION

Why do we need a book on writing melodies? There are any number of books currently available that deal with every conceivable aspect of music. Some of these books discuss rhythm, some tackle harmony, and there are all too many learned treatises about the many facets of arranging and composing music.

Oddly, there is virtually no information available about how to write pleasant tunes that the average person can sing and play. Most writers describe melody writing as if they were coaches trying to teach pitchers to throw curve balls before they've bothered to show them how to hold a baseball or hit the strike zone.

Sometimes it's more difficult to teach someone to do something that is relatively simple than to deal with more complex information. There is an old story about Mark Twain being asked to deliver a speech with very little notice. Twain asked whether the speech was supposed to last five minutes or an hour. The person who invited Twain was somewhat confused by the question, assuming that it would take a long time to prepare a lengthy speech. Twain then explained that he could easily deliver a long lecture without much preparation, but that summing up a complex series of thoughts in five minutes would take him weeks to prepare. My goal in this book is to give melody writing the five-minute treatment — to describe complex processes in as simple a way as I can.

The purpose of this book is to teach you how to construct melodies and how they fit into the overall songwriting process. In order to make this material as clear and useful as possible, I will avoid dwelling on technical matters.

For whom is this book intended? It's for the hobbyist or beginning songwriter who might need some basic instruction in constructing good melodies. And it's for writers who are further along in their writing, to help them avoid repetition and to encourage them to expand their experiments in constructing melodies. From this book, you'll learn how to read and write musical notation, find out the different ways melodies can be constructed, and master the intricacies of rhythms and chord progressions.

Before I get into the actual discussion of melodies, I should point out that the guitar and keyboard are the ideal vehicles for writing melodies. Both of these instruments lend themselves readily to playing chords and to creating (to an extent) rhythmic patterns or *grooves* (the parts played by rhythm instruments such as the bass or drums in a band). So if you play either the guitar or the keyboard, you will have a small orchestra at your fingertips.

Futhermore, both of these instruments allow you to sing along to what you are playing. This is not true of brass or wind instruments, and other instruments, like the bass, allow you to play only a single melodic line, not to create chords.

Because of all these factors, this book will explain specific musical matters with reference to the keyboard or the guitar. It has always surprised me how few music theory books use the guitar to illustrate the concepts they discuss. This book is designed to be equally user-friendly for guitarists and keyboard players.

For more information about melody writing, write to me, Dick Weissman, at 240 S. 39th St., Boulder, Colorado 80303.

Chapter One

What Is a Melody?

A melody is a tune, the part that you sing if someone asks you to sing "Three Blind Mice," "Eleanor Rigby" or any other song. In an instrumental piece, it is the single line of the structure that you can hum or whistle; it makes no difference if it's a symphony, a complex jazz suite, a nursery rhyme or a country and western tune. Some dictionaries refer to the melody as the *air*, while others call it the *tune* of a song.

If you have ever taken a music theory class, you know that the melody can be divided into smaller sections called *phrases*, and these phrases can be broken down into what textbooks call *motives* or *motifs*. What does all of this mean?

You're undoubtedly familiar with the opening part of the Beatles' "Hey, Jude." The words "Hey, Jude" and the two notes and the rhythm they are set to constitute a motive: a recognizable, if minute, musical theme that identifies the song.

If you break down familiar songs in this way, you'll notice that motives are often surprisingly simple. They may consist of two or three notes that are repeated, rearranged in different rhythmic patterns, or repeated in a different order. Sometimes, a single note is repeated several times, such as in the opening portion of John Denver's "Rocky Mountain High." But motives don't all follow one particular pattern. They may consist of notes that are close together, or they may involve jumps in the melody, such as in "Feelings" or "Send in the Clowns."

In the children's song, "Skip to My Lou," no single simple musical motive characterizes the song; rather it consists of a series of musical phrases. The music for "Skip to My Lou" (Figures 1-1a and 1-1b) is written out in three ways: in musical notation, in guitar tablature and in keyboard tablature.

Even if you are unable to read music, you should be able to follow the notes using these keyboard diagrams. The numbers are written in sequence 1, 2, 3, etc., telling you the order in which you should play the notes. The number 1 is the first note you play, 2 is the second note, and so forth, though the rhythm is not indicated.

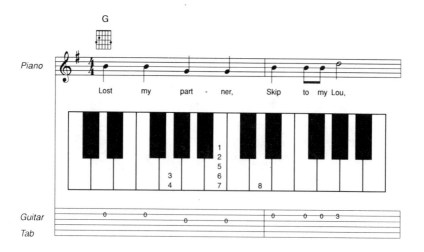

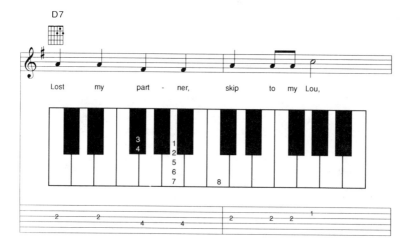

Figure 1-1a.

If you examine this tune in great detail, you can see that each verse has four lines written below:

- Lost my partner, Skip to my Lou (line 1)
- Lost my partner, Skip to my Lou (2)
- Lost my partner, What'll I do? (3)
- Skip to my Lou, My darlin. (4)

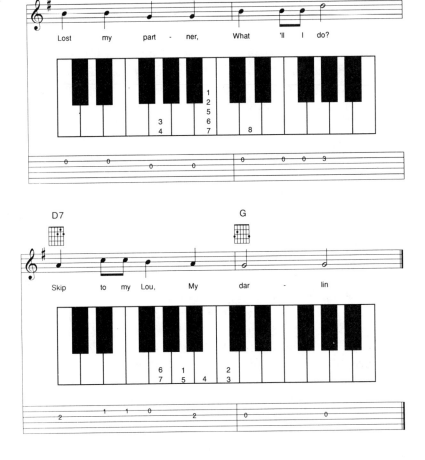

Figure 1-1b.

Further examination shows that these four lines really contain only three different melodies, because the melody of the third line is exactly the same as the first line. If you look carefully at this tune, you can also see the logic of why it is constructed this way. Try to interchange the second line with the first. It doesn't work in the same way. To put it another way, the first line leads very well into the second line, but if you try to sing the second line first, it doesn't seem to want to lead into the first line. Similarly, the fourth line brings you back to the beginning of the tune, ready to proceed to the next verse. Constructing a good melody is like building a house — you need to start out with a solid foundation and build from there.

If you try to change the melody around, substituting phrases for one another or restructuring the melody notes, chances are you will see that the tune is organized in a very logical and simple way. That's why we can easily remember it. Take some songs that are familiar to you, choosing some very simple melodies, and try to do the same thing. Change the order of the notes, even try to change the rhythm of the entire tune. Substitute melody notes if it amuses you. Once you have done this with three or four songs, you will have a new respect for the role of melody in the construction of a song.

WHY IS MELODY IMPORTANT?

Think of any song you enjoy. If you have any songbooks, take a look at a song you like. If you don't have a songbook available, take one of your CDs, cassettes or albums that contains a printed lyric sheet and choose a song to look at. Forget that you know the tune and associate it with the lyrics of the song. Imagine that someone has commissioned you to write a different tune to the lyric. As you attempt to put a new melody to the lyric, you ought to develop a new-found appreciation for the way lyrics and melodies work together.

Below is a list of the aspects of melody writing that make the melody itself crucial to the development of a song:

- Most people will not remember a lyric apart from the tune.
- People *may* remember the tune without recalling the lyric.
- A good melody will readily lend itself to inventive musical arrangements. These arrangements may include such elements

as a lead guitar line, a rhythmic groove, horn or string parts, or additional background vocals. A lead guitar line may duplicate the melody or actually be another melody that the guitarist or musical arranger invents. Horn and string parts are usually built around the melody, but, like background vocals, they may provide harmony parts that add more flavor to the melody itself. A rhythmic groove sets the melody in a rhythmic context and may provide an element of excitement that the melody suggests but does not emphasize.

- A particularly attractive melody can be arranged in a variety of musical styles and can be performed by many different artists.

It is quite possible for a song to become successful without a good melody, if it has a great rhythmic groove or inventive lyrics, or if it is performed by a remarkable singer. Starting with a good melody makes a song more fun to create and sing, and gives the song a better chance for success and longevity. Any financial success is, of course, an additional bonus, but everyone I know who writes tunes really enjoys the process of writing.

HOW MELODIES RELATE TO MUSICAL AND LYRIC STRUCTURE

When you hear a song on the radio or on a recording and you start to sing along with it, you are singing the melody. The other vocal parts on the recording are the harmony parts. Very few people walk around singing a harmony part unless someone else is around to sing the actual melody.

Harmony parts may be sung above or below the melody. Sometimes the melody line itself is in a high vocal register, and there are harmony parts that go even higher. The Beach Boys and Air Supply are two vocal groups who use this technique, which is also common in bluegrass music. Other vocal groups who sing adventurous multiple harmony parts include the Four Freshmen, Manhattan Transfer and Take Six.

The average person will not be able to sing melodies that are written in a high vocal range or involve jumping back and forth from a normal vocal register to a high vocal part. If you are trying to write melodies that the average person can sing, it is a good idea to avoid these "in the stratosphere" tunes.

Certain lyrics will almost always call for specific melodic styles. For example, if you write a romantic love lyric, you don't want

the singer to scream it in a very high register or croak it in the
low bass style of groups like the Statler Brothers or the Coasters.
You will probably want the melody to sound pretty and provide
an emotional connotation that suggests romance or a romantic
situation.

If you are writing a song protesting one of the ills of society,
such as racial inequality or another form of injustice, chances are
you will deliberately write a melody with an unpleasant edge to
it, one that will have a sense of urgency, a commitment to the
subject matter, or even an angry quality. Many of Bob Dylan's
early protest songs, such as "Masters of War" or "Hard Rain's
Gonna Fall," have this sort of jagged quality designed to underline
the seriousness of the subject matter. These melodies drone on
in a style closer to talking than to singing. The effect that you
strive to avoid in writing a romantic ballad is exactly what you try
to emphasize in a protest song—anger, or perhaps even hatred.
Using angry or talk-like melodies forces the listener to focus on
the lyrics of the song.

RHYTHM 'N' GROOVE

Rhythm is a very significant aspect of music, especially in contemporary American popular music. Rhythm influences melodies in
ways that are not easy to define. Think of the way a singer like
Ray Charles sings the words *baby* or *yeah*. These words are
phrased not as if they possess one or two syllables; the artist
extends them as long as he wishes. *Bay-ay-ay-ay-by* or *yea-ay-ay-
ah* might be the result. This sort of phrasing may be determined
in the actual writing of the song or it may represent an improvisation by the recording artist that was not part of the original tune.

Consider some other ways to deal with the rhythm of a melody.
Imagine that your melody is in 3/4, or waltz time, with three beats
for every measure or bar of music (see chapter six for more on
rhythm). Imagine a melody that might go with Figure 1-2.

Figure 1-2.

Without worrying about a specific melody, sing one note for each word (if you can't think of a melody, just sing the same note for each word). Make sure each note comes exactly on the word, not before it or after it. Tap a steady beat with a pencil to establish the rhythm. Be sure to go slowly at first, so that you know exactly where the beat is. Notice that the melody sounds stiff and "square," since you are phrasing exactly on the beat.

Now try the same lyric and the melody and phrase it as shown in Figure 1-3. Remember to tap the beat and go slowly.

Figure 1-3.

Notice how this very slight change in the rhythm gives an entirely different feel to the song. Instead of sounding stiff and metronomic, there is a slightly jazzy swing to the rhythm. A few examples of songs that "push" the beat in this way are the old rock standard "Wake Up Little Susie" and the folk-country hit "City of New Orleans."

In Figure 1-3, you are singing slightly ahead of the beat. Try the same experiment, but this time sing some of the words just after or behind the beat (Figure 1-4).

Figure 1-4.

Examples of melodies that drag slightly behind the beat are Bob Seger's "Against the Wind" or the Moody Blues' rock classic "Nights in White Satin."

By singing in front of or behind the beat you can add a feeling of fluidity to a melody. Songs in which every word falls exactly on the beat tend to be "square," or rhythmically dull.

WRITING TO THE RHYTHM

It is also possible to write a song by starting with a rhythmic groove. The actual rhythmic emphasis or the powerful pulse of the song can practically dictate the form of the melody. This rhythmic impetus can come from the drumbeat created by a drummer or a drum machine, or from the accent patterns used by a musician when he strums a guitar. When a really powerful groove is created, both the melody and lyric can take shape directly out of the song's rhythmic feel. In many contemporary songs, the rhythm may well be the most important and "catchy" part of the song.

MUST I PLAY A MUSICAL INSTRUMENT TO WRITE MELODIES?

There are many people who are capable singers but don't play a musical instrument. Likewise, since a melody is simply one musical line, you don't really need to play a musical instrument to write your own melodies. You simply need to come up with some musical phrases that go with one another, and then remember what these phrases are. If you can sing, hum or even whistle, you can write a melody. To aid your musical memory, you can either tape record the melody that you created or, if you have the necessary musical training, you can write down the melody in the form of musical notation.

If you continue to frequently write melodies, you probably will be motivated to learn basic keyboard or guitar, even if you never play these instruments professionally. It is simply easier to deal with melodies if you can play one of these two instruments. However, you should not become overly dependent on an instrument. You should always be able to write melodies in your head no matter what situation you happen to be in. A melody can occur to you anywhere—at a party, on an airplane or, for many people, while driving a car.

Some writers don't bother to write down or record melodies. They assume that they will remember any melody worth recalling. In other words, if the melody can't be recalled, then it probably wasn't any good in the first place. I disagree with this view because it presumes too many circumstances that can't be controlled. For example, if you wait too long before trying to recall your melody, it may not return to you. If you are under extraordinary stress or are traveling or become busy or involved in other matters, your memory of the tune may fade. So jot it down or make a tape. After all, you can always erase a tape or discard any musical doodles if you decide that you don't like them.

INSPIRATION VS. CRAFT

Is writing a melody the result of some mysterious creative process (inspiration), or is it a consequence of writing, more writing and rewriting? The word *craft* usually refers to the editorial work the songwriter does in modifying and changing the original melody into its finished form. Writers will probably give many different responses when asked if their songs result from inspiration or from the editing process. In fact, a writer may find that melodies to different songs arise from different levels of inspiration, or from dogged perseverance. Just as lyric writers run into "writer's block" (the inability to create new material), you may find at some point that either you are unable to write more melodies or that you are writing new melodies that sound very much like your older tunes.

I don't think it's possible to separate inspiration from craft in an effort to solve these problems. When inspiration fails or lags, it is possible to resort to craft as a way of working yourself out of your creative doldrums. Make no mistake, any writer, no matter how inventive, will have periods of creative drought where he simply cannot come up with anything worthy of his skills or ambitions. It is during these periods that the writer benefits from either taking time off or temporarily limiting his ambitions to simple goals, such as rewriting a small part of a song that is essentially completed or adding a missing part to a melody that is almost finished. This editing time can also be useful in the general process of self-evaluation, something that all writers should do to improve their work.

Sometimes a writer is almost a vehicle for a song that is coming from some other source, a song that seems to write itself. Often that song will rush out almost as a complete entity, but in a sort of rough and incomplete form. That is inspiration. But then craft comes into play: Through careful and meticulous rewriting, the writer will fashion this uncut gem into a finished diamond. This part of the creative process is hard work, not inspiration. Sometimes a song is like a puzzle that you find yourself unable to complete. The solution may come days, weeks or months later, or you may discard most of a melody but use a fragment of it in another song.

Chapter Two

Where Do Melodies Come From?

elodies come into being in a number of ways and from a variety of sources. Below is a list of ways from which melodies can emerge in the writing process.

- Chord progressions
- Hook phrases or lines
- Rhythm: beats, repeated or changing grooves
- The writer's instrumental style, a line suggested by a guitar or keyboard part
- The composer's head, emerging from a specific or general feeling
- A visual image, especially if the music is for a movie or a play
- A bass line
- The nature of a lyric
- An existing melody, but not an exact imitation of it

CHORD PROGRESSIONS

A chord progression is a logical sequence of chords that progress from one to another. For example, in 1950s rock and roll, the chord progression of C A-minor D-minor-7 G7 C was used in many songs, including "All I Have to Do Is Dream," "Donna, Donna," "Heart and Soul" and "Blue Moon." Figure 2-1 shows the necessary chord diagrams for keyboard and guitar. Remember, play all notes marked on each chord.

Although rhythm will be discussed later in this chapter, it should quickly become obvious to you that the style of the melody you play is going to have a close relationship with the rhythm.

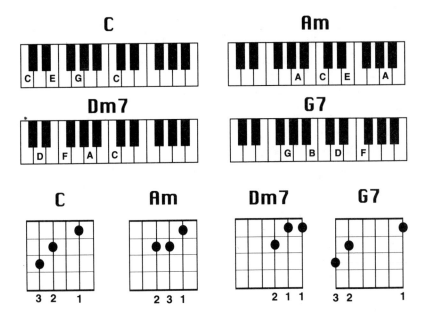

Figure 2-1.

For example, using this same chord progression, play C /// Am / // Dm7 /// G7 /// C. (A slash means you should repeat each chord once. In other words, play C four times, Am four times, etc.) Next take the same group of chords, but play them as follows: C / Am / Dm7 / G7 /. Then play them as triplets, three times within each beat or pulse, as follows: C C C C C C Am Am Am Am Am Am Dm7Dm7Dm7 Dm7Dm7Dm7 G7G7G7 G7G7G7. The rhythm should sound like this: *Da*-da-da, *Da*-da-da, *Da*-da-da, *Da*-da-da. 123, 123, 123, 123.

This triplet feel is quite typical of 1950s rock and roll, as performed by such vocal groups as the Platters or more recently by the Nylons or Sha Na Na. By changing the rhythm of the chords, you will undoubtedly end up with a different melodic feel than when you were playing each chord four times.

You are not playing a melody at this point, but you are playing a chord progression most people recognize because of the many 1950s rock songs that used that progression. You will probably start to *find* a melody from the chords as a result of playing this simple progression.

WHERE DOES THE MELODY COME FROM?

The easiest way to find a melody is to play the root, the note that is the name of the chord, as the top note of the chord. In the progression that you just played, the necessary notes are C, A, D and G. You can play them on the keyboard in descending order or you can play C, descend to A, then jump up to F and G (as in Figure 2-2).

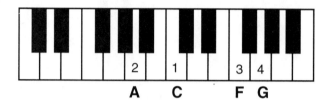

Figure 2-2.

The next step might be to connect the notes, or have a sort of melodic bridge between the closer notes. This would produce the melody C C C C C B A A A A A A A D D D D E F G G G G G G (Figure 2-3).

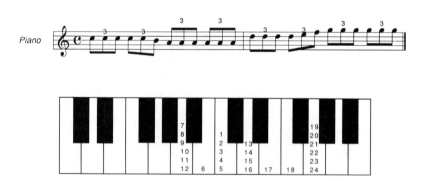

Figure 2-3.

On the guitar the same melodies would work as in Figure 2-4.

Note that in this particular chord progression, the sequence of melody notes works better on the keyboard, because you can easily arrange your chord so that the highest note you play in a C chord, for example, is the note that names the chord. The top notes of each guitar chord, however, are not necessarily the mel-

An octave lower than piano is playing

Figure 2-4.

ody notes. If you play open-string chords in the normal part of the guitar fingerboard, the top note of a C chord is an E and not a C. Don't worry if this seems confusing, because in chapter nine there will be a more extensive discussion of this problem.

You should now begin to understand how melodies arise out of chord progressions and how playing chord progressions in different keys may inspire different melodies. Try playing the following chord sequence in the key of D: D / A / G / / /. Play this progression a half dozen times or more until it sticks in your head. Figure 2-5 shows the necessary keyboard and guitar diagrams.

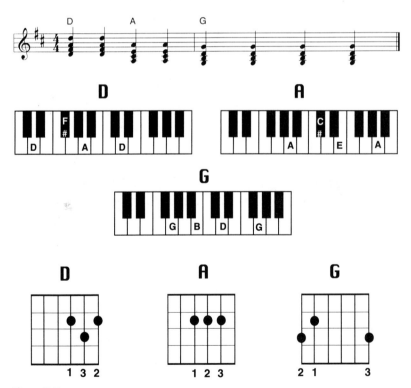

Figure 2-5.

Next, try the chord sequence D major to E major, using those two chords only (Figure 2-6).

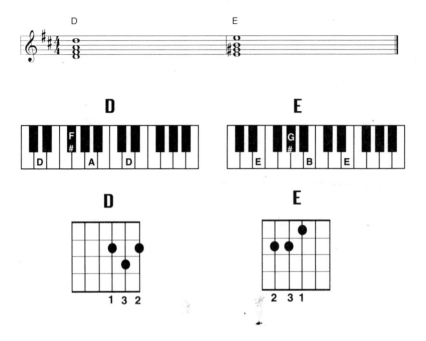

Figure 2-6.

Play only these two chords and see what melodies you can create from the notes. Then experiment with different rhythms and accents. If you find that playing guitar or keyboard distracts you from hearing the melody notes, record the chords and play them over and over. A simple tape recording enables the writer to focus entirely on the melody, without the distraction of singing or playing.

If you are playing guitar and are using the typical chords shown here, you will notice that by simply strumming the chords in sequence a melody will almost magically transport itself into your head. On the keyboard, it is a bit more complicated, because even though you are playing a specific chord sequence with your left hand, you have a vast menu of note choices for the right hand that will all go with the chord. For example, staying just with the D chord, you can play D, F-sharp or A (Figure 2-7).

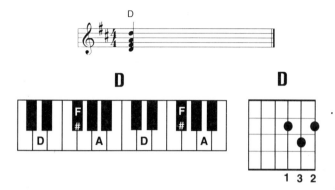

Figure 2-7.

Because of this variety of choices, deriving melodies out of chord progressions is, in some ways, easier to do on the guitar than on the keyboard. Piano players are able to separate the functions of the left and right hands without much difficulty. When you play the guitar both hands must work more closely together. In chapter eight, you will see that there are other things about the keyboard that make guitar players jealous.

Now that you have seen in a preliminary fashion how melodies evolve from chord progressions, when you listen to some well-known artist-writers, you'll easily understand that often they come up with their melodies simply from strumming a series of guitar chords. If you listen to Neil Young's songs, for example, you may agree that many of them sound like they were created by strumming chords, then finding the melodies in the chord progressions.

HOOKS

A hook is a particular phrase or fragment of a melody or lyric that is designed to pull the listener into the song. Skilled keyboard or guitar players can often come up with melodies or fragments of melodies simply by creating catchy little guitar or keyboard figures that seem to transform into the melody of the song. Eric Clapton's "Layla" contains a great example of a melodic hook that grabs the listener and almost physically involves him in the song.

The hook gives the average listener something to remember, whistle, hum or marvel at. It provides the focus for a song that sets it apart from every other song he has previously heard. Many writers think writing a hook is annoying and perhaps even juvenile. It isn't the goal of this book to develop complex discussions of aesthetics; rather it is to bring reality to the attention of prospective composers and songwriters. Like it or not, the hook is a central part of the pop song experience.

Developing Hooks

How can you learn to create good hooks? Pay particular attention to the introductions to songs; whatever the musical style, you can often identify a song after hearing just the first few bars. Don't try to make things unduly complicated. Remember, most consumers are not musicians, and what they tend to like and remember is a simple figure that is repeated numerous times during a recording. This may be exactly the opposite of what you, as a musician, enjoy. Musicians spend so much time listening to, composing or performing music that they probably want to write something unique and unusual. But be careful that your songs don't go over the head of the average listener. A friend of mine says there are two types of music: music for listeners and music for musicians.

Creating a hook early in the writing process is a lot easier than trying to find room for it in a song that you have already completed. Here are two approaches to studying hooks and learning how to create them.

1. Work backwards from a song to a hook. Take a song that you are familiar with and try to create an introduction to the song that will serve as a hook. Pay attention to the melody of the song, but don't feel obligated to reproduce it exactly.

2. Reverse the process above, going from a hook to a melody. Come up with a melodic figure that is interesting enough that you enjoy singing or playing it over and over. While you are in the process of developing the hook, don't think about writing a song. Imagine that you are re-creating a well-known song and have chosen to spin a new variation of it for your introduction.

RHYTHMS

Here is a brief look at the relationship between rhythms and melodies. One of the best ways to understand rhythm is to take a song that is familiar to you and try to play it in different rhythms. For example, if we take our old friend "Skip to My Lou" and change it to a waltz time, or 3/4, it will look like this:

Flies in the	*Buttermilk,*	*Skip* to my	*Lou,*
1 2 3	1 2 3	1 2 3	123

There are three beats in each group of words. Notice how different this feels from the way you would normally sing or play this song.

Using a 3/4 rhythm will provide a sort of lilt to the melody that will remind you of an old-fashioned waltz. If you stay in 3/4 time and put a strong accent on the first beat of each of the three-beat triplets, the song will have a German "oom-pah" feel to it.

Be careful not to write a melody in an automatic way, one that comes easily to you, rather than one that expresses the content of the lyric in an effective and appropriate way. Ask yourself what sort of feeling you are trying to get across with the melody.

The rhythmic feel of a song is tied to the melody in terms of an overall context. Remember the exercise in chapter one, singing on the beat, in front of or behind the beat? If you place strong accents on particular parts of the rhythm, your melody and vocal phrasing will be affected.

MELODY AS A FUNCTION OF INSTRUMENTAL STYLE

A melody can emerge from the writer's imagination or from the way his fingers find a particular hook, chord progression or random set of notes on a keyboard or guitar. When a writer has a very specific instrumental style, his melodies will tend to emerge out of the uniqueness of his instrumental work. James Taylor is a good example of an artist-writer who has a particular way of playing the guitar. The melodies seem to come out of the guitar style, rather than the other way around. When the listener hears the sound of the guitar on one of Taylor's records, he is usually prepared for the mellow sound that will almost invariably follow.

Neil Young has two very different guitar sounds, and the style of melodies that he uses with each one is distinct. Young's acoustic style is a kind of country-rock strumming. His electric guitar work features a lot of distortion and anger, and he will write that sort of song when he plays his "buzz-sound" on the electric guitar.

Billy Joel also has two sounds. In Joel's ballad tunes, such as

"Just the Way You Are," we anticipate, and usually get, a lush, chord-rich piano introduction, setting up a ballad feel. If Joel chooses to inject a song with more of a rock feel, the piano work is much more chord-oriented in a simpler way, with strong rhythmic attacks.

If you have developed your own instrumental style, either because you are an experienced player or, for some reason, you've invented something of your own through trial and error or rigorous study, you have a unique advantage in writing melodies.

There are advantages and drawbacks to a writer having such a strong instrumental style that the listener immediately recognizes it. Some of the advantages are:

• The writer knows what direction the song will take quite early in the writing process. Because of the guitar or keyboard style, with its consequent harmonic or rhythmic emphasis, the song almost has a tendency to go where it wants to go, rather than requiring the composer to direct it.

• The audience will recognize and identify with the instrumental style and find a certain gratification in this identification. Of course, if this process occurs too often, the artist becomes too predictable, and people may lose the desire to hear new songs that are simply resurrected old songs.

• When the audience knows and likes the style, a specific instrumental style can set a mood. A long, lush introduction to a song from Billy Joel tells the audience that a ballad is on its way.

Some disadvantages of having a well-developed and identifiable instrumental sound include:

• The style may totally define the writer's range, so that people say, "All of Artist X's songs sound the same."

• Such a style can constitute an artistic prison for the writer, one where growth becomes difficult to achieve. Who is to say that James Taylor doesn't truly yearn to write a song in the style of Van Halen, or vice versa?

• Repetition is almost inevitable when a guitar or keyboard player becomes extremely fluent in a specific genre, whether it's fusion, rap or traditional country music. Over time the audience may become bored with what was once a unique and attractive device.

COMPOSING IN YOUR HEAD

Try this experiment: Write a melody, any melody, right now, but stay away from your guitar, keyboard or any other instrument. If nothing comes to mind, imagine that you are writing music for a film, and the melody needs to express some particular feeling. The feeling might relate to something personal, such as love, or it might be pictorial, a tune intended to convey a peaceful ocean breeze blowing on clear, unpolluted water. Or it may be anything you want to write.

Try to analyze how this melody is different from the tunes that you write with a musical instrument. Here are a few things that may come out of this experiment:

• You become aware of how dependent you are on your particular musical instrument as a crutch that enables you to somehow come up with a melody.

• You realize that melodies may develop quite differently when you stop concerning yourself with chords. Just as the easy availability of chords on the piano or guitar makes it easier to write songs, it may limit the shape of your melodies. You may discover some melodies that have a new twist or emphasis when you try to find them in your head without instrumental assistance.

You may feel a terrible sense of insecurity about where the melody is supposed to come from, or in what direction you can take it. Try to ignore this feeling in order to get through the experiment without spending too much time intellectualizing about what is happening.

There will be times when you will be away from any musical instrument — in a car, on an airplane or on vacation. Think of writing away from your insturment as an investment in your musical future.

VISUAL INSPIRATION

Imagine that you have been assigned to write a melody for a movie scene that takes place in the California desert. Setting this picture in your mind will immediately lead to certain melodic ideas that will change rapidly if the next assignment is a scene that depicts teenage gang violence in Los Angeles. If the song involves particular places, time periods or feelings, you will write your melody to match these elements. Jimmy Webb is a writer who excels at creating melody-word pictures in such songs as "By the Time I Get to Phoenix," "Galveston" and "Up, Up and Away." So, one possible source for melodies is to create a picture in your mind and then write a melody that goes with it. This is exactly what you must do to write music for the movies, television or the theater.

WRITING FROM A BASS LINE

If you can, recall how "You've Lost That Lovin' Feelin' " sounds, either the original record by the Righteous Brothers or the tribute

Play an octave lower. Written in treble clef for easy reading.

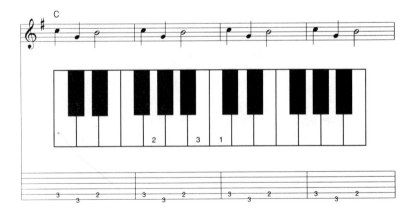

Figure 2-8a.

record by Hall and Oates. Notice how the bass line sets up the entire melody of the song. On either the bass strings of your guitar or with your left hand on the low notes of your keyboard, try to come up with a bass line that leads you into a melody.

For example, try the bass line in Figures 2-8a and 2-8b, using this rhythm: one beat, one beat, two beats. In other words, the first two notes are held for one beat each, the third for two beats.

Now play it again and try to sing a melody over what you are playing.

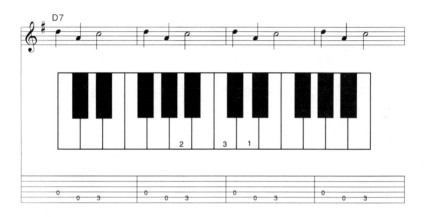

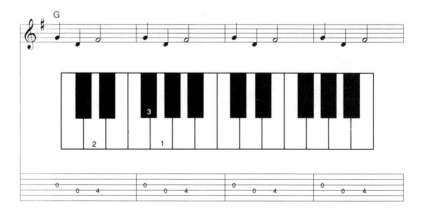

Figure 2-8b.

To get an idea of how important the bass line can be, change the rhythm as follows: half note, quarter note, quarter note. In other words, reverse the sequence of the rhythm from short, short, long to long, short, short. Notice how this will change the impetus for the melody.

Imagine that you are writing a waltz, a tune in 3/4 time, and change the bass notes to three even notes in each bar, or take the same bass line and invent your own rhythms. You will find that every time you change the rhythm of the notes, it will change the feel of the melody you are writing. This is another example of how something very simple can result in a series of complex and sometimes unexpected changes in the direction of a melody.

If this bass line bores you, make up your own bass line. Be careful to remember the exact rhythms of the notes, so you can change them, and observe how that affects your melody. It's a good idea to tape record the bass line and to write the melody while listening to it, without having to be occupied with playing your guitar or keyboard.

HOW LYRICS CAN DEFINE A MUSICAL DIRECTION

Some songs are written by two or more people working simultaneously on the words and music. Other songs are written by two people who work independently of one another, one writing the words and the other the music. Sometimes the lyricist presents the composer with a completed lyric, and other times the composer may complete a melody and then present it to the lyricist. No matter how you work, the lyric is going to have some effect on your music. It may determine some of the following elements:

• The rhythm of the words may define the rhythm of your melody.

• The lyric may refer to a particular locale or a phenomenon of nature like a beautiful sunset. This will tend to push the composer into reflecting the locale or sentiment in the music. For example, most people think of the sun as a positive thing, not a sorrowful one, and the music will logically move in the same direction.

• The complexity of your melody may be dictated by a lyric. If the lyric is extremely intricate or deep, the chances are that you will try to make the melody take up that challenge.

- If the lyric represents a particular musical style, like rap music or a country music weeper that seems to call for fiddles and a pedal steel guitar, the direction of the entire musical part of the piece is predetermined.

- If you are writing music for a play or a movie, you will have to pay attention to the script. Although there may not be any lyrics, you will be influenced by the acting, the camera work, the pace of the action and the intensity of the actors' performance.

- It is also possible to contradict the nature of a lyric with your music or to write against the action in a play or movie. In other words, you might write a happy tune to a very sad lyric, or a sad tune to a happy lyric. This tends to draw more attention to a song, which in a movie or theater piece may or may not prove to be a good idea. Sometimes an artist will perform the song in a manner opposite to the way you wrote it, such as Barbra Streisand performing the opening section of "Happy Days Are Here Again" as a dirge, going against the content of the lyric.

MELODIES INSPIRED BY AN EXISTING MELODY

You can write a melody that is intended as an imitation of a particular musical style or of an existing melody. This is most frequently done when writing movie or theater music or when a songwriter inadvertently or deliberately borrows a part or all of someone else's tune. Obviously any composer can borrow or steal melodies, but it is not legal to use someone else's melodies without permission unless they are in the public domain. It is a common, though incorrect, belief that it's acceptable to "borrow" up to four bars of a melody, but nothing in the copyright law allows this, and it is dangerous and unwise to consciously lift *any* portion of another composer's work.

In reviewing the sources of melodies, it is clear that there are so many different methods of inspiration that you ought to be able to draw on some new ones no matter what your experience has been up to now.

Chapter Three

Where Do Songs Start?

WRITING TO LYRICS

There is no one way to write songs. It is possible to start with the words, the music, or even the rhythm of a song, and to plug in the other necessary elements from there. In contemporary pop music, collaborators often come up with the words and the music simultaneously and contribute some of each of these elements. In older forms of pop music, especially before the rise of rock and roll, there was a precise division of labor between lyricists and composers, and we still find this separation of roles in the writing of Broadway shows. (Stephen Sondheim is the great exception, writing both words and music to his shows.)

If a lyricist presents you with a finished lyric, the chances are he already has an idea of a musical direction for the melody. A lyric celebrating romantic love is clearly going to call for a melody that is different from a lyric written about a baseball team. In other words, the subject matter, the nature of the story and the plot development will often dictate your choice of a melody. The nature of a rhyme scheme or the accent pattern of a lyric may also influence the direction of your melody.

For some composers, having these elements dictated before they begin is a bit of a hindrance and they may feel that their creative input has been severely limited. Other composers might take such a project as a challenge.

BEGINNING WITH A TUNE

This reverses the process described above, with the composer writing a specific melody that the lyricist must then match with a lyric. The composer must always pay attention to the length of the melodic line. Just as it may be difficult to compose a melody to fit a lyric whose lines are irregular in length, it is hard to match a lyric with a disjunct melody. A very pretty melody or a very jagged one will certainly dictate the direction of a lyric, and so will an insistent or unusual rhythm. If you write a melody in 5/4 time (five quarter notes to the measure), the lyricist will probably have to struggle to match the musical accents of your melody.

From a composer's standpoint, the advantage of writing the melody first is that you are free to establish your own direction. The disadvantage is that, unless you are writing an instrumental tune, you cannot ignore the lyricist's need for a melody line that can be comfortably fitted with a lyric.

WRITING SIMULTANEOUSLY

For collaborators, the great advantage of writing the words and music simultaneously is that it provides instant feedback for each partner. This enables the words and music to evolve together and ensures a better chance that the collaborators will be moving in the same musical direction. Also, working together moves the song along more quickly and also provides input from each collaborator on what works and what doesn't. Working together may enable the composer to get past his own questions about a melody or to establish a slightly different groove or accent pattern as the words evolve. Similarly, it gives the composer some input into the direction of the lyrics.

In a good collaboration, both writers are working on the words and the music, even when both acknowledge that one writer is stronger in one of these areas than the other one. It also leads to a quicker understanding of when a particular song may be a dead end, perhaps something that contains a couple of good ideas but isn't a coherent whole. If the two parties work separately, it may take several weeks before this is obvious to both of them.

COLLABORATION WITH A LYRICIST

Over a long period of time, a good collaboration may lead to successful, long-term growth for both writers. Elton John and Bernie Taupin come to mind, as do Thom Bell and the late Linda Creed. It is also possible to collaborate with different writers for different projects, as long-term hit composer Barry Mann has done, writing with his wife Cynthia Weill and with Dan Hill and other lyricists.

COLLABORATIONS AND PARTNERSHIPS

In some rock and country bands, all of the people in the band collaborate on the songs. In these situations, it is not unusual for some members of the band to simply create grooves, like bass or drum parts. These are really contributions to the arrangement of the song, as opposed to actually composing the song itself. Sometimes, the actual writers in these groups feel that these contributions are of great value to the evolution of the song; in other cases, it is more of a democratic decision, where the group has decided to share all rights to the songs. In the Beatles' songs, Lennon and McCartney shared the ownership of most of the group's songs, even though one of them typically served as the editor to the other writer.

I sang for three years with John Phillips, who went on to start the folk-rock group the Mamas and the Papas. John likes to write songs late at night, and he often uses another person as a sort of soundboard, bouncing ideas off them and encouraging them to make their own contributions to the songs. He does this as a way of keeping his creative juices flowing, and he gives his co-writers credit and part ownership of the songs. In effect, he is sharing the rights of his songs simply to keep his creative process flowing.

Jay Graydon described in the Los Angeles Songwriters Showcase magazine *Musepaper* his collaborations with songwriter-producer-arranger David Foster. Foster writes very quickly and he basically uses Graydon as an editor or song doctor. Jay's task is to affirm or reject Foster's steady stream of ideas. Although Graydon acknowledges that he is never too sure of what he has actually contributed to one of their songs, in Foster's eyes Graydon has made a useful contribution to the writing process.

Most collaborators who maintain long-lasting partnerships split their success 50-50, whether or not their contributions to the songs are exactly equal. For further information about collaborating agreements and other business details of writing songs, see John Braheny's fine book, *The Craft and Business of Songwriting* (Writer's Digest Books).

FILM AND COMMERCIAL COLLABORATIONS

In film and TV commercials, collaboration is often dictated by the people in charge of the project. For example, in commercials the composer often works with a copywriter from the advertising agency that represents the product. The copywriter often writes the lyrics for the commercial. This collaboration may not be one that the composer has chosen, but it may "come with the territory."

In films, there are several sorts of collaborations that occur. One is a collaboration with an arranger-orchestrator. Although many film composers are perfectly capable of writing the orchestral parts for their music, they often don't have the time to do so. In these cases the composer will usually write sketches that suggest orchestral parts, but leave it to the orchestrator to notate the precise musical arrangement. Some orchestrators are so experienced in writing for large orchestras that the composer may rely on them to provide a good bit of the orchestral parts. In these cases, the composer limits herself to writing specific melodic themes, and the orchestrator does the rest.

There are some film composers who only write melodies and do not have the technical training to orchestrate their music. They are obligated to work with an orchestrator, unless the director is willing to accept a score that is performed on synthesizers by the composer.

Chapter Four

What Defines a Good Melody?

t is easier to come up with some written criteria to define a "good melody" than it is for any two people, musicians or nonmusicians, to actually agree on what makes a melody good or bad. I'll try to set forth some of the things I believe define a good melody, with the full understanding that the reader may agree or disagree.

A melody must be easy to remember. It should stay in the listener's head, be "catchy" and sneak up on you. For example, you may find yourself singing a tune from a television commercial. You didn't try to learn the tune, if fact you may not even like it, but there you are, walking around the house or driving the car singing the damn thing.

The melody should be recognizable to nonmusicians. The average person ought to be able to sing your tune with comparative ease.

The melody should lend itself to a variety of musical treatments. I once played a recording session in New York in which an entire album of a particular Oldsmobile commercial was recorded. It was arranged in twelve different musical styles: There was a Hawaiian version, a country and western arrangement, rock and pop versions, and eight others. The point is that it was possible to play and sing this tune in all these styles and retain the tune's own special quality (whatever that was).

Some songs have melodies appropriate for a particular musical artist or genre, but they don't work if someone tries to convert them to a different style of music. For example, I find it hard to imagine the Beatles "Hey Jude" arranged in a traditional country and western style (although there is an interesting instrumental arrangement of it by an offbeat bluegrass studio band called Area

Code 615). The late Roger Miller's "King of the Road" probably wouldn't make much of a soul serenade, although I suppose anything is possible. I'm sure you can think of a heavy metal, rap, country, pop or folk tune that you cannot imagine being performed in any other musical style.

When a melody is tied to a very specific musical style, obviously the song's longevity and earning potential will be restricted or tied to the popularity of that style. So, certainly from an economic standpoint, it is desirable for a song to have the sort of melody that lends itself to many different interpretations. What makes one melody readily convertible to another musical style, while another tune is firmly entrenched in a very specific musical idiom?

Lyrics With Universal Appeal

First of all, we must pay some attention to song lyrics. "Bridge Over Troubled Water" started its life as a hit record by Simon and Garfunkel; later Aretha Franklin's version became very successful in its own right. The song is about loneliness and communication, which are obviously concerns that most people share. If you are writing a song about a sports event that took place in a town in Iowa, it is unlikely that anyone who lives outside the immediate area will find your song appealing.

Is It the Lyrics or Is It the Melody?

But what about the role of the melody? When Aretha Franklin sings a melody, she doesn't so much change it as decorate it with vocal slides, interjected phrases or different accent patterns. Art Garfunkel, on the other hand, is a straightforward ballad singer whose interpretation comes from the texture or color of his voice rather than from creating melodic variations.

Is It the Different Chord Changes?

Part of the question of whether a song can be arranged in a different musical style involves the question of whether a song lends itself to the use of alternative chords. Jazz musicians call these chords "substitutions." *Any* song can be arranged in this fashion, but some will sound ridiculous outside of their original context. I doubt that you would enjoy hearing "Three Blind Mice" played with many unusual chord modifications.

In fact, the average listener will have difficulty grasping a melody that is harmonized with complex chords. By "complex" I mean the sort of chords that you see in modern jazz transcriptions, such as G-minor-7#9. A jazz singer may love such a piece, but the average person will find it forbidding.

Below is a checklist of some of the elements that allow a song to be successfully converted from one musical style to another:

- The lyric has universal meaning (like "Bridge Over Troubled Water").
- There isn't a strong stylistic identity to the song, such as a religious or patriotic connotation (e.g., "God Bless America").
- The chord pattern can be reworked without any obvious or jarring differences (like a children's nursery song).
- The melody doesn't have specific characteristics that tie it inseparably to a specific style, such as blues notes (the notes E-flat and B-flat in the key of C, for example), causing the listener to immediately identify a song as a blues song.
- The melody is strong enough so that people will enjoy hearing it again and again.
- The melody should have some special quality that sets it apart from previous melodies by the composer or others, but should not be so odd or unique that it will prove impossible for the audience to understand. This speaks to the problem of "music for musicians" vs. music for the average listener. Many musicians only enjoy music that is way over the head of the average person. Remember that for most people, music is a pleasant diversion and they don't want to devote too much time trying to understand it. If you write melodies that fly too far over the head of the average person, most likely that is exactly where the melodies will go — over the consumer's head.

On the other hand, people enjoy a tune that has some little touch that separates it from other tunes. It is a fine line balancing inventiveness with commerciality, one that is not easy to walk.

- A melody should be enjoyable to sing. Think about the times you rode in a car and sang the songs everyone else seemed to know. Think about the songs you sang at parties, picnics, or whenever your friends got together with a guitar.

Some melodies are enjoyable to sing because they stick in your head; others have pretty or distinguished melodies. Others may be almost sing-song and are fun because they are like nursery rhymes.

• The melody should be in a normal vocal range. Most people are not comfortable singing a song that spans much more than an octave (a range of eight notes). If you write songs that have giant melodic skips, upward or downward, the average person will have trouble singing them.

Certain singers have very broad vocal ranges, like Mariah Carey or Cyndi Lauper. These artists deliberately try to write tunes that exploit their vocal abilities. If you are a great singer going after a record contract and intend to record all your own songs, you needn't worry about what the average person can sing. However, if you are simply a songwriter and not a performer, you are going to greatly limit the potential market for your work if only a magnificent singer can reproduce your melodies.

• A melody may create a sense of time, place, mood or even geography. A melody can transport you to Istanbul, Greece or Africa, even without a lyric. Specific musical styles can transcend the environment of the listener, and certain melodies announce that they represent the ragtime era, folk blues or mountain string band music. Musical styles have specific mannerisms that relate variously to melodies, singing styles, instrumentation, phrasing, rhythm and so on. Once again, in writing movie music, these are crucial elements for getting the audience's minds off their own surroundings and into the movie's setting.

• A great melody should have enough staying power that it transcends the immediate contemporary musical style it was recorded in. We call such songs "standards," meaning that we can expect to hear them for years to come in different musical styles or treatments, recorded by a variety of different artists over time.

• The rhythm of the melody should reinforce the notes or "tune" and should reinforce the impact of the melody. Think of how important the rhythm of tunes like "Begin the Beguine," "I've Got Rhythm," "Sunshine of Your Love" and "Tennessee Waltz" are in the overall context of the melody. To underline this point, tap out the rhythm of these songs on a table with a pencil and *then* sing the melodies. Try to change the rhythms of these songs and notice how the melodies no longer seem to work.

• The melody of the verse and the chorus should be distinctly different from one another, and the melody of the chorus should be the strongest tune in the song. For the moment, it's sufficient to say that the chorus of a song is what most people remember, so it needs to be the strongest part of your melody. (More about form in chapter five.)

• A great melody fits a lyric to perfection. Think of some of your favorite songs and try to imagine a different melody written to the same lyric. Why do great songs marry excellent lyrics and fine melodies? Perhaps the answer is that these are the exact qualities that define a great song. Most people will lock in on either the melodies or lyrics in a song. They do not appreciate both of these elements to the same extent. In rock and roll, since rhythm is such an important part of the song, the melody has a great advantage over the lyrics. However, there has to be at least a section of the lyric that people can remember and relate to.

• Some melodies simply fit the style of a particular artist like a fine, handmade suit. If you have a unique vocal style, it may enable you to write songs that people will enjoy hearing you perform, even though other artists may never record these songs. The problem is that a "unique" style is exactly that, and for many writers this uniqueness exists more in their own ego than in the reality of popular taste. It is best to imagine other people singing your songs even if your goal is to be a recording artist as well as a songwriter.

• A melody that is universally accepted is easy for the average person to grasp. It is the tune that the person hums coming out of the theater as opposed to the fifteen other songs in the play or movie. A flexible melody that can be arranged in many different musical styles and still retain its identity and its own special qualities will have a far greater chance for success. A new melody should be individualistic enough to stand on its own but not so weird or bizarre that it's difficult to understand.

These remarks apply to music that is destined for the mainstream marketplace. If you are writing for a specific musical idiom, such as modern jazz, where the audience is more musically sophisticated, there will be room for a higher degree of musical complexity or inventiveness in your work as a composer. If your work is intended for the mass audience, then simplicity is an important aspect of its character.

It is useful to get as much experience as possible in writing music of all sorts for many different audiences. This will enable you to respond to whatever musical demands are made on you in the future, whether they are to write a complex music score for a film or a Top 40 country song.

Chapter Five

The Form of Popular Music

Popular music is generally written in a consistently specific way. The different sections of a song consist of the verse, the chorus and sometimes, although not always, the bridge. The verse is the opening portion of the lyric that begins the song. The melody of the verse usually sets the groundwork for what is to come.

A FORM

The simplest song form contains only verses and is usually called "A form." That's because the letter "A" is used to identify a *section* of the song (in this case, the *only* section — the verse). The verses use a single melody that is repeated throughout the song. There is no chorus at all.

The obvious problem with A-form songs is that they tend to get boring. Their primary advantage as a form is that, because there is only one repeating melody, it is generally simple to remember the tune to the song. Consequently, one of the places that you will find the A form is in the children's songs, such as lullabies, older traditional songs like "Frère Jacques" or in folk songs.

Occasionally, an A-form song makes its way onto the pop music charts. The Nitty Gritty Dirt Band's first hit record, "Buy for Me the Rain," is an example of an A-form song. It had three verses, and the first verse is repeated at the end of the song. This song is seldom heard today, except when the Dirt Band is in a nostalgic mood!

Another example of an A-form song that was a big hit is Gordon Lightfoot's "The Wreck of the Edmund Fitzgerald." This song was written in the style of an old English ballad, and it was designed to feel like a traditional folk song. Since traditional music was never intended to be used for commercial purposes, the emphasis was placed on the story told in the ballad rather than on the melody or the performance by the singer. The subject of this song was a shipwreck on the Great Lakes, much as a song written in the sixteenth century might have concerned a great battle or the reign of a noble king. Therefore, the choice of an A form was quite appropriate to Lightfoot's vision of the story. The form was cleverly disguised by the musical arrangement and production techniques used on the record. It started out very simply, but, as the rather long song developed, different musical instruments were brought in at various parts of the songs. It may well be that Lightfoot had the orchestration of the recording mapped out in his head while he was writing the song. But, whether or not this was true, the fact is that the song was another rare example of an A-form song becoming a big hit record. I doubt that any other recording artist would have chosen this song as a "commercial" release if Lightfoot hadn't recorded it himself.

Many blues songs are written in an A form, with no chorus. Often these songs don't tell a specific story, but are simply a group of verses that reflect the singer's attitudes about a specific situation or emotion. Sometimes the verses are traditional and are used over and over in different songs put together by different singers. Since the mood is emphasized more than the story (which would have a beginning, middle and ending), the A form can be quite effective in a traditional blues song.

AA' FORM

AA' form consists of a series of verses (the A section) with a repeated chorus (the A' section) usually sung after each verse. The chorus uses the same melody as the verse in this form. If the song is lengthy, sometimes the chorus will be sung less frequently. This can be done by using the chorus after two consecutive verses instead of always alternating verse, chorus, verse, chorus. Another possibility is to double up on some of the verses as the singer gets deeper into the song. The reason for doing this is to take the listener's attention away from the constant repetition of the same melody.

"This Land Is Your Land" by Woody Guthrie is an example of an AA' song that repeats the same melody, as is our old friend

"Skip to My Lou." In both of these songs, the melody for the verses and the chorus are quite similar, but not precisely identical.

The advantages and drawbacks of this form are simlliar to the A form, except that, with the same melody repeated in both the verse and chorus, it becomes really easy to remember the song. This is a great advantage in teaching a song to young children, but the average adult will find the constant repetition boring. The longer the song, the greater chance of boredom setting in.

AB FORM WITH TWO MELODIES

This is one of the dominant forms in popular music, no matter what the musical style. In this AB form there are verses (the A sections) that repeat the same melody with a different lyric in each, and a chorus (the B section) that has its own melody and lyric that repeats.

Songs that use the AB form are usually organized in an AABA order, such as Kathy Mattea's version of Nanci Griffith's "Love at the Five and Dime" or the Beatles' "Michelle." Different combinations are possible, such as AABABA or AAABAB. In these forms, the writer makes the listener wait before going to the chorus. Examples that use these forms are Hall and Oates's "Maneater" and the Eagles' "Lyin' Eyes," respectively. Many of Lennon and McCartney's songs *start* with the chorus. Examples are "She Loves You" and "Hard Day's Night."

It is crucial in this form that the melody of the chorus be the more memorable of the two melodies. It is also most often the part of the song that contains the title, usually either at the beginning or the end of the chorus.

Here are some other characteristics of the chorus that you will tend to find in this form:

• The chorus is usually in a higher vocal range than the verse. It is generally accepted that the high part of the vocal range, especially the male vocal range, is more exciting than the lower range. This was true of such groups as the Beach Boys, Air Supply and Yes, and is also true of many of heavy metal bands where a song's climax is sung in a higher vocal range, often screamed in anguish.

• It is virtually a given that the title of the song will appear in the chorus and may well be repeated several times.

- The chorus is also the place in the song where there may be other vocal parts, sung in harmony with the lead. These parts may actually be recorded by the same singer, or they may involve other members of the group or hired background singers, who either do not sing on the verses or sing only background syllables such as "ooh" or "ahh" or echoes of the words in the verses themselves.

- One of the primary goals of pop songs is to involve the listeners so they will not only remember the melody of the chorus but actually sing it to themselves or with their friends.

- Usually records are designed so that if there is a fade ending with a portion of the song repeated over again, it is the chorus that gets repeated.

The AB-form song with separate melodies for verse and chorus is still widely used in all sorts of pop songs, whether they are rock, country or some other style. The advantage of this form is that, because there are two melodies to work with, it is relatively easy to maintain the interest of the listener, especially if the song has a great chorus to it. Because the chorus is repeated throughout the song, the listener has enough chance to learn and absorb it, and yet the verse provides some melodic relief. The verse should build interest, and the chorus becomes like an old friend that the listener welcomes every time she hears it.

If the song isn't lengthy, there may not be disadvantages to this form. If the song is particularly long, however, even two melodies may not provide enough spice or interest to keep the listener involved and amused. This brings us to the last basic form, ABC.

ABC FORM—VERSE, CHORUS AND BRIDGE

Some writers are fond of writing lengthy songs that have complex plot lines and take a long time to resolve. Many of these songs add a third part to the verse-chorus form called a bridge or release. It has a new melody and an additional lyric and is usually only sung once during the course of the song.

The function of the bridge is to provide a slight surprise or bit of fresh air to a lengthy melody. A good example of a song with a bridge is Jimmy Driftwood's "The Battle of New Orleans." This song retells the story of a three-day battle that took place at the end of the War of 1812 between the U.S. and Great Britain. Be-

cause of the epic nature of the subject matter, the song is necessarily rather lengthy. To keep the interest level up, Driftwood inserted a bridge and, in fact, repeats it later in the song. This is a comparatively unusual way of using a bridge part, but because the melody used in this instance is brief and rather attractive, it is very effective. A more typical use of bridges can be found in numerous Beatles' songs, such as "You Won't See Me" or "I've Just Seen a Face." In these songs, the bridges come after several verses and choruses, providing a slight change of pace.

Sometimes the reason for using a bridge is not because the song is long, but because the writer simply wants to present a new point of view or has come up with a melodic fragment that she wants to include. It is common for the bridge to be shorter than either the verse or chorus, sometimes just a line or two to add some new element to the song: a new melody, a surprising shift of point of view in the lyric, or some striking instrumental hook line.

A bridge can also express a shift in a song's narration. Possibly the verse and chorus told the story from a female point of view, and the bridge reflects the man's side of things, or vice versa. A bridge can also be used to express underlying doubts. Maybe the verse and chorus asserted a strong point of view, say a man singing that he will never leave the female character in the song. The bridge might humanize the picture by expressing a conflicting thought or point of view, or simply reflect some confusion not expressed in the lyric. If the lyric of the bridge contains a shift in the point of view, the melody should match this change of feeling or context.

INNOVATIVE FORMS

A great way to study song form is to look at the Beatles' music. In "Eleanor Rigby" there is a bridge but no chorus. Because there is no chorus, Lennon and McCartney start and end the song with the bridge. Other unusual techniques that the Beatles used include beginning songs with choruses and changing key between a verse and a chorus. If a song is sufficiently interesting or powerful, or if the artist-songwriter is already famous, it is quite possible to break many of the "rules" of songwriting and still write a successful song. In theater pieces or movie music, it is possible to pull off even more innovative song forms.

SONG FRAGMENTS

I once wrote a single-verse song for a play. Anything longer would have interrupted the dramtic flow of the play in the particular spot where this song occurred.

For the same play I wrote a duet between the male and female leads that used an ABCD form. Each character's song had a verse and chorus, using a total of four different melodies. At the end of the song, both of them sang the chorus of the woman's song.

THROUGH COMPOSED MUSIC

Art songs are songs usually set to famous poems and sung by vocalists with operatic voices. In some of these songs, each portion of the song uses a different melody. There are no repeats at all. I keep waiting for some avant garde rock group to come up with a song that uses this form — a sort of stream-of-consciousness style analogous to Pink Floyd's use of instrumental music.

OTHER ASPECTS OF SONG CONSTRUCTION

Hooks

Almost all popular songs use hooks: recurring lyrics and/or melodies designed to hook the listener into the flow of a song and get him involved with the tune or story line. A phrase like "I Can't Get No Satisfaction" is clearly the major melodic and lyric hook in the song of the same name by the Rolling Stones. Similiarly, in the country standard "The Green Green Grass of Home," it is that phrase and that part of the melody that most people will remember when they think of the song.

Some songs even have a *pre-hook*, a section that leads into the actual hook. A pre-hook usually appears just before the beginning of the chorus, and like the chorus itself is a recurrent phrase that typically has an ascending melody. As an example, John Braheny cites the "You're trying hard not to show it" portion of the Phil Spector, Barry Mann and Cynthia Weill hit "You've Lost That Lovin' Feelin'."

Intros

Nowadays, a crucial part of a song is the introduction. This may consist of a guitar figure, a bass lick, a drum part or even a background vocal. The next time you listen to the radio, notice how you can generally recognize most songs even before the lyric starts, because of the catchy introductory instrumental figures. Sometimes a whole song can flow out of such introductory material, but more commonly it simply sets the tone for what will follow.

At one time, a producer or arranger may have come up with an intro or orchestration ideas. But now, it is increasingly common for songwriters to come up with these little parts themselves. When the songwriter makes a demonstration tape of the song, it is a tremendous plus to have these elements in place, even though a demo is supposed to be a rough version of the song. Later, when the songs are produced in first-class studios, the producer of the session may have studio musicians to duplicate or expand on these ideas.

No one can set up absolute rules that will bring you commercial success. Nevertheless, it is important that you study the basic forms used in popular music and understand their function. Once you achieve some notoriety as a songwriter, you can begin to experiment and bend the forms to fit the needs of your particular talent and goals.

Chapter Six

Rhythm and Grooves

UNDERSTANDING RHYTHM

Many writers who spend a lot of time developing their melodies and rewriting their lyrics only deal with rhythms when they have a problem. Maybe they are unable to fit a melody into a rhythm pattern that seems comfortable for most of the song—somehow it may not work with a particular line or section of the tune. While you are reading this chapter, try to think like a drummer. In other words, assume that the rhythmic element of your songs is the most important single aspect of them.

Time Signatures

If you look at any musical example or piece in this or any other book, you will notice that a set of numbers appears on the musical staff immediately after the sharps (#) or flats (♭) that follow the clef sign. The clef sign is the symbol at the extreme left of every line.

The numbers that appear to the right of the clef may read 2/4, 4/4, 3/4, etc. The bottom number indicates a unit of time. When that number is a 4, it represents a quarter note. If the time signature reads 6/8, or 12/8, it means the basic unit of time is an eighth note.

The top number indicates the number of notes that make up a musical subdivision called a *bar* of music. A 4/4 bar indicates that there are four quarter notes in each bar. That is the rhythmic subdivision of the music. Bar lines are indicated by vertical lines that are placed at the end of each bar (Figure 6-1).

Strong and Weak Beats

An important aspect of writing melodies is determining where the melody sits in relation to the rhythm of a piece. Whether the

Figure 6-1.

melody falls on strong or weak beats, in front of the beat or behind the beat, or right *on* the beat itself will also influence the form and direction of your melody.

Try the following experiment: Set up a 4/4 rhythm, with four beats for each measure of music. You can do this by playing chords on the piano or guitar, or by tapping out time with a pencil, or by using a metronome that clicks off beats in various tempos. Keep the beat going and sing a song that you have written, or any song that you can easily recall. If possible, use a cassette recorder and record the singing along with your timekeeping.

After you have recorded the song, play it back. Where does the melody fall? Do all the notes come exactly on the four beats of each measure, or do some of the melody notes fall between the four beats? Is there a rhythmic emphasis on the melody note? In a 4/4 bar there are four beats, each of them is a quarter note. Emphasize the first and third beats of the measure, then try the same thing but emphasize the second and fourth beats.

In most blues or soul-oriented music, the emphasis is strongly on the second and fourth beats of the measure. In the older forms of country music, the accents usually fall on the first and third beats of each measure. Try to figure out where the emphasis naturally falls in your melody.

Now that you have analyzed a song in this way, take the same tune and deliberately shift the beat around. If the emphasis was on the first and third beats, sing it so that the accents fall on the second and fourth beats. Once you are comfortable with this experiment, take it to another level of difficulty by changing the accents so they fall between the beats instead of right on them.

The purpose of moving the accent patterns around is to get you to examine whether you tend to write all of your tunes in a rhythmically similar pattern. If your accents tend to always fall in the same places, it may make your melodies sound similar, even if the actual notes and the range of your tunes varies. Performing this sort of rhythmic analysis will also provide you with some n sources of melodic inspiration and direction.

Developing Grooves Without Technical Assistance

Take a 4/4 rhythmic pattern, four beats for each bar of the music. Now, let's say you're writing a simple blues song, using the chords in Figure 6-2.

This is a simple twelve-bar blues pattern, one that you could imagine B.B. King or any other blues singer singing. Try playing the pattern with each chord exactly on the beat and no accent. Count 1 2 3 4, being careful to count the beats evenly. You may want to tap your foot to help you keep time.

Now take the same pattern and accent the first and third beats of each bar. Now you have **1** 2 **3** 4   **1** 2 **3** 4, etc. To make it easier to understand all of this, sing or hum a melody to a lyric, such as the following example:

C
Went to the river, tried to get a - cross,
1   2   **3** 4 **1**   2   **3** 4   **1** 2 **3** 4 **1** 2 **3** 4
F
Went to the river, tried to get a - cross,
1   2   **3** 4 **1**   2   **3** 4   **1** 2 **3** 4 **1** 2 **3** 4
G7   F   C F C   G7
Gonna keep tryin', I'm gonna be the boss.
1   2   **3** 4 **1**   2   **3**   4 **1** 2 **3** 4 **1** 2 **3** 4

Now that you've accented the first and third beats of the bar, try the same lyric and tune, but accent the second and fourth beats of each bar, as follows: 1 **2** 3 **4**   1 **2** 3 **4**, etc.

Notice how different the same melody sounds when you accent one set of beats in place of the other. Next try a more difficult approach: Play the four beats evenly without an accent and try to sing the melody just before the beat. Sing the first word just before the first beat of the song.

Once you have mastered this, reverse it and sing right *after* the first beat of the song.

At first you will probably find this continual shift of rhythms very annoying, but once you have mastered it, you should be able to add a new element of rhythmic flexibility to your songs. You will also have grasped the notion that, if the words of one verse

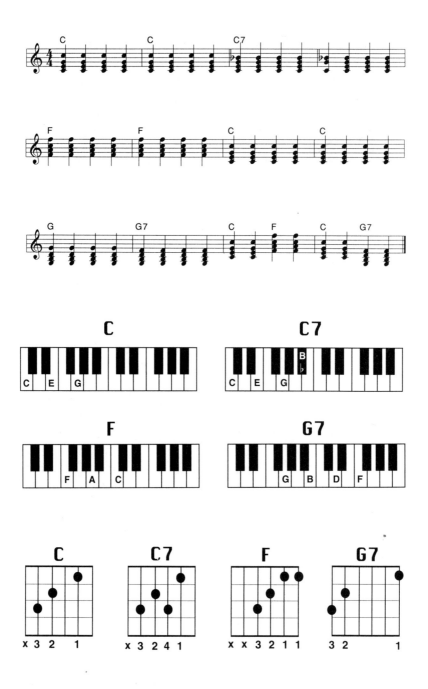

Figure 6-2.

don't exactly fit into a melody that works quite well with the previous verse, a simple shifting of the beat, holding a note or shortening it, enables you to retain the basic structure of your melody and fit in words that didn't seem to work before.

One note of caution: If each verse requires you to bend the melody in this fashion, then you may need to go back and refine your lyrics. Too many changes in the melody make it hard for the listener to remember the tune.

Take a few minutes and listen to some excellent singers who enjoy bending melodies, like Ray Charles or Aretha Franklin. Notice how they not only bend rhythms to make lyrics fit, but also change melodies that do fit into rhythms in order to create an element of surprise or excitement. It may take you a long time to become as skilled as these artists are in creating rhythmic changes, sliding and bending melody notes and changing accent patterns, but in the meantime you will probably start writing more interesting and varied tunes.

Cut Time

Sometimes a song is written in 4/4 time but is performed at a very fast tempo. For the convenience of the musicians, the song is counted with two beats as the rhythmic subdivision, even though there are actually four beats in each measure. This is known as cut time, and when musicians play in cut time you will notice that their feet are only tapping two beats for each measure of music. Cut time is indicated by the symbol C with a line through it: ¢. The C stands for "common time," another way of referring to 4/4 rhythms. This symbol will appear in the music just after the key signature, on the first line of the music (Figure 6-3).

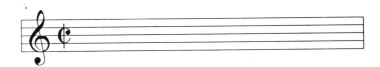

Figure 6-3.

Relating Rhythm to the Message of Your Song

Not only does rhythm relate to and influence the melody of your song, it also must be relevant to the lyric. For example, if you are writing a song urging students not to drop out of school, you will want to keep the rhythm firm and insistent. If your chorus uses a phrase like "Stay in school, don't be a fool," you will obviously want to put a strong accent on the words *stay, school* and *fool*.

On the other hand, if you are writing a song about falling in love while floating on a raft in the South Seas, you will probably use as few accents as possible, trying to follow the concept of the lyric with a dreamy, floating sort of melody.

Exotic Rhythms and Percussion

In the last five years or so, such artists as David Byrne, Peter Gabriel and Paul Simon have used drummers and percussionists from various parts of the world on their recordings, and these musicians use a variety of exotic percussion instruments. There are two aspects of the use of exotic rhythm instruments that deserve your attention as a composer.

First of all, many of these recordings feature different sizes and shapes of drums that come from various parts of the world. Many African percussion instruments have some sort of rattle built into them, so that the rattle is part of the sound of the instrument. African, Arabic and Greek hand drums have also become quite popular. The use of these unusual percussion instruments has opened up a new world of sound in the domain of popular music.

The other aspect of using drummers from different parts of the world is that in many countries rhythms like 5/4, 7/8 and 5/8 are not considered to be especially unusual or difficult. Music from any part of the world is readily available at most large record stores, and I recommend that you listen to some of this music, and experiment with it in your songs.

Developing a "Metronome Sense"

When musicians who do not normally play with one another get together, the results can be surprisingly good or bad. Much of their ability to play together successfully is based on their ability to share rhythmic concepts. Certain drummers, for example, may consistently speed up, and some others may lag behind the beat. It is a good idea to buy an electric metronome and practice playing or singing with it. Many young musicians find that they have specific rhythmic deficiencies that can be corrected by practicing with a metronome.

Mixed Meters

There are many reasons why studying Beatles' songs in depth is an excellent tool for the aspiring songwriter. One of these reasons is the Beatles' use of time changes in the course of a song. A few examples of these time changes are in Lennon and McCartney's "Strawberry Fields Forever," "Good Morning, Good Morning" and "A Day in the Life."

Another place to find meter changes is in film scores and television commercials, where the meter changes are often a function of the changing action on the screen.

USING TECHNOLOGY IN CREATING GROOVES

Probably no events in recent history have had as significant an impact on music as the advent of the computer and the development of MIDI, Musical Instrument Digital Interface. MIDI enables different brands of computers, digital musical instruments and other types of electronic devices to transmit data to each other.

Before we delve into a discussion of the various techniques involving computers and MIDI instruments, it might be helpful to provide some basic background. Here is a brief description of several of the commonly used tools of the electronic musician:

A *sequencer* is a device that records and stores musical events and transmits the data to various MIDI instruments and other MIDI devices. It operates in much the same way as a multitrack tape recorder, except that it enables the user to alter information the way a word processor does, copying or deleting events such as notes or musical phrases. It has cut and paste functions and can quantize, or correct, rhythmic errors or inconsistencies of a performance.

A *drum machine* is a sequencer that contains prerecorded drum and percussion sounds that can be arranged in a variety of patterns. They can subsequently be linked together to form more complex rhythmic structures. Most drum machines can be triggered from their own front panel, synthesizer keyboard, an octapad or other touch-sensitive controller using drumsticks or even bare hands or fingers.

A *synthesizer* is a device that generates sound in a variety of fashions. Early analog models relied on oscillators to produce a tone, while the new generation of digital synths produce sounds by a complex process of wave-form reproduction and combination. A true synthesizer allows the user to not only make major alterations to the sounds programmed into it but also program completely new sounds.

A *sampler* is a device that records a small portion of a pre-existing sound and stores that sound in its internal memory and subsequently on a computer disk to be played back via its own keyboard or an external controller. Once this data is stored in the sampler it can be altered just as any synthesized material can.

A *sound module* primarily plays back sounds and/or samples that are already programmed into it. It does allow the user to make alterations to tone characteristics, such as attack and decay, resonance, filter frequencies, adjustments to pitch, etc.

Aside from the data that can be stored in the internal memory of each of these types of devices, it is also possible to load extensive sound libraries into the memory of these machines, creating a virtually unlimited number of sounds.

A *work station* is a keyboard instrument that incorporates a synthesizer and/or sampler and sequencer all in a single device. The ideal work station is in fact a self-contained MIDI studio. Work stations provide a vast selection of sounds, including a wide variety of drum and percussion samples. You should go to your local music store and see demonstrations of these devices to find the programs best suited to your needs.

Using the Technology in Pop Songs

Sequencers provide a unique level of flexibility for a composer who is used to working with piano or guitar. If you are writing a song where the rhythmic groove is of primary importance, you will probably start with a drum pattern or bass line. If you are writing a ballad, you will probably want to work out the chord patterns first.

Let's assume you are writing a "groove" song with a sequencer. In this type of music, you will begin with a small fragment of two to four bars. This section will be looped or repeated over and over to give you a foundation to build upon. You will then have a rhythmic pattern that affords you the luxury of playing along. I recommend that you let the drum pattern play and begin improvising a bass line along with it. Once you have a bass part, you can begin to use the sequencer to help with some of your composing. For example, make a copy of the pattern of the bass notes and transpose it to different keys. Experiment with different patterns until you find the one that works best for your song.

It is important to understand that your drum pattern will probably not be the final version of your drum arrangement. Once the song is finished, you will probably want to alter the pattern so that each section of your song will have a specific drum part. You may also want to add fills (lead-ins) so that the drum part is not so obviously mechanical or repetitious. Of course, in some forms of music, like rap, a repetitious drumbeat may be an integral part of the song, but even then you may find it advantageous to develop the drum part beyond your original two- or four-bar pattern.

Groove songs can also start with a bass line. Just as when you started with the drum part, you will want to develop a two- to four-bar bass-line pattern. Next you will add a drum pattern. In most pop idioms, the bass and drums need to be closely related, and they form the foundation of the song. Once you have developed the bass and drum line, you will want to add other parts, such as piano lines, background parts, etc., before you actually write the melody. The number of added parts will vary from one composer to another, or from song to song. At times, simply having the bass and drums worked out will be enough to suggest an appropriate melody. In other instances the rhythm track needs to be virtually complete before you come up with the melody line.

Generally speaking, the more active your rhythm track, the simpler your melody should be. For example, say you're working on a melody in 4/4 time where the basic unit of time is a sixteenth note. Each beat will have four sixteenth notes if you continue that feel throughout the song. Figure 6-4 shows the way four bars of music with a sixteenth note pattern will look.

If we break up the beat and start to use eighth and quarter notes in addition to sixteenth notes, the pattern will look like Figure 6-5.

The less active the rhythm track, the more room there is for a complex melody.

Syncopation

A final weapon in our rhythmic arsenal is the use of syncopation. In syncopation, accents are placed *off* the beat instead of on

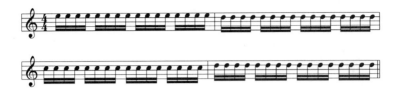

Figure 6-4.

Figure 6-5.

the beat. In a 4/4 bar of music, notes might come between the beats (Figure 6-6).

The first note is a dotted quarter note. A dot increases the value of a note by half, so the dotted quarter note gets one and a half beats. The second note (an eighth note) is *tied* to the third note (a quarter note). The tie means you hold the first note down for the time value of both notes—you don't play the second note. So in this example, the eighth note tied to the quarter note is held for one and a half beats. Try to feel an underlying pulse of eighth notes. Instead of counting 1 2 3 4 for the four beats in a measure, count "1 and 2 and 3 and 4 and." The "attacks" are on 1, the "and" after 2, and on 4. Accenting the "and" instead of the "2" is syncopation.

Figure 6-6.

The "Rules" of Rhythm

These suggestions about rhythm are guidelines, and some of the most interesting music that has been written has made a point of violating them. They should be seen as a point of departure. Rules are based on common sense, and through trial and error you will probably come to similar conclusions.

Chapter Seven

Organizing Your Melodies

A key is the tonal center of a song or piece of music. If you play guitar or keyboard, there are probably certain keys that you favor, simply because the chords are easy to play, or you have played in these keys so often that your fingers find the correct chords without much thought or strain.

LOCATING THE KEY OF A SONG

There are a number of methods you can use to determine the key of a particular song. Ninety-nine percent of all songs end on the chord that is the same as the key of the song. In other words, if the last chord of a song is a G chord, the chances are that the song is in the key of G. How can you tell what the name of the chord is? If you look at a piece of sheet music, the chord name will usually be written over the last few notes of the song. If you are able to read music, you will notice the last chord of the song contains the notes G, B and D.

There are two exceptions to this rule. First of all, there are a small number of melodies that do not resolve at the end of the song; the endings sound "up in the air." The old folk songs "I Know Where I'm Going" and "The Wagoner's Lad" are two examples. Three other examples are "Four Strong Winds," the pop-folk favorite by Canadian folksinger-songwriter Ian Tyson, which has been a hit three or four times now; the Nitty Gritty Dirt Band's old hit "Buy for Me the Rain"; and Sylvia Tyson's "You Were on My Mind," a hit in the mid-sixties by We Five. Notice that all of these songs are either traditional folk songs or songs in folk-rock style.

The other instance where the key cannot be identified from the last chord occurs on many pop records, where the ending is electronically faded. In this situation the ending phrase is re-peated over and over and the producer arbitrarily decides to fade the music in a particular place. The sheet music of such songs will usually be printed with a repeat sign and an indication that the ending fades indefinitely. Under these circumstances, you should treat the end of the last printed line as the actual ending of the song, even though the recording itself may not end in that specific place.

KEY IDENTIFICATION CHART

Sharps	Major	Relative Minor
0	C	A minor
1	G	E minor
2	D	B minor
3	A	F# minor
4	E	C# minor
5	B	G# minor
6	F#	D# minor
7	C#	A# minor
Flats		
1	F	D minor
2	B♭	G minor
3	E♭	C minor
4	A♭	F minor
5	D♭	B♭ minor
6	G♭	E♭ minor
7	C♭	A♭ minor

Identifying Keys

The above chart will enable you to identify the key of a song from its music notation. Just after the G clef at the beginning of each song there is key signature. It shows the sharps and flats, if there are any. The number of sharps or flats determine the key of a song. There is one complication: Each key signature can represent two different keys, a major key or its relative minor. To identify whether a key is in major or minor, look at the last chord of the song. Once again, 99 percent of the time, that chord will identify the key of the song (Figure 7-1).

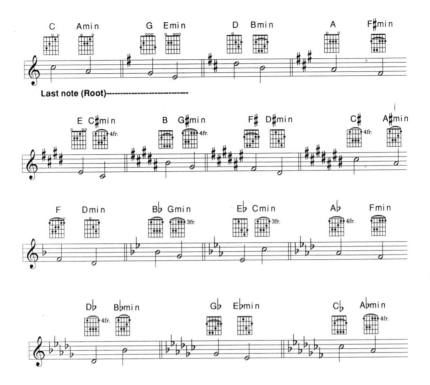

Last note (Root)------------------------

Figure 7-1.

Generally speaking, it is a good idea to avoid writing songs in keys that have more than four or five sharps or flats. Another thing you need to consider is that a song may be in a key that is quite suitable for your voice but is difficult for someone with a different vocal range.

RANGE

Many popular songs cover a musical range of only about an octave. If a song is written in the key of C, this will include the notes from middle C to the C an octave higher.

How High Can They Go?

If you listen to recordings by singers or groups like Whitney Houston, Mariah Carey, Michael Jackson, the Beach Boys or Yes, you may wonder whether you should be writing songs that have large melodic leaps in them and go up in the vocal stratosphere.

The fact is that most singers don't have the tremendous vocal ranges of these artists. You may think your song is perfect for, say, Whitney Houston, but if she is not the one who ends up singing it, you will have written your song right out of the market. A more typical singer with a normal vocal range will not even attempt to sing your song.

Try to sing your songs yourself. If you are having trouble reaching the high or low notes (unless you are a particularly poor singer), the chances are that most singers will think twice before trying your melody.

Making Appropriate Demos

Following the same logic, when you make demos of your songs, don't use singers who do vocal tricks, like making huge vocal skips and singing a specific verse in a higher vocal register, that are beyond the average professional singer. Remember, the more accessible your songs are to a reasonably good singer (and to the general public), the greater your chances are of getting them recorded. If you are lucky enough to get a song recorded by a brilliant singer in a recording session supervised by a skilled record producer, it's likely that they will rearrange your melody and highlight it in a way that you will enjoy and appreciate. Don't try to do their job for them.

SCALES

A scale is a group of notes that cover an octave of music. Octave refers to two pitches that are eight notes apart (from C to C, for example). Notes that are an octave apart sound alike because they are related mathematically. Before you become convinced that this book has suddenly turned into one of those horrendous treatises on music theory, go to your keyboard or guitar and try this experiment. On the guitar play the fifth string (the second lowest in pitch or the second one from your right thumb). Figure 7-2 is a diagram of the guitar showing the names of the strings and the first five frets on each string.

Place the ring finger of your left hand on the fifth string at the third fret. (The frets start at the top of the guitar neck.) Pluck the string and listen to the pitch that sounds. Then play the second (B) string, fingering it with the index finger of your left hand at the

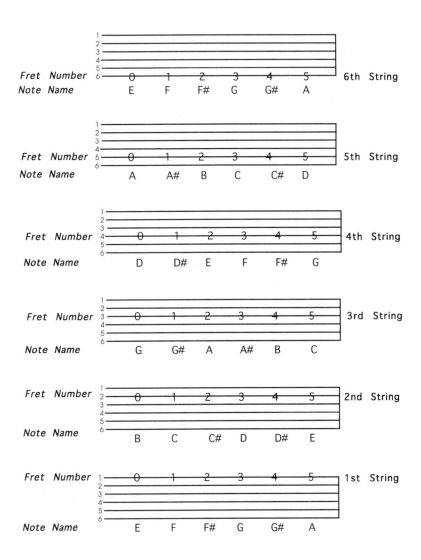

Figure 7-2.

first fret. These two notes are both Cs, but they are an octave apart.

If you play piano or any keyboard instrument, finger middle C, and C an octave higher (Figure 7-3). These two notes are an octave apart.

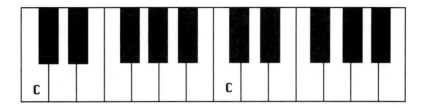

Figure 7-3.

Major Scales

Through a series of notes, we can now connect these octave Cs and create a major scale. The actual notes will be C D E F G A B C. On the guitar they are fingered as follows (also see Figure 7-4):

C   Fifth string at the third fret
D   Fourth string open
E   Fourth string, second fret
F   Fourth string, third fret
G   Third string open
A   Third string second fret
B   Second string open
C   Second string, first fret

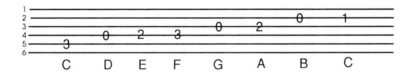

Figure 7-4.

In music notation the notes look like Figure 7-5.

Figure 7-5.

On a piano keyboard, play the notes in Figure 7-6, from left to right.

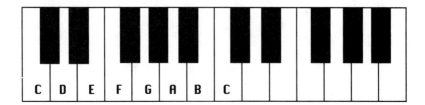

Figure 7-6.

This is a C major scale. If you have ever taken music lessons, you have probably practiced playing major scales. Note that in a major scale there are set distances between the various notes:

C to D   A whole step, two frets on the guitar
D to E   A whole step, two frets on the guitar
E to F   A half step, one fret on the guitar
F to G   A whole step, two frets on the guitar
G to A   A whole step, two frets on the guitar
A to B   A whole step, two frets on the guitar
B to C   A half step, one fret on the guitar

Note that between the third and fourth and seventh and eighth notes of the major scale is always a half step, or a distance of one fret. All other notes of the major scale are a whole step or two frets apart. On the keyboard, a whole step includes a distance that covers a black and a white key, while a half-step involves going from white to black, black to white, or the two places (E and F and B and C) where there are consecutive white keys without black keys.

Minor Scales

If you go back to page 55 where we talked about key signatures, you will see that the minor key that has the same signature (no sharps or flats) as C major is A minor. There are three kinds of minor scales: the natural minor, the harmonic minor and the melodic minor. The natural A minor contains the notes A B C D E F G A. Just as with the C major scale, there are no sharps or flats. Figure 7-7 shows these notes on a piano keyboard.

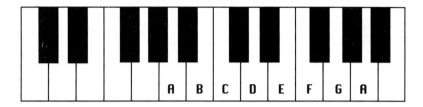

Figure 7-7.

On the guitar the notes are as follows (also see Figure 7-8):

A   Fifth string, open
B   Fifth string, second fret
C   Fifth string, third fret
D   Fourth string, open
E   Fourth string, second fret
F   Fourth string, third fret
G   Third string, open
A   Third string, second fret

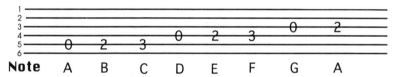

Figure 7-8.

The harmonic minor scale is the same as the natural, except that the seventh note, the G in A minor, becomes a G-sharp. Figure 7-9 shows this on the piano.

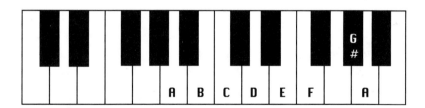

Figure 7-9.

On the guitar instead of playing the third string open, finger the third string at the first fret (Figure 7-10).

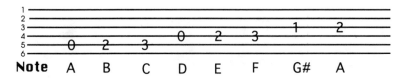

Figure 7-10.

This brings us to the melodic minor scale. The first five notes of the scale are the same as the natural or harmonic minor. As shown in Figure 7-11, when you get to the sixth note, the F becomes an F-sharp, and the G becomes a G-sharp, as the scale ascends. (F-sharp, on the guitar, fourth string, fourth fret; G-sharp, third string, first fret).

On the piano, play as shown in Figure 7-12.

When the melodic minor descends, the G-sharp and F-sharp are removed and become G and F natural, respectively (Figure 7-13).

The Importance of Scales in Melody Writing

It is important that you understand how scales are used so you can comprehend the relationship between notes and chords. This

A Melodic Minor (Ascending) - Guitar

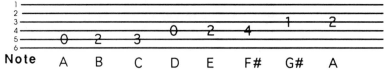

A Melodic Minor (Descending) - Guitar

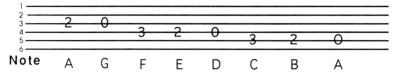

Figure 7-11.

A Melodic Minor (Ascending)

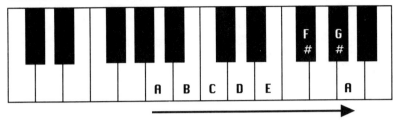

A Melodic Minor (Descending)

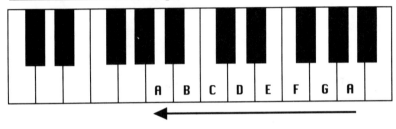

Figure 7-12.

will help you to understand why some melodies sound so good and others seem disjunct and difficult to sing. This information may be new to you; if so, it will become clearer as you read the next two chapters.

Scales are occasionally used in melodies in an absolutely literal way. For example, the opening line in the traditional Christmas

A Melodic Minor (Ascending)

A Melodic Minor (Descending)

Figure 7-13.

carol "Joy to the World" is nothing more than a C scale played in descending order, C B A G F E D C. This is a descending C major scale. The old tune "Three Blind Mice" also uses a major scale, but it is not quite as literal. All the notes are used but not in consecutive order. Figure 7-14 shows the opening portion of "Joy to the World" using the descending major scale.

Figure 7-14.

MODES

The Greeks used a system related to scales called modes, which are sequences of notes that are like scales, except that each mode has the half and whole steps in different places. Many folk songs are written in modes, and sometimes they don't use all of the notes in the mode. I have underlined the notes that have a distance of a half step between them.

Ionian	C D <u>E F</u> G A <u>B C</u> (like the major scale.)
Dorian	D <u>E F</u> G A <u>B C</u> D
Phyrgian	<u>E F</u> G A <u>B C</u> D E
Lydian	F G A <u>B C</u> D <u>E F</u>
Mixolydian	G A <u>B C</u> D <u>E F</u> G
Aeolian	A <u>B C</u> D <u>E F</u> G A
Locrian	<u>B C</u> D <u>E F</u> G A B

Pages 66-67 show diagrams of the various modes for guitar and piano. It is important that you realize that modes do not have to start on a particular note. They are based on the distances between the notes — the half steps as opposed to whole steps. The Dorian mode, for instance, could start on a G. The quality that identifies it is that the half steps (on the guitar, distances of one fret) are between the second and third and sixth and seventh notes of the mode. If you start a Dorian mode on a G note, the notes will be G A B-flat C D E F G (Figures 7-15a and 7-15b).

Although modes are sometimes used in popular music, they

are found more frequently in traditional folk songs. Since the Ionian mode is the same as the major scale, I won't give you any examples of songs written in this mode; any large songbook will have dozens of examples. Examples of songs in other modes are:

Dorian	"Scarborough Fair"
Phyrgian	Often used in Flamenco (Spanish gypsy music)
Lydian	Can be found in the music of Bela Bartok
Mixolydian	American folk songs like "Old Joe Clark"
Aeolian	"When Johnny Comes Marching Home"
Locrian	Rare

OTHER SCALES

There are dozens of other scale forms. Not all scales have eight notes; there are five-, six- and seven-note scales as well. The five-note scale is called the pentatonic scale. Children are often taught music through the use of five-note scales because there are fewer notes for them to remember.

If you use a five- or six-note scale in creating your melodies, these songs will be easy to remember, but they will also tend to be somewhat monotonous because of their musical simplicity.

If you study music of other cultures, you will find that there are scales that use different skips between the various notes. These kinds of scales are distinctive but sound peculiar to people brought up on the western scale forms.

INTERVALS

Intervals are the distance between one note and another. Although you may never have thought about organizing your own melodies in such a formal way, it is useful to recognize the sound of different intervals. You should also be aware that large melodic leaps on either an upward or downward direction may be awkward to sing, though they may be suitably dramatic for some particular musical or lyric message. A song that opens with a rather startling melodic leap is Mel Torme's "The Christmas Song," better known to most people as "Chestnuts Roasting on an Open Fire." The first two notes of the song are the same note, an octave apart.

Each interval has a distinct sound. Skips are defined as follows, strating once again from C, and diagrammed for guitar and keyboard (Figures 7-16a and 7-16b).

Dorian Mode

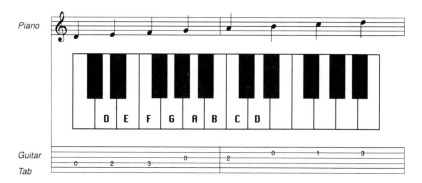

Phrygian Mode

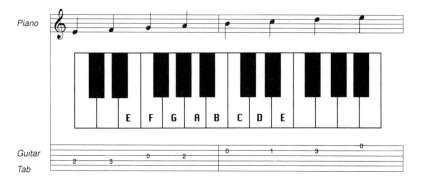

Lydian Mode

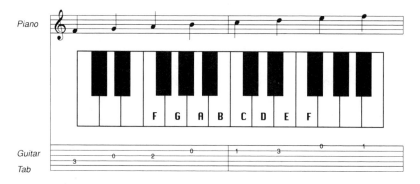

Figure 7-15a.

Mixolydian Mode

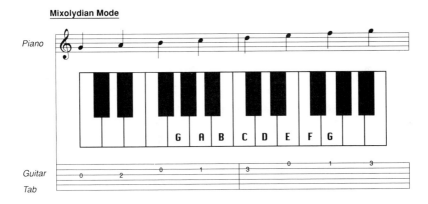

Aeolian Mode

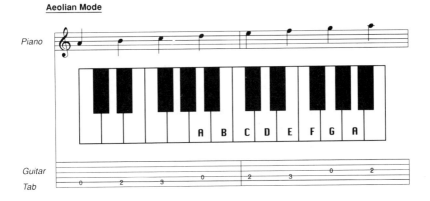

Locrian Mode

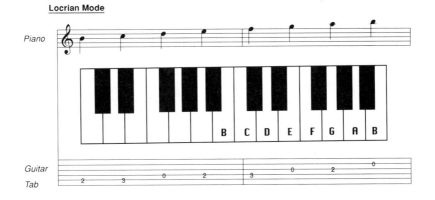

Figure 7-15b.

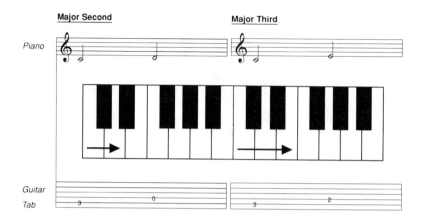

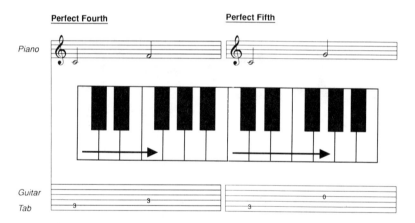

4ths and 5ths are refered to as "Perfect" instead of "Major."

Figure 7-16a.

C to D   A major second (the first interval in a major scale), the first two notes of the song "People."

C to E   A major third (thirds are the most common interval in vocal harmony).

C to F   A fourth (a sort of hollow sound—the interval used in the fox hunter's call), beginning of "Here Comes the Bride."

C to G   A fifth (a rather hollow sound, used in various older folk tunes).

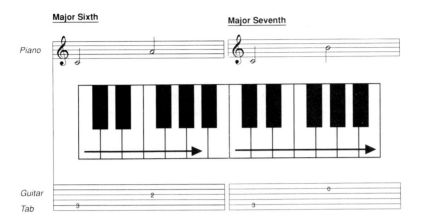

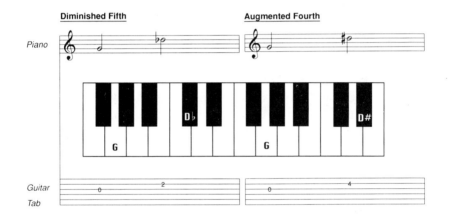

Figure 7-16b.

C to A   A major sixth (first two notes of "My Bonnie Lies Over the Ocean.")

C to B   A major seventh (sounds unresolved – the B wants to go up to the C above it).

Note that intervals can also be minor. C to D-flat is a minor second, C to E-flat is a minor third, C to A-flat is a minor sixth, and C to B-flat is a dominant seventh, C to F-sharp is an augmented fourth, and C to G-sharp is an augmented fifth. These intervals are harder to hear, because they sound a bit dissonant or nonmelodic on first acquaintance. They were often used in the popular music of the 1930s and 1940s. If you listen to these intervals on a regular basis you will become used to their sound.

Certain intervals, like fourths and fifths, are often found in English or American folk songs, and intervals of a third or a sixth lend themselves to vocal harmony. The early Beatles' records and the recordings of the Everly Brothers used a good deal of vocal harmony in fifths. This same sort of harmony singing is found in some traditional English folk song performances and in harmonies sung to American folk songs from the southern Appalachian Mountains. A classic example of singing in thirds is found in the vocal work that goes with Mexican mariachi music.

The reason for discussing all of this is not to attempt to force your writing into a particular style, but to make you aware that certain sounds are characteristic of specific musical styles.

CHORDS

Chords are groups of three or more notes played at the same time. They are readily playable on keyboards or guitar. They are more difficult to find on an electric bass and simply don't exist on instruments like the flute or trumpet. A major or minor chord, such as C major or A minor, has three notes representing the first, third and fifth notes of the scale. For C major, these notes are C, E and G; for A minor, A, C and E (Figure 7-17).

Groups of chords that go together in a sequence are called *chord progressions*, and they will be covered as we go into some depth about writing with a piano or guitar. In addition to the major and minor chords, there are countless variations of these chords that contain additional notes. If you have ever owned a chord book for guitar or keyboard, you've seen dozens of chord combinations, although too often the authors of these books don't explain what these chords do.

CRITIQUING YOUR OWN WORK

How can you evaluate your own melodies? One way is to tape record yourself singing and playing them and listen to the tape. You should record your songs anyway, because if you write a good number of them, you won't be able to remember them all.

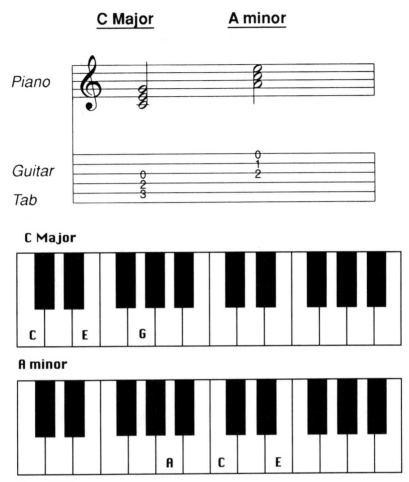

Figure 7-17.

Another way to evaluate your songs is to have friends sing your tunes. This is particularly useful if you are not a good singer. You should pay attention to whether other people have problems singing your melodies. If they are having trouble with your tunes, the chances are that your melodies are difficult to sing and you will have a hard time getting other people to record them. Some questions to ask yourself in critiquing your own melodies include:

- Do you have an easy time remembering the tunes?
- Do you find that many of your songs sound alike?
- What about the rhythms of your songs? Do they vary or are

you locked into the same style song after song?

- If you write on a keyboard, have you tried writing on guitar, or vice versa? Have you ever collaborated on melodies where you write on guitar, and the other melody writer uses a keyboard?

Chapter Eight

Creating Melodies on the Keyboard

CHORDS AND INVERSIONS

In this chapter, you will learn how chords and other aspects of melody writing relate to the piano or other keyboard instruments. There's more information about reading music in chapter thirteen if you need it.

Piano music will be shown here in conventional music notation and in diagram form, with the letter names of notes indicating where to place your fingers. You should be able to follow all of the information in this chapter whether or not you are able to read music. Guitar players who have no interest in keyboard instruments can skip to chapter nine, but even if you have the simplest sort of inexpensive keyboard, this chapter should be useful to you.

Figure 8-1 shows three versions of a C chord. The first chord has a C in the bass, and any sort of music theory books will describe it as being in *root position*. The notes of the chord are C, E and G. The second chord contains the same notes in a different order: E G C. This is called a C chord in first inversion. The third chord contains the notes G, C and E and is a C chord in second inversion. *Inversion* is simply the process of using the same notes of a chord in a different order. The bass note is different in each of these chords, and the note that has been displaced is then played an octave higher. If you play the notes of the chord from left to right with your left hand, the first note in the left hand will be the first thing you hear. The sound is going to be different when a chord is inverted than when it is played in root position. In addition to changing the sound of the chord itself, inversions are also used to make chord changes flow more easily. For example, play a C chord in second inversion (Figure 8-2) and then

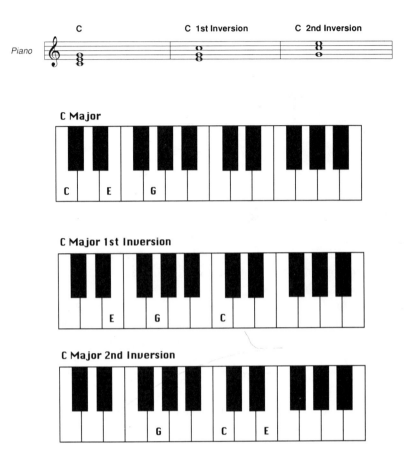

Figure 8-1.

change to an F chord in root position. Notice that the bass line is moving by a step.

To show you how inversions can be a real source of melodic inspiration, play the following chord sequence: C, E minor, F, G (hold each chord for two beats).

Now play the same chords but use these inversions: C, E minor in second inversion (B in the bass), F in first inversion, G (Figure 8-3).

Now play the melody in Figure 8-4 over both sets of chords: C, E, D, C, A, B (play in numerical order).

Notice how different this melody sounds when the chords are inverted, instead of all being played in root position. Now take some chord progressions that are familiar to you and play them

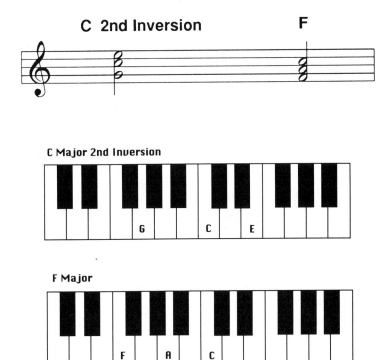

Figure 8-2.

with the chords inverted, so that the bass line moves as smoothly as possible. In other words, try to avoid jumps in the bass note. Try playing C Am Dm7 G7 (Figure 8-5).

Now try the chord progression G D C, found in some country tunes. This is the reverse of the more common G C D chord progression. If you play the D chord in first inversion (F-sharp in the bass) and then play the C chord in first inversion (E in the bass), notice how easily the left hand moves from one chord to the next (Figures 8-6 and 8-7).

Adding Notes in Chords

It is quite common, especially on keyboard instruments, to add a dash of color to a chord by adding notes to a basic chord, or to substitute these notes for part of the chord. The two most common notes to add are the second or fourth notes of the scale. On

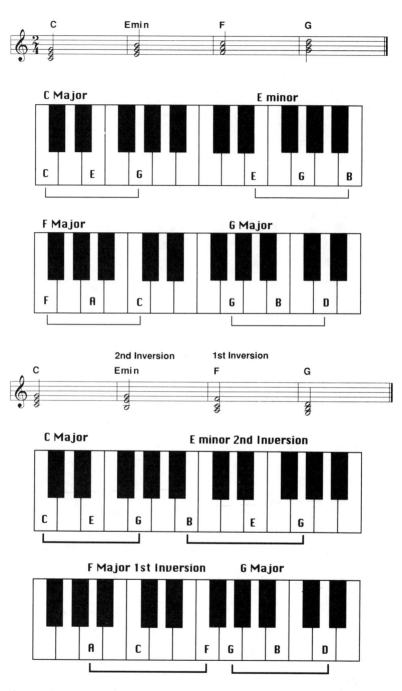

Figure 8-3.

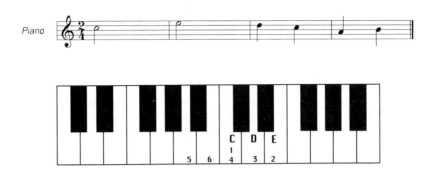

Figure 8-4.

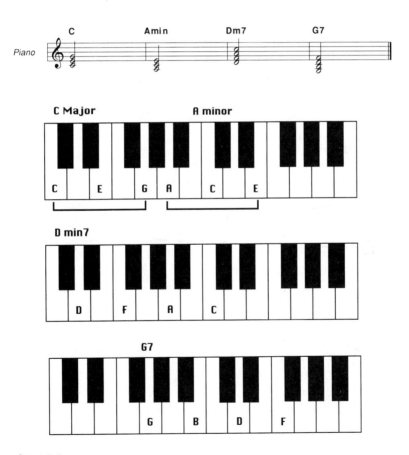

Figure 8-5.

a C chord, an added second is a D, and the fourth is an F. The fourth is said to be suspended because it has a feeling of being "up in the air," that usually resolves back to the third (the E). A C suspended fourth could be played C F G, with the F then returning to the E note. A common addition to a C chord is a C6, where you simply add an A to the C E G notes. Take some chords that are familiar to you and try adding these notes to those chords.

Substitutions

In addition to adding notes to chords, it is also possible to substitute one or a series of chords for a chord. Adding notes to chords is a process that is usually referred to as chord alteration. In substitution, you are actually substituting one or more chords for other chords. This technique has been highly developed in modern jazz tunes, where sometimes there are so many chord substitutions that the original melody of the song becomes unrecognizable. Try this simple example of a chord substitution for the blues: Play a C chord for eight beats. Now take the same eight beats but play two beats each of the following chords: C Dm Em C. This is an example of chord substitution.

Left Hand-Right Hand

The piano is the only instrument where either hand can actually play independently of the other one. This cannot be done on the guitar, where it is impossible to use one hand without involving the other one. It is quite possible to come up with a perfectly adequate one-handed piano part without being concerned about the other hand. Experiment at the keyboard by playing one hand at a time. This will help you realize why playing the keyboard is so enjoyable and at the same time so unique. If you need any further evidence, listen to Ravel's "Piano Concerto for the Left Hand." As the title indicates, this entire piece uses only the left hand and was written for a veteran whose right hand had been amputated because of a war wound.

Try playing a melody with your right hand. It doesn't matter what the melody notes are. The point is that with one hand you can actually pick out a melody. One way of creating melodies is to find a melody and then set a series of chords to it. Another way is the exact opposite: Have the melody come out of the chords you are playing. Play a chord such as C Em/B F/A G, or some of

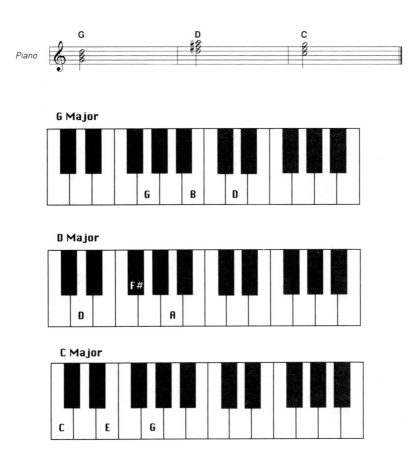

Figure 8-6.

the chord progressions that we have already mentioned, and see if any melodies emerge from the chords. (Note: Em/B means that B is the bass note of the chord. In other words, it's an Em chord in second inversion.)

Bass Lines and Pedal Points

A pedal point is a constant tone in the bass that continues to play through a series of chord changes, even though the bass note may not be part of the chord that is played. Pedal tones are usually designated as follows: Am/A G/A F/A E/A G/A. The note to the right side of the slash sign (/) is the bass note. If you play this sequence it will sound vaguely familiar to you because it is the

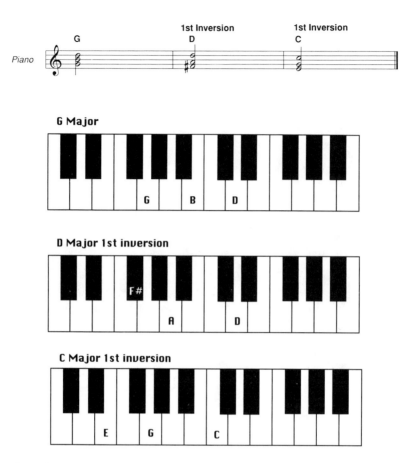

Figure 8-7.

sort of thing commonly used for television or movie music when the composer wants to create a feeling of ambiguity. Because the bass note is constant, the chord changes are masked, and there will be a series of unresolved chords that don't seem to have a particular destination. Pedal tones are fun to experiment with, but when they are used too often, they tend to create a feeling of sleepy anguish in the listener, a sort of "Is anything going to happen in this tune?" feeling. Jim Webb is a master at using pedal tones, and if you examine the music for some of his songs, like "By the Time I Get to Phoenix," you will find ample and well-executed examples of pedal tones.

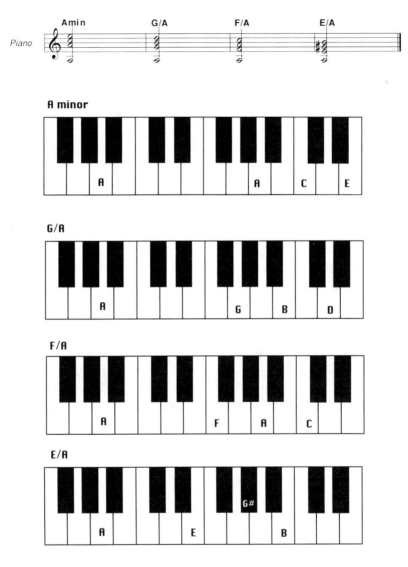

Figure 8-8.

If you play the Am G F E chord progression, you may find that once again a melody will come forth out of the chord sequences you are playing. Think of pedal tones as yet another color in your musical artist's palette (Figure 8-8).

TONE AS A WAY OF DEVELOPING CRAFT

As a keyboard player, you will want to develop every possible resource to keep your melodies as fresh as possible. If you are playing an acoustic piano, use the pedals to sustain notes, or to make musical phrases louder or softer, more or less intense. If you are working with an electronic keyboard, try to explore every possible tonal and rhythmic resource that your particular keyboard possesses, whether it is a prepatched sound or one you come up with yourself. Use the drum patterns on the synthesizer in the same way. Try to write tunes that fall outside the styles you are comfortable with in an effort to expand your horizons. A useful exercise is to attempt to write songs that imitate existing songs or musical styles, just to see whether you can grasp the essence of these styles.

You will find that varying the tone and intensity of your keyboard attacks will actually influence the direction and motion of your melodies and enable you to find new musical directions. Often a musician's musical limitations are largely the result of his own lack of experimentation rather than a lack of talent.

One last suggestion: Use your tape recorder and spend some time listening to the results of your experiments. Some of them will undoubtedly be more successful than others. If you don't continue to grow and to expand your musical horizons, you will ultimately become bored with your music. There is really no reason why you should allow this to happen.

Chapter Nine

Creating Melodies on the Guitar

I f you are a keyboard player who doesn't play the guitar and you aren't interested in learning how, you may want to skip over this chapter. Before you leave this section, however, you might at least try to play a little guitar, because the sound and feel of it may take your melodies in new directions. Another reason to take a look at this chapter is that, if you play keyboards in a band that has a guitarist, it will help you understand the chord voicings that are available on a guitar fingerboard that don't exist on a piano keyboard.

GUITAR CHORDS

Open String Chords

The easiest chords to play on the guitar are chords that use a combination of left-hand fingerings and the open strings of the guitar. "Open" means that the right hand plays these strings without left-hand fingerings.

For example, play the E-minor chord in Figure 9-1. Place your fingers where the diagrammed dots are, in this case on the fifth string at the second fret and the fourth string at the second fret.

Now, with your right thumb or with a pick, strum across all the strings of the guitar. The sixth, third, second and first strings are all played open, but the left hand is fingering the fifth and fourth strings. Sometimes a chord is played with open and closed strings, but the player does not play certain strings in the chord. Take a look at the diagram of the D chord in Figure 9-2. Notice the X under the sixth string. This indicates that the player should not play that string. If you wonder why, go ahead and play it, and you will hear that the open E note doesn't sound good with the rest of the chord.

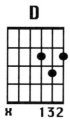

Figure 9-1.

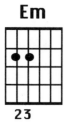

Figure 9-2.

Chords on Top Four Strings

Another common way of playing chords, especially in the higher positions of the fingerboard, is to play them on the top four strings of the guitar. This is particularly effective if you are playing with at least one other musician or with a band. The sound of the high strings is somehow particularly "guitaristic" and will cut through the sound of the rest of the band. This is equally true for acoustic or electric guitar, although obviously the texture of the sound will vary according to what sort of guitar you are using. What you will lose is the bass notes, because you are omitting the sixth and fifth strings of the guitar.

Moveable Chords

A moveable chord is a chord fingering pattern that can be moved up the fingerboard from one fret to another without changing the fingering of your left hand. Each time you move the chord up one fret, the chord becomes a half tone higher. In other words, a moveable C chord would be a C-sharp if moved up one fret, a D if moved up two frets, etc.

Figure 9-3 shows an F chord fingering, diagrammed first in normal position as a four-string F chord, and then at the fifth fret, where it is actually an A chord.

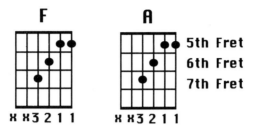

Figure 9-3.

In addition to playing chords on the top four strings, it is also possible to play chords that use the fifth, fourth, third and second strings of the guitar, but omit the sixth and first strings. Don't finger the sixth or first strings with your left-hand fingers, and also be careful *not* to play them with the right hand.

Try the chord in Figure 9-4, derived from an A chord. In the positions marked here, this is a C chord. To put it another way, this is a C chord derived from an A fingering pattern.

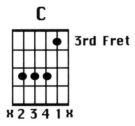

Figure 9-4.

It is also possible to play chords on the lowest strings, the sixth, fifth, fourth and third strings. This is somewhat unusual because the chords are bottom heavy, and on many guitars, when you move up the fingerboard, the bass strings may be out of tune if the neck isn't straight or the frets are not properly aligned.

Barre Chords

This leads us to six-string chords, or chords that use the first finger of the left hand to form a barre. In these chords, the first finger must fret all six strings firmly, and the rest of the chord is added just as it would be used without the barre.

Figure 9-5 shows a diagram of an E-minor chord.

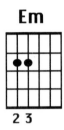

Figure 9-5.

Use the first finger of your left hand across all six strings of the guitar. Now add the E-minor chord shown above, moved up one fret (Figure 9-6).

Figure 9-6.

The trouble with barre chords is that, unless you are using very light strings, the barre will tend to make your left hand and wrist tired. This is especially true of acoustic guitars and is worse on twelve string guitars.

You can accomplish the same thing that a barre does by using a *capo*, a mechanical device that changes the key of a guitar by simply placing it on the fingerboard. For example, if you are playing in the key of E but find a song too low in pitch for your singing voice, you can place a capo on the second fret and you will actually be playing in the key of F-sharp.

Jazz Guitar Chords — Six, Four, Three, Two

One more kind of chord voicing you should be familiar with is a format used extensively in jazz rhythm guitar, most notably by the late Freddie Greene, long-term guitarist with the Count Basie Band. In this style of playing, your left hand deadens the fifth string, and you also avoid playing the sixth and first strings. The way you deaden the string is to let the fleshy part of your finger drape across the string so that it mutes the sound. Try the Am7 (Figure 9-7).

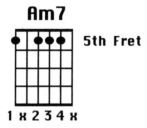

Figure 9-7.

In the jazz rhythm style, not only are notes deadened, but the right wrist snaps the chord, so that the attack is very clipped and rhythmic. This is one of the most difficult styles of guitar to master, so don't be discouraged if your initial attempts to play chords in this style don't sound very good.

To give you some sense of the differences between all of these styles, I have diagrammed the sequence G to A minor showing the open-string chords, the four-string chords, the barre chords, and the jazz style chords (Figure 9-8).

CHORD INVERSIONS

Chord inversions on the guitar can be found in two ways. Either you simply choose which strings to play in the basic chord formation, or you move the chord up the fingerboard. For example, take the E-minor chord. In Figure 9-9, I have marked which inversion is available, based on which string you choose to play.

If you play all six strings, you are playing the chord in root position, or with an E in the bass. To play the first inversion (G in the bass) you are restricted to the third, second and first

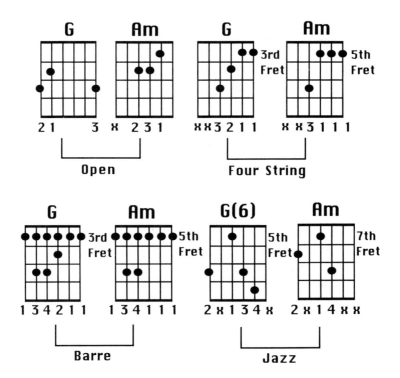

Figure 9-8.

strings. You can play the second inversion (B in the bass) by starting the chord with the fifth string.

Another way to play the first inversion is to change your left-hand fingering in a way that puts a G in the bass (Figure 9-10).

To accomplish the same thing up the neck, play a D-minor chord, moved up the neck two frets to make it an E-minor chord. By playing the fourth string, the chord becomes a first inversion of the E minor with G in the bass (Figure 9-11).

Figure 9-12 shows a second inversion E minor (B in the bass).

Unfortunately chord inversions on the guitar are not as easy to find as they are on the keyboard, and the sound is much less dramatically different than the sound of a chord inverted on the piano. This accounts for some of the difficulties that pianists and guitarists can have working together. Piano players need to understand that an inversion that is quite simple for them to find may be awkward to finger on the guitar. When the pianist is playing a

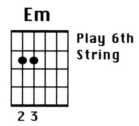

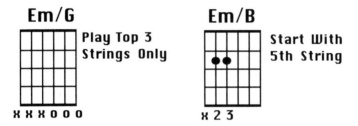

Figure 9-9.

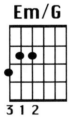

Figure 9-10.

chord inversion and the bassist is following it as well, if the guitarist is not playing the inversion, an unpleasant thick texture to the sound results, almost as if someone were playing the wrong chord. This will be particularly true if the guitarist is playing the part very emphatically on an electric guitar, against a loud electric bass line and a highly amplified keyboard.

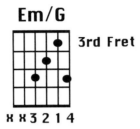

Figure 9-11.

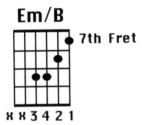

Figure 9-12.

Finding Chord Inversions

The secret to finding chord inversions on the guitar involves two things: First, you need to understand chord structure; in other words, you have to know what notes are in a chord. Second, you need to learn the notes on each string of the guitar all the way up the neck, from the lowest to the highest frets.

Since this is not an instruction book on guitar method, I have only tried to explain what chord inversions are and to give you a few examples of them. There are many excellent guitar instruction materials available in book form or on audio- or videotapes, and I strongly recommend that you look into them. If possible, take lessons from a teacher who understands the fingerboard and play with other musicians as much as you can.

Doubling Notes in the Chord

When a guitarist plays a big open-string chord, like a G chord, there will be some notes in the chord that are doubled an octave or even two octaves higher.

In Figure 9-13, two octaves of G notes are being played on

sixth, third and first strings. B is played on the fifth string and on the second string, and D on the fourth string. A different sound can be obtained by slightly changing the fingering of the chord. In Figure 9-14, I have eliminated one of the B and added a D.

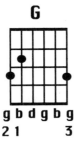

Figure 9-13.

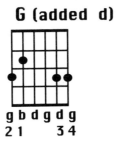

Figure 9-14.

Try experimenting with different chord fingerings. This will enable you to make your chords more interesting. Figure 9-15 shows some diagrams of different ways to modify a G chord. This should give you some indication of how to add extra notes to familiar chords. Remember, the final judgment of what "works" and what doesn't depends on whether a chord sounds good with a particular melody.

Adding Notes Not in the Chord

In addition to reorganizing chord fingerings so that different notes of the chord are doubled, it is also fairly easy to add other notes to chords to create a feeling of extra color or musical interest. For example, the suspended fourth is a chord very commonly used in all sorts of songs. It was particularly favored by Roger

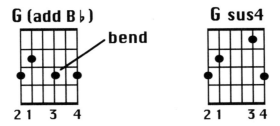

Figure 9-15.

McGuinn and the folk-rock group the Byrds. Figure 9-16 shows a D suspended fourth, often indicated in chord books as a "D sus4."

Figure 9-16.

The fourth in the suspended fourth chord generally goes back to the third of the chord, in this case the F-sharp found on the first string at the second fret. The suspended note provides a kind of ringing harmony, which adds a little dash of color. If you listen to any folk-rock recordings, you will often hear the suspended fourth, especially with the D chord.

Another note commonly added to chords is the second; in an A-minor chord, this is a B. Try the A minor added second in Figure 9-17.

Neighbor Notes

In the case of the suspended fourth and the added second notes, both are close neighbors to the chords they have been added to. The only true test of whether they will work with a particular melody is to try them out and see if you like the sound. If you have written a very active melody with many melodic leaps or

Am (add 2)

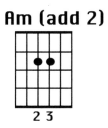

2 3

Figure 9-17.

skips, you probably will not want to use these added notes. However, if your melody is relatively static, the use of an additional touch of color in the chords can provide a bit of welcome depth to it. Avoid using any chord device too often, because what started out as a fresh and lively device can quickly turn into a cliché.

HOW CHORDS AFFECT THE MELODY

By this point you are probably thinking that all of this stuff about chords is fine and good, but isn't this supposed to be a book about writing melodies? Go back to the diagrams of G and A minor and play each version of that chord pattern. Try to invent your own melody over the chords. I think you will immediately see the point. For example, the jazz guitar chords will work with a soul or jazz sort of melody, or even a ballad, but the open-string chords will suggest a country or folkish sort of melody.

Each left-hand style of fingering chords will change the musical style of your song. In fact, using different fingerings in the left hand will even affect the melody itself. When you feel as though you are trapped in a creative rut, try playing one of these chord styles that is a bit unfamiliar to you. I think you will find very fertile ground for writing new kinds of melodies and for increasing your general knowledge of music and the guitar.

Pedal Points

A pedal point is a constant tone in the bass that continues to be used as the chords change. Even though the pedal tone might sound ugly or dissonant if played with a single chord, as part of a group of chords, it provides a sort of constant sound that clouds the harmony of a tune and leaves the listener with a feeling of suspense. Pedal tones are usually written as follows: Am/A G/A F/A E/A etc. The A is the pedal tone or bass note (Figure 9-18).

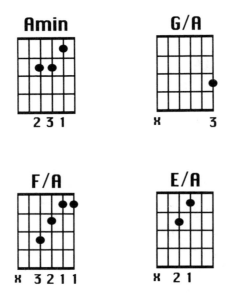

Figure 9-18.

Pedal tones are very effective when used infrequently, and they can be very effective on the guitar. Pedal tone sequences can be difficult to find on the guitar, however, depending on the nature of the chord shape that is being fingered in the left hand. They are particularly effective when used with open strings, as in the example above. Notice that the A note is an open fifth string that requires no left-hand fingering. Open strings have a particular ringing sound that adds an almost harpsichord-like quality as a constant tone against the chord changes in this example.

Bass Lines

It is quite possible to come up with melodies simply from bass lines playable on the bass strings of the guitar, with or without chords. Try the following simple bass line, diagrammed and notated in Figure 9-19: GGBEED GGBEED etc.

Figure 9-19.

As simple as this bass line is, you ought to be able to come up with a melody that will go with it. You may want to change from the straight bass line by adding some chords, so you may want to modify some of the notes in the bass line. One possible change is to drop one of the E notes, another is to add an E' at the end of the figure. In either case, this is a very easy example of the possibilities that can be opened up with a bit of ingenuity in using bass lines. As you become more adventurous, you can add other notes much as you did in modifying chords.

Two-Note Figures in Place of Chords

It is possible to substitute two-note chords in place of full chords. As with pedal tones, this will create a feeling of tension that may lead into a melody. I used the two-note chord sequences in Figure 9-20 in a song written about the late Karen Silkwood. Try this sequence.

Try to create your own melody from this series of two-note figures.

Figures like the introduction to the Silkwood song can also be used in writing heavy metal songs. Because you are leaving out the middle note of the chord, there is a feeling of uncertainty that lends itself to dramatic vocal performances. Although it is possible to play these two-note chords on piano, the effect is not quite the same. Every instrument has its own special qualities, and the ring of guitar strings is quite different from what can be accomplished on a keyboard.

TYPES OF GUITARS

There are many different kinds of guitars. The two basic types of acoustic guitars are the nylon-stringed, wide-necked guitars (classical and flamenco) and steel-stringed, narrower-necked gui-

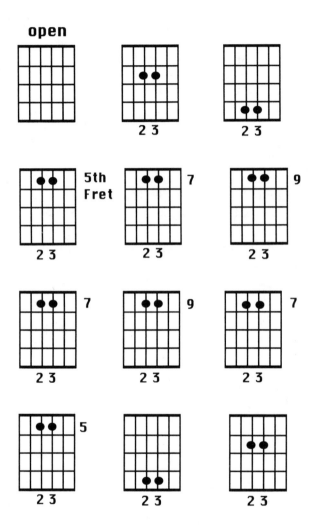

Figure 9-20.

tars. There are also F-hole guitars, which are ideal for playing jazz and are sometimes modified by adding pickups that allow them to become electric guitars. In the last five years, more and more nylon- and steel-string, round-hole acoustics are being made with built-in pickups that enable them to be played as electric guitars.

Electric guitars are made in hollow-body and solid-body styles. The hollow-bodies are semi-acoustic, and the solid-bodies will not sound if they are not plugged into amplifiers. Most players who become reasonably good guitarists own more than one guitar, and many own five or six. Other guitars that are relatively easy to find are electric and acoustic twelve-strings; slide guitars, which usually have resonators; and the dobro, the guitar's close relative, which is played with a metal slide. The dobro is a sort of acoustic pedal steel guitar.

Each guitar is especially appropriate for certain styles of music, depending on the sound quality of the guitar and the musical direction of your song.

RIGHT-HAND STYLES

There are many right-hand styles of playing the guitar that more or less match different styles of music. These right-hand techniques include:

- Playing with a flat pick
- Playing with the right-hand fingernails (used by classical and flamenco players)
- Fingerstyle without nails (used by many folk and country players)
- Fingerstyle with thumb and finger picks (used by blues and country pickers)
- Flat pick and fingers (used by country and some jazz players)

A Quick Guide to Right-Hand Patterns

This section includes a number of right-hand picking patterns. Try these at your leisure; don't try to memorize all of them at one time. As you go through these strums, you will probably find some more appealing than others, and some will provide more of a challenge. The suggested right-hand positions are recommendations. Feel free to modify them according to the size and shape of your hands and your technical abilities.

Thumb and index patterns. These are pretty much the same as the sort of thing you do with a flat pick. The thumb picks single notes, usually in the bass, and the index finger brushes up and down across the strings. Here are several examples to be used in 4/4 or 2/4 time:

Pattern No. 1: Thumb plays a bass note (sixth, fifth or fourth string), followed by index finger brush across the rest of the strings, from lowest to highest (fourth string to first string).

Rhythm: Even (two quarter notes or two eighth notes — Figure 9-21).

Thumb and Index Patterns

Pattern 1 (Rhythm Only)   **Pattern 2 (Rhythm Only)**

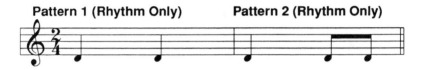

Figure 9-21.

Right-Hand Position: The right hand can be arched, or you can rest your little finger on the pickguard, or just beyond the sound hole if your guitar doesn't have a pickguard.

Pattern No. 2: Thumb plays bass note as in Pattern No. 1. Index finger brushes down as above, then the index finger brushes back.

Rhythm: Quarter note, eighth note, eighth note (long, short, short — Figure 9-21).

Right-Hand Position: Same as Pattern No. 1.

Thumb and index patterns are good basic guitar strums that can provide a simple accompaniment for your singing. The same patterns can be used with a flat pick.

Arpeggio Patterns. Arpeggios are sequences of single notes played by the thumb and index, middle and ring fingers of the right hand. They usually begin with the bass note. This style is typically found in classical guitar and has a soft, sensitive sound.

Pattern No. 1: Thumb plays bass string (sixth, fifth or fourth string). Index finger picks up on third string (up means toward you). Middle finger picks up on second string. Ring finger picks up on first string.

Rhythm: Four even eighth notes. Repeat the pattern in 4/4 time (Figure 9-22).

Arpeggio Patterns

Figure 9-22.

Right-Hand Position: Keep your right hand arched. Each note should be clear. If you are used to playing with a pick, it may be uncomfortable for you to use the ring finger at first. Stay with it!

Pattern No. 2: (Arpeggio for 3/4 time) Thumb plays bass string and first finger picks up on third string. Middle finger picks up on second string, then ring finger picks up on first string. Middle finger picks up on second string. Index finger picks up on first string.

Rhythm: Six even eighth notes (3/4 time—Figure 9-22).

Right-Hand Position: Arched, as in Arpeggio Pattern No. 1.

Arpeggio Variations

It is possible to create dozens of variations of the arpeggios shown above. To vary the patterns you can double the note your thumb plays using one of your fingers on a higher string; you can pause between different notes making some of the notes shorter or longer; you can start with the fingers instead of the thumb; or you can change the order of the notes. An example is to play thumb and index, ring and middle finger, in that order. These patterns will sound just a little bit different from one another.

Travis or Fingerpicking Styles

Another right-hand technique uses alternating thumb notes and works particularly well with country or folk music. It is often referred to as "Travis picking." This name honors the late Merle Travis, one of the primary influences on this picking style. As with arpeggios, you can figure out dozens of variations, but Figure 9-23 shows a basic pattern.

Delay almost imperceptible

Think of as

Figure 9-23.

Thumb plays low bass note (sixth or fifth string). Middle finger picks up on first string. Thumb plays high bass note (fourth or third string). Index finger picks up on second string.

Rhythm: Four eighth notes, but the first and third notes play right on the beat and the second and fourth notes lag just behind the beat. This style is used by such artists as the Indigo Girls; Gordon Lightfoot; Peter, Paul and Mary; and Chet Atkins.

Right-Hand Position: Usually the ring finger is rested lightly on the pickguard or just above the sound hole.

Variations on Fingerpicking

It is possible to fingerpick with the thumb and index finger alone, or even to use the right finger. If you experiment with the ring finger, you will have to arch your right hand. This is a challenge if you are playing at a fast tempo.

Strum Techniques

Strum techniques enable the player to provide rhythm along with the melody parts. Sometimes the melody is avoided and a percussive rhythm part is created by doing two things: (1) The player deadens the strings of the guitar with the left hand immediately after strumming the guitar. This is accomplished by raising the left-hand fingers off the chord immediately after you hit it. Another way to deaden the strings is to touch the strings with the palm of your right hand immediately after you have strummed them. This can be done at the same time the left hand mutes the strings or *instead* of muting the strings with the left hand. (2) The player actually hits the wood of the guitar with the fingernails of the right hand. This is typical of South American music.

If you are interested in these rhythmic strumming styles, I suggest that you listen to recordings of as many South American guitarists as you can find. It is easier to execute these techniques on nylon-string guitars; steel strings tend to break your fingernails if you play hard for extended periods of time.

Right-hand picking sytles greatly influence the shape of a melody as well as the general musical direction of a song. The more picking styles you know, the more variations will appear in your melodies.

One last note: There are many shapes, sizes and thicknesses of flat picks, and there are also plastic and metal finger and thumb picks, some of which come in different gauges of thickness. Experiment with all of these tools, because you can never predict when the very slight change of musical tool might lead you down an entirely new creative path in writing melodies.

Chapter Ten

Understanding Musical Styles

WHAT IS STYLE?

Defining musical styles could easily result in a book as large or larger than this one, but let's take a look at musical style and address the question of how melody itself is a component of musical style. Along with the elements of rhythm, harmony and melody, certain musical characteristics seem to define the nature of specific musical idioms.

The Blues

Let's take the blues as an example of a specific and well-documented musical style. What are the musical characteristics of the blues?

1. A specific scale is used for most blues. Instead of the C-major scale, CDEFGABC, the blues scale is CDEb FGABbC. The third and seventh notes of the scale are flatted or lowered a half step.

2. Most blues, especially older styles, have a lyric and musical format that consists of three lines. It breaks down like this: The first line is a statement; the second line repeats the music and lyrics of the first line, with possibly the suggestion of an answer and the third line concludes the thought set up in the first two lines. It has a different tune from the first two lines.

Here is an example of a blues lyric:

I never get a letter, never get a letter from you,
You know I never get a letter, never get a letter from you,
I still seem to love you, no matter what you say or do.

Notice the slight variation between lines one and two. Singers like Ray Charles may play with the words by throwing in little vocal phrases or mannerisms, like "well now," "whoa" or "yeah yeah," as though they are actually speaking to the listener. So another aspect of the blues is a direct and almost conversational style, as though the singer were actually sitting in the room with the listener.

Traditional blues generally had twelve bars of music played in 4/4 time. However, if you go back and listen to blues by such traditional singers as Blind Lemon Jefferson or Lightning Hopkins, you will find that some of their verses contain extra beats or even extra whole bars of music. The form of a specific musical style is rarely as rigid as the way the style is defined by music critics, or for that matter by anyone else who tries to analyze and classify music. In other words, there are aspects of style that are internal, that are part of the idiom, and that enable a particular performer to transcend the boundaries of a musical style and yet still be faithful to the essence of it.

WHAT DETERMINES STYLE?

Each musical style has its own particular logic or sets of musical or lyric conventions. Below is a brief discussion of stylistic mannerisms correlated with some examples of contemporary musical styles:

1. Does the style have specific vocal sounds or other unusual qualities such as blues notes, yodels or use of the falsetto voice? Blues notes are typically found in blues and blues-influenced music, yodels are occasionally used in country music, and falsetto (upper register vocal range) is characteristic of gospel music but is also found in the work of such pop/rock vocal groups as the Beach Boys or Air Supply. In heavy metal music, many singers almost talk-shout in a very high register.

Alan Lomax, a world-famous ethomusicologist, classifies all vocal styles as open- or close-throat singing. Open-throat singers sing very freely and with great power; closed-throat singers tend to have a pinched vocal delivery that sounds constricted or muffled. For example, open-throat singing is characteristic of black gospel music, while traditional country music is often sung with a pinched, closed-throat sound.

2. What are the rhythmic characteristics of the music? Bossa nova (Brazilian) music frequently uses syncopation. In syncopation the rhythmic accents in the music fall on the off beats, the places between the clicks of a metronome, or between your foot taps. Heavy accents on the second and fourth beats of a measure are typically found in soul-influenced music. Rap music features such strong percussion that melodies are actually secondary to the rhythm.

3. Are there specific chord progressions or ways of using chords that identify the style? In bebop, it is common to substitute complex chords that contain additional notes for the original chords of a song. Chords like C7♭5 (C, E-flat, G-flat, B-flat) are part of the language of bebop (Figure 10-1).

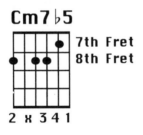

Cm7♭5

7th Fret
8th Fret

2 ☓ 3 4 1

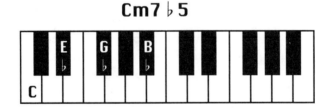

Cm7♭5

C E♭ G♭ B♭

Figure 10-1.

4. Are there certain time signatures that seem to be found over and over in a style? For example, 3/4 time is used in Viennese dance music (waltzes), and 5/4 and 7/8 time signatures appear in Greek music. African music often uses multiple drum parts that westerners find difficult to follow because there is more than one rhythm going on at the same time.

5. Does some sort of dance style define both the rhythm and the melody? Waltzes are always in 3/4 time and generally use

tunes that are pretty and light. Violent or dissonant musical contributions are not appropriate to this style, unless the musician is trying to satirize it.

Many South American music styles are intimately connected to specific dance beats or styles, and certain rock styles (from 1950s rock to rap music) are also connected to specific dance steps.

6. The instruments used in a piece of music may also partly define musical style. Think about the sound of fiddles or pedal steel guitars in country music, synthesizers in disco, horns in jazz, and strings in symphonic music.

The elements that define musical style include rhythm, harmony, instrumentation, vocal and instrumental range technique, dances and the traditions of the styles themselves. Innovative musicians may change the direction of musical style, but they rarely invent a completely new style of music.

Chapter Eleven

Arranging Music

THE DIFFERENCE BETWEEN A SONG AND A RECORDING

Although virtually all books about songwriting insist on the importance of a song as the essential ingredient of a successful record, the fact is that many record producers, music publishers or artists cannot "hear" a song unless it is presented in a form that is close to a finished production.

A song itself is complete when it has a melody and a complete lyric. The chances are that you have never heard a recording that contains these elements without any additional embellishments. Today's recordings contain numerous elaborations and extensions of the "raw" song. These relate to almost every aspect of the song itself: the rhythm or groove of the song; the harmonic structure (chord progressions found in the song or additional background vocal harmonies); and the addition of many or a few acoustic or electronic instruments to provide color, texture or variety. Besides these elements, the performer or her musical arranger may have added numerous "hooks" to provide the listener with further aural stimulation.

Because so many of today's songwriters are also recording artists, arrangers or even record producers, it is very difficult to separate the elements of a basic song from the embellishments added during the recording session. The songwriter needs to be aware of how songs become finished records, because on first listening, a song presented with a solo vocal accompanied only by guitar or keyboard is likely to sound dull and unimpressive even to many skilled professionals in the recording industry.

These days, many songwriters make very sophisticated demonstration tapes, or "demos," of their songs to play for people in the industry. These demos represent the sound that the writer would like to see happen when a big-name artist has selected his song for recording. There is no question that having a well-equipped home studio and a high level of musical skill at your command, or available to you through the services of friends and acquaintances, is a tremendous bonus to your songwriting talents. Even though it may have little to do with your own composition process, this is a reality of the contemporary music business.

Although it is true most of the time that the song is the heart of a record, we can all think of numerous examples of hits that are minimal songs from the standpoint of the inventiveness or talent represented in their lyrics and melodies. A great performance, arrangement or production can certainly compensate for a song that is something less than wonderful. Still, a really well-crafted song tends to be recorded again by other artists, which can inspire you to write even better songs. But no matter how good your song is, for it to have any commercial success, someone has to record it.

MUSICAL ARRANGEMENTS

Musical arrangements on recording sessions are created in a variety of ways. Sometimes "head arrangements" are used, which involves using information that evolves at a recording session by tapping into the brains of the musicians playing on the session. Usually the performer, a key musician in his band, or the record producer performs a sort of overall editing function in a head arrangement, selecting an idea here, omitting one there or combining different musical concepts to complete the arrangement.

What an Arranger Does

A more formal way to treat the arranging process is to hire a musical arranger who writes out all the vocal and instrumental parts and gives them to the musicians and singers. These musical performers then sight-read the music, sometimes changing it slightly under the guidance of the arranger and/or producer. Since most studio musicians are good sight-readers, this process happens in short order in a well-organized recording session.

One way to find an arranger is to consult the recording studio. Never hire an arranger unless you have heard some examples of her work.

Introductions, Fills, Breaks and Endings

Every part of a finished musical arrangement contributes to the success of a song. It is important to your career as a songwriter that you grasp all of the various parts of the recording process that transform a song into a hit record. As you develop an understanding of this process, you will be able to play your demos so they become closer to the way a good record sounds. The more you analyze this process, the better you will be able to work with other musicians and singers to improve the quality of your demos.

The *introductions* to your songs are extremely important, because if they are well constructed and unique, they will capture the attention of the listener from the first note or rhythmic groove of the song. Think of some of your favorite recorded songs and how you immediately recognize them when they are played on the radio. If the introduction to your song is boring, the listener or radio station music director won't bother listening to the rest of the recording.

Fills are brief instrumental passages that fill out and add spice and a sense of originality to the music of a song. They typically occur between a verse and a chorus or between one verse and another verse. They may also occur at the end of a line or when a note is held by a vocalist. Certain musicians have an amazing knack for adding very brief fills that bring a sense of color and movement to a song. Fills are an invaluable element to the success of a record.

A *break* is an instumental solo. It is usually placed about two-thirds of the way through a song. While a good fill usually involves understatement, a break is a chance for a particular instrumentalist to play a dazzling solo based on the melody of a song, taking the tune to another level. Breaks are often improvised, relying on the skills of a particular player to highlight a song and bring musical excitement to it. A good example of that sort of break is Eddie Van Halen's famous guitar solo on Michael Jackson's recording of "Beat It."

The *ending* of a song provides still another opportunity to bring more vocal or instrumental colors into play. This is especially true of a fade ending, where a musical or lyric phrase is repeated over and over, but often with variations that may actually be more interesting than the original melody of the song.

Vocal Harmony

Vocal harmonies add strength, color and general musical interest to a song. In certain vocal groups like the Nylons or Crosby, Stills, Nash and Young, the vocal harmonies may provide the essential sound of the group. In other words, the vocal harmonies may be more interesting than the sounds of a particular soloist.

Although we usually think of vocal harmonies as being a sort of background canvas for the lead singer, the harmonies can provide different rhythmic figures, other melodies sung against the main part, or use syllables instead of words to underline the rhythmic feel of a song. Sometimes the syllables created (e.g., "Do Ron Rons") may actually be what the listener remembers about the song's lyric, rather than the actual words.

Many of these vocal parts are ad-libbed in recording sessions by the background singers. There are many background singers who seem to have a natural ability to create these parts instantaneously. It is also possible to hire a music arranger to write these parts out, but this will require that the singers be able to read the music at sight.

In addition to the role of vocal harmonies, it is possible to strengthen a song by literally doubling or even tripling a vocal part. This can be done by having the singer re-sing the same part, or the double can be done electronically by recording the original vocal onto another track of the tape.

Rhythm Sections

In certain styles of music, especially rap or any sort of dance music, the rhythm section parts may be the most crucial part of the song's appeal. The rhythm section is typically the drummer and bass player, with a rhythm guitar and/or keyboard player often included. Grooves can be created by live musicians, by electronics through sampling or the use of drum machines or other devices, or through a combination of live musicians and electronics.

If you are using a live rhythm section for your demo recording, you need to be aware of certain key elements that will enable them to work well together. In particular, the drummer and the bass player must have a sort of shared rhythmic concept in terms of overall feeling and accents. The bass player and the bass drum need to make accents together. Certain rhythm section players play very slightly behind the beat, and others play slightly in front of it. If you put a bass player and drummer together who come from opposing schools of thought on this subject, you will be in for a long and unpleasant session. Similarly, certain drummers have a tendency to speed up the rhythm ever so slightly. If the other players don't follow suit, you will end up with a very nervous-sounding instumental track.

If you are hiring musicians for a recording session, ask the bass player and drummer if they have worked together on other sessions and have respect for each other's playing.

Quite a few records or demos use samplers, drum machines or sequencers. If you are using a drum machine, get a drummer to help you program the machine so the patterns played are not too repetitious or colorless. Most drummers are going to understand how to create these colors better than an average musician or songwriter would. Sequencing is a useful tool if you have a small home studio with MIDI capabilities. You can actually create multiple rhythm parts and then bring them to a studio and re-record them on a multitrack machine. Again, beware of using cut-and-dried patterns that bore the listener.

Samplers are a means of using orchestral parts without hiring live musicians. These devices contain musical parts stored on computer chips that can be called up and programmed according to your own particular taste or musical vision. Many people will never know the difference between sampled parts and live musicians, but there may be a slight lack of instrumental color or sound that comes from the playing of individual live musicians. Also, presets on many synthesizers, especially the lower-priced ones, often sound like organs, no matter what the presets say the sound is supposed to be.

All of these electronic devices are useful for song demos because they present a cost-effective alternative to spending large amounts of money in the recording studio.

Strings and Horns

If you are using strings or horn sections on a recording, the chances are that someone will have written out instrumental parts for them to play. Once again, this is the role of the music arranger, unless you have the ability to write these parts out yourself.

Strings add an element of depth and sophistication to a song, especially on a ballad, whereas horns tend to add excitement and a jazz or rhythm-and-blues feel. Examples of classic string arrangements are Thom Bell's charts for many of the Philly-International records produced by Gamble, Huff and Bell with such groups as the Ojays and Harold Melvin and the Bluenotes. I particularly recommend that you listen to the Ojays' recording of "Backstabber" to get an idea of the kind of color and emotion that a well-executed string arrangement can bring to a song.

Musical Styles

The style of a musical arrangement often will place a song in a particular genre. The arrangement may well be of equal or greater importance to the lyric or melody in making this identification for the listener. The musical elements that enable the listener to identify the style involve elements of rhythm, the instruments played on the record and the vocal style of the performer.

Vocal style is certainly one of the key elements in making this identification, particularly if the singer has a strong style that immediately brings a certain musical signature to the attention of the listener. A Ray Charles or Aretha Franklin vocal would bring a "soul music" identification to any song they sing, regardless of the song's initial melody or the intentions of its composer.

Similarly, we identify a heavy rhythmic emphasis on a record with a dance groove. Drums on a country record, even a country-rock record, don't sound like dance-groove productions by L.A. and Babyface that involve multiple percussion and rhythm parts mixed in a very prominent way.

And the presence of certain instruments immediately brings a certain identification to a recording. Country fiddle has an extremely specific instrumental color, as does the slide guitar. A large string section almost invariably makes a song into a ballad in the ears of the listener.

Somewhere down the line, your goal should be to play your demo for a music publisher or record producer. It is important for a songwriter to be aware of these musical aspects, because if you demo a rock song without drums, for example, many music publishers won't hear the song as a rock song. Remember that many of the people who work in music publishing and for record companies don't have a formal musical background, so if your demo doesn't contain a particular style or groove, they will have difficulty hearing the song in the way you may have intended it.

There is a famous and oft-repeated story about movie producer Samuel Goldwyn that illustrates how people have specific impressions of music that may be erroneous or based on limited information. The story goes that Goldwyn was doing a movie to be shot in France and he immediately called the film's composer and insisted that the musical score would require French horns. Keep that story in mind whenever you prepare a demo of your song and wishfully believe that, "Oh, he'll hear it as a rock song with my acoustic guitar demo." Don't attribute a particular level of insight or expertise to someone in the business unless you *know* they have these skills.

THE SONGWRITER AS MUSICIAN

If you are a reasonably good guitarist or piano player, get in the habit of making your demos with little instrumental fills or figures. If you can do that, you will have a much greater chance of getting your songs recorded. Paul Overstreet, for example, is a reasonably good guitarist and a superb commercial songwriter. He seems to have that special talent for placing a catchy little guitar figure in the intro of his songs or between the lines.

Record producer Allen Reynolds, who produces Garth Brooks, told me he used songwriter Pat Alger on some recording sessions even though there were many better studio guitarists available. Reynold's reasoning was that Alger had lived with his own songs for a long time and had developed little guitar figures over a period of months. No one working in a recording studio has the luxury of devoting that kind of time to coming up with a guitar part. Reynolds also had the feeling that Alger knew and felt his own songs better than any "hired hand" would know them.

Try to develop your own ability to create piano or guitar fills, hooks or grooves. Listen to such writer-performers as pianists Mark Cohn, Herbie Hancock, Bruce Hornsby or Carole King, and guitarist-writers like Curtis Mayfield, Paul Overstreet or James Taylor. Try to re-create their fills and listen to your own playing on tape. In a little while, you ought to be able to figure out how to create your own musical trademarks that will help to get your songs recorded. If you get good enough at it, you may also be able to get work playing on the sessions. At a current minimum rate of about $250 a recording session, that isn't a bad idea.

Chapter Twelve

Writing Instrumental Melodies

O utside of jazz and classical music, the market for songs has always exceeded the demand for instrumental music. Nevertheless, films, television shows and the theater all provide a significant market for instrumental music. Since the 1980s a strong demand has surfaced for New Age and "New Acoustic" music as well. There are some instrumental New Age albums that have sold over a million copies.

Most successful instrumental music has specific melodic themes that people enjoy and remember, much as they recall the melodies to hit songs.

SUITING MELODIES TO INSTRUMENTAL STYLES

Specific melodic structures or devices may be especially suited for certain styles of music. The melodies found in New Age music tend to be rather "floaty" or abstract. Rather than a "melody" — a simple specific series of notes that the listener recalls — an entire figure of guitar or piano arpeggios may be repeated many times in order to convey a mood. In rhythm and blues, soul music and jazz, melodies often involve improvisational elements or attitudes where a melody is seldom repeated in exactly the same way from one verse to the next. This is not entirely an aspect of performance abilities, because the composer's plan for the structure of the melody will enable this improvisation to occur.

Jazz melodies are often quite complex and involve the use of numerous chords. In many cases these melodies are difficult for the average person to reproduce, because the average person doesn't readily hear these complex structures.

In rock guitar instrumentals, there is a strong emphasis on showcasing the player's speed. The composer must have a basic knowledge of tuning of the guitar, and of what is easily accomplished and what is difficult even for the advanced player.

In folk and country instrumentals, too, the ability to execute a particular melody at a fast tempo may be an important matter, but there is also some emphasis on the "catchiness" of the melody.

The fiddle, guitar and banjo are all tuned differently, so something that's easy to play on one instrument may be quite difficult to execute on another one. If a fiddle player writes an instrumental piece for his instrument, it may or may not transfer easily to the guitar.

Certain instrumental melodies are showpieces to demonstrate instrumental versatility. "Orange Blossom Special" is a fiddle tune that meets that description, and there are many similar examples. A tune like "Wildwood Flower," a staple of acoustic guitar music, is simple and easy to remember and represents the opposite approach—something that even an elementary guitar player can master.

If you want to write music for a particular instrument that you don't play and don't know very much about, you should study a method book for that instrument or buy one of the numerous books on arranging that explains the range and characteristics of that instrument. These books will also tell you how the instrument is tuned and what key the player will be playing in. For example, if you want to write a part for a trumpet player and your tune is written in the piano key of C, you need to write the music in the key of D. Trumpet is a transposing instrument that is actually pitched in B-flat, so a trumpet D note is a keyboard or guitar C. The transposition of music to concert keys, so that all musicians are playing in the same key, is a fundamental part of learning how to arrange and orchestrate music.

IMPROVISATIONAL ELEMENTS

In many styles of music, improvisation is a key element in determining the longevity or value of a piece of instrumental music. Improvisation is perhaps *the* key element in jazz, but it also plays a significant role in blues, folk, country, rock and New Age music.

One way to determine whether your melodies are suitable for improvisation is to actually try to improvise on them yourself. Look for the following factors:

- Is there a clear, concise melody to work from?
- Are there spaces or held notes in the melody that lend themselves to adding additional notes?
- Is it fairly easy to find other chords that work with your melody?
- Are there sections of the melody that require techniques specific to the instrument that you wrote for? For example, it is easy to bend notes on the guitar, but this is not possible on an acoustic piano.
- Is the chord progression so interesting that the player will immediately find a fountain of ideas gushing forth beyond the structure of the original melody?
- Does the melody clearly fit into a particular musical style so that the average musician knows "where to go" with his improvs?

INSTRUMENTAL MUSIC FOR FILMS, TV, COMMERCIALS AND THEATER

The music in films is always subordinate to the picture. Unlike pop music where the composer is free to choose her own direction in terms of style or groove, the film's action dictates the direction of the music.

The advent of technology has enabled the contemporary film composer to "preview" his score for a producer or director prior to the time an actual orchestral scoring session takes place. This preview is often referred to as a "polaroid" and it gives the composer the opportunity to demonstrate portions of a score for the approval of a producer or director, who may then ask for changes in the score. Because this prerecording was done in a home studio, the changes can be made with minimal expense. On the negative side, the time spent making polaroids can take the composer away from his real task of composing music for the film. This is particulary difficult if time pressures to deliver the score are tight, as is often the case.

The development of technology has also created unique and exciting opportunities for composers to create electronic scores for films. There are several commonly used hardware and software packages designed to aid the composer and music editor with the timing and synchronization of music to film.

Tempo

Not only does each specific scene of a picture have a particular flow or rhythm that suggests a tempo, the picture as a whole has a flow or rhythm that tends to set the overall mood or style for the entire score. A film like *Out of Africa* features expansive cinematography and a pace that slowly builds through the entire film. It is not only a classic love story between a man and a woman, but also a love story that involves the main character's feelings about Africa. These factors affect the concept of the score. Even the action scenes are scored in a melancholy and sweeping fashion. In a film like this, there is a tendency not to follow the action on the screen as literally as one would do in a film like *Lethal Weapon*. In a straight action picture, the composer's goal is to use the music to keep the action moving, even when the action on the screen seems to stop.

In both types of film the overall pace of the picture sets the style and mood of the score. It is essential that the composer always be aware of what is going on in the film. For example, if there's a car chase with a great deal of action, the music will need to be active with a fast tempo, and various musical elements will punctuate the action on the screen. If one car suddenly pulls out of sight and stops, should the music also stop? This would depend on a number of different factors, especially what is going to happen next. If the chase continues even though one car has stopped, the music might change slightly to reflect that change in the action. In most cases, you would want the music to remain active so that the audience will still have the feeling that the chase is continuing. Another way of dealing with the same situation would be to keep the music active so the score continues to build tension.

The style of a particular director, or the type of picture in production, may also affect the decision as to whether the composer should match the action on the screen in the film score. If the music follows the action too closely, it may give the picture a cartoon or comic-book look. This might work in a picture like *Superman*, and might even contribute to the fantasy aspects of the picture, but in a more realistic picture, this type of scoring might seem ridiculous.

There are instances when it might be desirable for the music to do the opposite of what is happening on screen. A good example of this can be found in a sequence from *A Clockwork Orange* when the main characters are riding at high speed in a stolen car. At first the music moves with the action, but as the car goes faster and faster, the music slows. This ultimately gives the viewer a feeling of even greater speed, even though the music is actually slowing down.

Melody

Many of the same considerations that govern the rhythm also hold true in determining what the melody should accomplish during a particular scene. Melody has a similar relation to emotion as rhythm does to action. For this reason, it is important to determine exactly what emotion a particular scene is striving to evoke. The composer then constructs the melody to help create that emotion. If you wish to underscore a sad emotion, a slow melody in a minor key will tend to suggest this feeling. To convey a heroic feeling, a majestic melody beginning with an interval leap of a fourth (C to F) or a fifth (C to G) can help to communicate this emotion. A feeling of joy can be evoked by composing a bright, perky melody in a major key. These are simplistic examples that should be tempered by common sense and instinct. Finding the right melody to effectively underscore a particular scene may be a little more complicated, but these examples will provide a starting place. As you work with these ideas, you will develop more sophisticated melodies for films.

Many composers use a device called a *leit motif*, a melody that represents a specific character. This melody is often repeated in the film score, but with different combinations of instruments, or played at different tempos or even in different meters. If there are two or three important characters in the film, it is possible to develop a theme for each one of them. In a film like *Star Wars*, there are themes for the heroes, the villains and even some of the comical animal characters.

The most significant composition in a film is the "main title theme." This is generally the first piece of music the audience will hear, and it will set the mood for the picture. This theme is also the glue that holds the film together from a musical standpoint, because it may be used in a variety of scenes. It is therefore important to develop a theme that can be manipulated in several ways to help portray different emotions. A well-crafted theme can be played fast during a chase scene, at a slow tempo to portray sadness, manipulated rhythmically and transformed from a "happy" major key to a "brooding" minor key. If the main title theme is a song, the same rules prevail.

The composer must pay special attention to the melody when a song is the main title theme. In pop music, a strong lyric or a great vocal performance may compensate for a weak melody, but in a film, the minute such a tune is heard without the lyric or the vocal performance, its weaknesses would become apparent.

Rhythm

One of the key problems in film scoring is to make a melody or even an entire song fit perfectly in a scene. The melody may contain the proper emotion but fail to fit the exact timing of the picture. There are several possible solutions for this problem. One is to change the tempo of the music so that it fits the exact length of the overall scene. This may work in some situations, but it also can adversely affect the way the music plays against the scene.

Sometimes slight alterations in a tempo will actually improve the way the music cue plays against the scene. However, when this does not work, the composer may find that "odd meters," or unconventional time signatures, can solve the problem. Let's say that a composition works well with the first portion of a scene, but halfway through the scene the music moves on before the action moves. If you extend a bar by just a beat or two, the music may fall into place with the picture. At other times you may have to resort to the use of something more unusual, such as 3/8 time or a 5/8 bar in the middle or end of a passage that was composed in 4/4 or 3/4 time. A skillful film composer will be able to work these techniques into the composition in such a way that the music seems to flow quite naturally with the picture without the listener being conscious of any rhythmic irregularities.

Commercials

When a composer writes music for commercials, the primary requirement is that a single line or theme be created that becomes identified with a particular product, "Like a good neighbor, State Farm is there" or "Stanley, we want to help you do things right" are particular themes that have been used for years by the manufacturers of these products. The challenge is to marry the tune to the words and to understand that the entire musical theme may run for only eight or ten seconds. Also, in commercials there is often a section called a doughnut, where music is scored at a barely audible level while an announcer speaks.

As with writing for film, the TV commercial requires working with the information on the screen. Certain products have established a happy image, an image of reliability, a "with-it," contemporary image, or an avant-garde, cutting-edge sort of feeling. A Volvo commercial that emphasizes safety and reliability is going to require a different type of music than a commercial emphasizing a car's speed or attractiveness.

Many commercials are fifteen or thirty seconds long. In television, a thirty-second commercial requires no more than twenty-eight-and-a-half seconds of actual music and/or copy, with the remainder of time representing the movement of the videotape. Obviously it is important to the advertiser that the consumer remember the product name and the advertising logo, so the melody must be constructed so that the consumer has that sort of instant recall.

In radio commercials, the lack of a picture makes the words and music even more important than on TV. Some commercials are used on both radio and TV, and some appear only in one medium.

In the largest music markets, the music for commercials is produced by large independent "jingle" houses; in smaller markets the composer may work directly with the advertising agency or even with the maker of the product.

Theater Music

Just as in film, music must play a subordinate role to the dramatic action in a play. Even in a musical, the music should not detract from the dramatic action on the stage. Unlike popular music recordings, theatrical music can exist in fragments, songs can be repeated, and mixtures of songs and incidental music may be used. Incidental music is instumental music used as background or filler for scene changes or other background use.

While musicians in film music are usually hired to fit around the needs of the composer, in a theatrical work the composer must be conscious to which roles may require more acting skills and which call for superb singing. A performer may be a wonderful actor but have a very limited vocal range. It is rare to find a performer who is equally skilled at acting and singing. In the more minor theatrical roles, the performers might be hired based on their musical abilities.

In the case of musical comedies, the composer, lyricist and the writer of the script are often three different people, but all are involved in the project from the very beginning. In this way, the work of the composer and the lyricist may influence the direction of the script.

When there are only a handful of songs in a play, the content of the lyrics and even the direction of the melodies may well be dictated by the play's author in much the same way that the director of a movie influences the work of the film composer.

Whether you are writing music for film, commercials or theater pieces, writing music to fit into other artistic mediums provides one of the most challenging and rewarding experiences available for a composer.

GETTING STARTED

In all of the mediums described in this chapter, the best way to get a start as a composer is to find a movie production company, advertising agency or theater company in your community. In most cities, the type of film work available is likely to be five- or ten-minute industrial films. These films promote a product or such things as a tourist resort and afford a young composer a good opportunity to learn how to write music to picture. Local advertising agencies and theater companies may provide you with a chance to get started in writing commercials or theater music. Consult the annual *Songwriter's Market* (Writer's Digest Books) for further information on opportunities for employment as a composer. (See appendix for information.)

Chapter Thirteen

Reading and Writing Music

Many books about music start out with extensive sections that explain how to read and write music. I have deliberately delayed presenting this material until the end of the book because, in my opinion, reading music is a useful tool for a musician, but not a required course of study that separates professional musicians from amateurs.

There were many incredible musicians like the Beatles or Wes Montgomery who didn't read music, and there are many more who can read music only slightly, but are spectacular players.

So what are some reasons why you would want to know how to read and write music?

1. It enables you to communicate with other musicians quickly and easily, without having to resort to the use of words to describe particular aspects of music.

2. It provides a language for musicians to describe what they do and to analyze other existing songs or musical works.

3. If you continue to develop your musical skills beyond simple reading and writing, it will enable you to write musical parts for players of other instruments. The ability to do written arrangements of your music will enable you to have your music performed according to your own taste. When you are unable to write music down, other musicians will make their own modifications to your ideas, adding or deleting whatever they choose.

Take a few minutes and go through the rest of this chapter. I think you will find that with a little bit of work and concentration you can learn how to read music. If it doesn't work out right now, come back to it at another time.

MUSIC NOTATION

The Treble Clef

Music is written on a musical staff that has five lines and four spaces. The names of the lines on a treble staff are EGBDF ("Every Good Boy Does Fine"), and the names of the spaces spell out the word FACE (Figure 13-1).

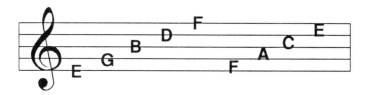

Figure 13-1.

The Bass Clef

All guitar music is written on the treble staff, as diagrammed above. The same staff represents the right hand of the piano. The bass clef is written on a bass staff (Figure 13-2).

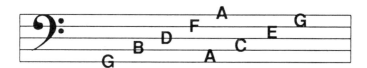

Figure 13-2.

Note that the lines on the bass staff are GBDFA and the spaces are ACEG. This is the staff where notes below middle C are written, the notes played by the left hand on the piano. Don't get discouraged if you find it a bit confusing to read two different clefs at the same time, one governing the use of the left hand, and the other controlling the use of the right hand. It will become more natural the more you practice.

Ledger Lines

Lines above and below the musical staff are called ledger lines. Figure 13-3 shows the most common ledger lines. Keep in mind that if you write many notes above or below the staff, an average musician may have some difficulty reading the music.

          C   B   A   G   F   E   G   A   B   C   D   E

E is the lowest note on the guitar

Figure 13-3.

Rhythms

In chapter six, you learned that a 4/4 time signature indicates that there are four quarter notes for each measure of music.

For now, the only other rhythmic information you will need concerns rests and dotted notes. The dot in a dotted note appears just to the right of the note. A dotted note extends the length of a note by half. In a 4/4 rhythm, a dotted quarter note is worth a beat and a half; a dotted half note will get three beats.

Rests are indications that a player is to remain silent. Figure 13-4 shows a whole-note rest, a half-note rest, a quarter-note rest and an eighth-note rest.

          Whole rest   Half rest   Quarter rest   Eighth rest

Figure 13-4.

Sharps and Flats

A sharp raises the pitch of a note. On the guitar it raises the pitch one fret, on the piano from one key to the next highest black key (except that between E and F and B and C there are no black keys). The key a piece is written in is indicated by the number of sharps or flats in the key signature, which appears right after the clef sign. Any song can be written in a major or a minor key, and Figure 13-5 shows what keys correspond to which flats or sharps in the key signature.

Figure 13-5.

Lead Sheet for "Go Tell Aunt Rhody"

The next page shows a lead sheet for "Go Tell Aunt Rhody." A lead sheet contains the melody and lyric of a song, with the chords written over the words. In addition to printing the music in notation, the music is printed in guitar tablature (string and fret numbers for guitar), and I have marked the keyboard diagram with the notes to be played in numerical order (though, you can't tell what the rhythm is from Figure 13-6).

Sight-Reading

Sight-reading is the ability to read music the first time you see it. It is a sort of automatic response that takes some practice to develop. Essentially, this is what studio musicians do: Walk in and read a written piece of music with few, if any, mistakes the first time that they see it. Naturally, if a piece is extremely difficult to read, it may require some rehearsal, even by skilled studio

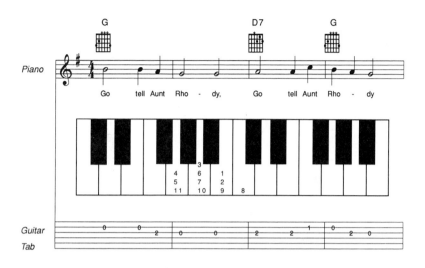

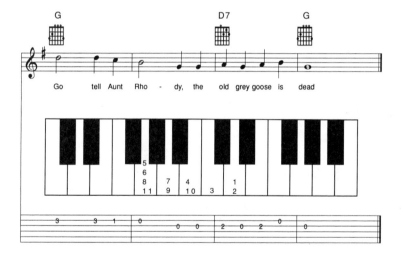

Figure 13-6.

musicians. Take a look at the written music of some songs that you know and play them through as though you were seeing them for the first time. The advantage of developing good sight-reading skills is that it enables you to read other people's music with minimal effort, or to write down your own music.

Sight-Reading Tips

When you see a piece of music for the first time, look at it from beginning to end. Play it through slowly, but *don't stop if you make a mistake*. Try to get the general concept of the piece before you look for any technical problems you may have in playing the music. The biggest impediment to developing sight-reading skills is a stutter-step approach. Once you have the general shape of the music in your head and fingers, you will have ample time to practice any section of the music that is giving you difficulties.

Another sight-reading tip is to pay particular attention to the rhythm. Nine out of ten problems in sight-reading don't come from a player's ability to play the notes, but from a lack of attention to the rhythm. Be sure you understand the time signature, establish a reasonable tempo, and pay particular attention to any melodic figures that are played on the off-beats. Many players who are quite comfortable playing syncopated (off-the-beat) figures cannot read these same figures when they see them in music notation. If necessary, mark the music with numbers $1+2+3+4+$ to help your eye identify which notes occur on the beat and which are played off the beat.

Try to do a bit of sight-reading of new music for ten or fifteen minutes each day at the start of your practice routine. You will be amazed at the improvement in your reading skills, and you will also improve your ability to write lead sheets.

Numbering Chords and Transposing Music From One Key to Another

It is a common practice to number chords based on what key they are written in. This helps to explain the relationship between the keys, and it also helps you to understand how to play a song in a different key. This is often a necessity if someone else is singing the song and has a different vocal range than yours.

If we take a C major scale, you will remember that the notes are:

```
I  II III IV  V  VI VII I
C  D   E   F  G  A  B   C
```

If you are playing a song in the key of C that uses the C, F and G7 chords, it becomes easy to visualize the same progression in any key, as long as you remember that the chords are based on the I, IV and V notes of the scale.

Below are the scales in all of the practical major keys, with the number of each scale note over the name of the note.

Key	I	II	III	IV	V	VI	VII	I
C	C	D	E	F	G	A	B	C
D♭	D♭	E♭	F	G	A♭	B♭	C	D♭
D	D	E	F#	G	A	B	C#	D
E♭	E♭	F	G	A♭	B♭	C	D	E♭
F	F	G	A	B♭	C	D	E	F
G♭	G♭	A♭	B♭	C♭	D♭	E♭	F	G♭
G	G	A	B	C	D	E	F#	G
A♭	A♭	B♭	C	D	E♭	F	G	A♭
A	A	B	C#	D	E	F#	G#	A
B♭	B♭	C	D	E♭	F	G	A	B♭
B	B	C#	D#	E	F#	G#	A#	B

Notice that if you are playing in the key of G, the I, IV and V7 chords will be G, C and D7. These relationships apply in any key and will enable you to transpose music quickly and efficiently.

NASHVILLE NUMBERS SYSTEM

In Nashville most music written for recording sessions uses the number system rather than musical notation. Instead of reading music notation, the players read the music through these mathematical relationships of the notes and the chords in the key.

Lead Sheets

A lead sheet (pronounced "leed") is a melody line of a song written out, with the lyrics written under the melody and the chords written above it.

There are several good reasons to learn how to write lead sheets for your songs. A lead sheet helps you to remember your own songs, and it also is a vehicle for communicating the correct melody and chord changes to other musicians. This is a useful tool at recording sessions or even for teaching members of your own band a new song.

The golden rule of lead sheet writing is that, if it looks complicated, then it is probably written incorrectly. The goal of a lead sheet is to make a musician of average skill able to interpret your song or instrumental piece. Writing lead sheets is not as difficult as most people think, although it does take a certain amount of time before you are able to do it at a reasonably fast pace. Try not to insist on capturing every single subtle nuance of your song in notation form. Other singers or musicians will probably add their own interpretations anyway. Figures 13-7 and 13-8 are examples of some lead sheets without the guitar tablature and piano keyboard diagrams. From now on try to read from the notation and to avoid using tablature or the keyboard diagrams. *You've learned how to read music.*

Soon You Will Be Comin' Back To Me

by Dick Weissman

Figure 13-7.

"Soon You Will Be Comin' Back to Me" is an AB-form song. Notice the following:

- The chorus is sung in a higher melodic range than the verse.
- The style of the song is bluegrass. The song actually was an instrumental piece used in a movie called *Beasts*. A singer-songwriter friend named Mary Flower suggested I write words for it, which I eventually did.
- The chord change G to F, I to flat VII, is characteristic of bluegrass music.
- It is doubtful that this song will ever get recorded in any other musical style, because the tune and lyric are so characteristic of the "high lonesome sound" of bluegrass.

"Look What They Done to Her" ("Karen's Song") is a more unusual song in a number of ways.

- It is an ABC-form song but each section is repeated twice, so that the bridge is not designed to fulfill its usual function of providing variations in a very long song.
- The A section of the song does not use chords, but is a series of fourths (the interval between D and G, for example). This is very effective on the guitar, which is mostly tuned in fourths, but is much more difficult to pull off with a solo piano. It is a device that is sometimes used in heavy metal music. The concept of borrowing a technique used in one style of music and placing it in another context can be very striking, if used judiciously.
- The chorus of the song is in a higher register than either the A or B parts, but is actually sung more softly. This is an effective dramatic device for a theatrical piece, but it would be unusual to use this technique in a pop record.

Modulation

Although a song may start out in a particular key, it is possible to change key during the course of the song. This is called *modulation*. In ragtime music, different sections of the music were often written in different keys. The same concept is used in most classical orchestral music.

It is also possible to raise the key of a song after each verse. This is often done in half-steps, so a song starting in C would go to C-sharp in the second verse, D in the third, and so forth. Most modern songwriters avoid these halftone modulations, because

Karen's Song

by Dick Weissman

Figure 13-8.

so many musicians who entertain in lounges have used this device to death. Sometimes a song modulates only in the last verse to achieve a dramatic effect.

It is technically possible to modulate to any key, but giant leaps tend to be jarring to the listener. In "I'd Love to Lay You Down," the hit song recorded by the late Conway Twitty, he modulated *down* from one verse to the next. Because his voice had a great bass-baritone quality, this unusual effect really helped the song.

OTHER MUSICAL MATTERS

As you continue to learn more and more about music, you will find that other aspects of formal music can be helpful to you in your writing. A *ritard* (short for *ritardando*) indicates that the singer should slow down. Ritards usually occur near the end of the song. They are not part of the melody, but can be an effective emotional device for emphasizing a particular part of a lyric.

Notes can be played or sung with different levels of intensity by musicians or singers. If a passage is marked *legato*, it means that the composer wants the music to be played very smoothly; if it is marked *staccato*, the composer is asking for the musician to play notes in a sort of broken or shorter attack.

Computer Programs for Writing Music or Other Forms of Musical First Aid

A number of computer programs will print out music. If you don't have a computer or access to one, you can hire a teacher or student at a local music school or college to write out the music for you. This will probably cost you twenty-five to thirty-five dollars a tune. In the major music business centers, this service is readily available, and many music publishers hire people specifically for the purpose of writing lead sheets. If you do hire someone to write out your music, make sure that it is neat and legible, and check to see that it is not overly complicated.

Further Aids to Study

The few pages presented here are not designed to enable you to play with the Philadelphia Orchestra. They very likely represent your first attempt to read and write music. Consult any one of the numerous music reading and theory books to extend your knowledge of formal music. The appendix lists a few of the many books that should prove helpful.

A FINAL WORD

The purpose of this book is to help you expand your melody writing in different musical directions. I've tried to cover the various characteristics of good melody writing, and to discuss such matters as the role of rhythm, piano and guitar styles and using modern technology to help you in your personal growth as a composer.

The best way to go about writing music is to write first and intellectualize later. In other words, don't be too critical of your work *while* you are doing it. The time for editing, rewriting, rearranging, filing or throwing away a song is after you have at least completed a rough draft of your work.

This book touches on subjects you may not have thought you were interested in, such as writing for film and theatrical productions. Who knows what opportunities may present themselves as you continue to write music? The best way to keep your own interest in music at a high level of energy and enthusiasm is to constantly experiment with different musical forms and styles. Listen to as much music as you can, and keep an open mind about musical styles.

FOR GUITARISTS

Homespun Tapes, at P.O. Box 694, Woodstock, New York 12398, is a great source for instructional audio- and videotapes. Happy Traum's Fingerpicking Audio and Video Series and his books for Oak Publications will help you in developing right-hand techniques. You may also want to look at my own *Alfred's Guitar Strums Handy Guide* and Mark Hanson's fingerpicking books for Oak Publications.

PIANO

John Mehegan's four-volume piano instructional books for Amsco Publications provide a comprehensive jazz piano course. Homespun Tapes has a *Dr. John Teaches New Orleans Piano* video. I've also found the Matt Dennis blues and ragtime piano books published by Mel Bay to be useful.

GENERAL MUSIC ASSISTANCE

There are a number of ear-training tapes on the market that should help you to recognize chord progressions and to improve your ability to hear various musical styles and patterns. I find Matt Glaser's six tapes (Homespun) to be especially useful in dealing with ear-training with a jazz focus. Most of the other available tapes approach it through classical music.

I urge you to buy some legal fake books, which include hundreds of songs by various composers. These ought to help you understand the range of melodies in the contemporary music world. *The Complete Beatles*, a two-volume set from Cherry Lane Publications, should be available at your local music store. Other fake books are published by Hal Leonard, Columbia Pictures Publications and Warner Brothers Music. They cover everything from turn-of-the-century tunes to the latest in rap, country and pop music.

BOOKS

There are many excellent books available on songwriting, although most of them concentrate more on lyrics and the business of music than on melody writing or musical matters. Below are a few of the books that I recommend.

> Braheny, John. *The Craft and Business of Songwriting*. Cincinnati: Writer's Digest Books, 1988.
>
> Citron, Stephen. *Songwriting: A Complete Guide to the Craft*. New York: Limelight Editions, 1991.
>
> Flanagan, Bill. *Written in My Soul: Rock's Great Songwriters*. Chicago: Contemporary Books, 1987.
>
> Lanfenberg, Cindy, ed. *Songwriter's Market*. Cincinnati: Writer's Digest Books, 1994.
>
> Sebesky, Don, *The Contemporary Arranger*. Van Nuys: Alfred Publishing Company, Inc., 1979. This is a book about music arranging that comes with recorded examples. It will help you understand the role of various musical instruments in the contemporary orchestra.

COPYRIGHT FORMS

Copyright forms are free. They are available from the Register of Copyrights, Library of Congress, Washington DC 20559. Form SR copyrights a tape and doesn't require any written music. If you can do your own lead sheets, use Form PA.

AUDIOTAPES

There is an excellent six-cassette audio series called "The Homespun Songwriter's Workshop." It is available from Homespun Tapes, Box 694, Woodstock, New York 12498, and features some useful tips on melody writing by hit songwriters Eric Kaz and Pat Alger.

INDEX

AA' form, 37
AB form, 38-39
ABC form, 39
ABCD form, 41
Accents, 19, 31, 44, 47
Adding notes to chords, 75, 78, 91-92
Advertising agency, 28
Aeolian mode, 64-65
A form, 36-37
Air, 3
Air Supply, 7, 38, 103
Area Code 615, 31-32
Arpeggios, 99, 113
Arranger (orchestrator), 29, 42, 107
Arranging music, 106-112
Art songs, 41
Audiotapes (recommended), 134

Ballad, 8, 36, 111
Barre chords, 86
Bass clef, 122
Bass lines, 12, 22, 24, 79
Bass players, 57, 94-95, 109
Beach Boys (The), 7, 38, 56, 103
Beatles (The), 30, 38, 40, 70, 121, 133
Bell, Thom, 27, 111
Bluegrass, 7, 129
"Blue Moon," 12, 44
Blues scale, 102
Blues song, 37, 45, 103, 114
Bossa nova, 104
Braheny, John, 28, 41, 134
Break (instrumental), 107
Bridge (musical), 39, 40
"Buy for Me the Rain," 36, 54
"By the Time I Get to Phoenix,"
    22, 80

Carey, Mariah, 33, 56
Charles, Ray, 47, 103, 133
Chord changes, 31
Chord progressions, 2, 12, 15, 17, 70,
    79, 90, 104
Chords, 14, 54, 56, 70, 73

Chorus (of song), 33, 37-40
Closed throat singing, 103
Collaboration, 27-29
Commercials, 29, 30, 118-119, 225
Composing in your head, 21
Computer music composing
    programs, 131
Copyright forms, 134
Copyright law, 25
Copywriter (in advertising agency),
    28, 29
Country music, 25, 30, 43, 93, 99, 103,
    111, 114
Craft, 11
Cut time, 47

Dance music, 111
Demo tape, 42, 57, 106
"Donna, Donna," 12
Dorian mode, 54-65
Doubling notes in chord, 90-91
Drum machine, 49, 108, 110
Drummer, 43, 48, 109-111

Editing songs, 11
"Eleanor Rigby," 3, 40
Electronic fade, 55
Endings, 107

Fade ending, 108
Falsetto, 103
Film, 28-29, 35, 115-118, 132
Fingerpicking (for guitar), 99-100
Flats, 60, 102, 123
Folk songs, 36-37, 70, 99
Form of popular music, 36-42
Franklin, Aretha, 31, 47, 111
"Frère Jacques," 36

"Go Tell Aunt Rhody," 124
Greek music, 104
Grooves, 43-53
Guitar, 2, 20, 83-101
Guitar, types of, 95-97

More Great Books to Help You Sell Your Songs

  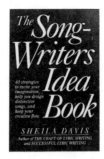 

Networking in the Music Business — Who you know can either make (or break) your music career. Discover how to make and capitalize on the contacts you need to succeed. *#10365/$17.95/128 pages/paperback*

Beginning Songwriter's Answer Book — This newly revised and updated resource answers the questions most asked by beginning songwriters and gives you the know-how to get started in the music business. *#10376/$16.95/128 pages/paperback*

Songwriter's Idea Book — You'll find 40 proven songwriting strategies sure to spark your creativity in this innovative handbook. Plus, learn how to use your unique personality to develop a song writing style. *#10320/$17.95/240 pages*

Making Money in the Music Business — Cash-in on scores of ways to make a profitable living with your musical talent (no matter where you live). This guide covers performing as a solo or in a group, writing music for the radio, jingles and more! *#10174/$18.95/180 pages/paperback*

1994 Songwriter's Market — Find the inside tips on how and where to place your songs in more than 2,000 up-to-date listings of song markets. Each listing includes submission requirements and tips from the buyer. Plus get helpful articles on the ins and outs of the music business. *#10342/$19.95/528 pages*

Successful Lyric Writing — Write the kinds of lyrics that dazzle music executives with this hands-on course in writing. Dozens of exercises and demonstrations let you put what you've learned into practice! *#10015/$19.95/292 pages/paperback*

- -

Comfortable Words
for Irina Ratushinskaya

Slowly the sugar dissolves in the tall glass of tea.
It is a hard oblong.

You can let go of your name, now, like a silver spoon
that looked after you. Little by little love will look out of you

as Kiev looks out of its windows at the unbelievable.
Three winters of barbed wire.

Try not to remember, try not to forget: you have inherited
the earth, your samovar.

For you it is obdurate as truth or Russia,
tongue-tied mother.

For you it is silver quiet.
Remote

Mordovia: slowly your heart will discover how to dissolve its
  oblong.

In March 1983 the Russian poet Irina Ratushinskaya was sentenced to seven years'
hard labour and five years' internal exile, accused of anti-Soviet agitation and
propaganda. Her crime was writing poetry. She suffered beatings, force-feeding and
solitary confinement in a 'strict regime' women's labour camp in the Mordovian
Autonomous Republic. In October 1986 she was unexpectedly released.

Wedding in the Port

Sometimes she wished they were travelling again:
at last they'd reach a big port on the brink of an ocean.
Simply, he'd put the ring on her finger,
and there'd be a priest at the ready, in the wavering light of the
    harbour.
She'd be certain: she would never betray him again,
would be kind to him always, and as tender
as the miraculous advent of spring.
She'd finally yield and consent, just to pay tribute
to his heart's lucidity, to an audacious passion
she could neither repel nor reciprocate.

Someone Else

It's drinks time, and we're gulping gin
and shuddering soberly.
It's summer time, the lenient evening
expands.

There's someone else I'd like to see
through the long window.
With enigmatic steps he'd cross the lawn,
then hurry up the marble stairs.
He'd cough as the door squeaked open.

He'd talk, resting his glass on his forearm
which would be tranquil, like a sleeping animal.
He'd stumble into stories,
and I'd curl up in the stony space
cleared by the sound of his voice.

Montecastelli Poem

He sang in another room
and in the silence when the song had ended
his eyelid fluttered on his hand,
his thoughts clustered in his side,
and his sigh forked inside me as a river forks.

■

The trees are rustling outside the open window.
I think I heard the same restless susurration
on the night she died, but I can't be sure.
There's nothing to do but light a cigarette
and stare at the eiderdown.

Nocturne

After a friend has gone I like the feel of it:
The house at night. Everyone asleep.
The way it draws in like atmosphere or evening.

One-o-clock. A floral teapot and a raisin scone.
A tray waits to be taken down.
The landing light is off. The clock strikes. The cat

comes into his own, mysterious on the stairs,
a black ambivalence around the legs of button-back
chairs, an insinuation to be set beside

the red spoon and the salt-glazed cup,
the saucer with the thick spill of tea
which scalds off easily under the tap. Time

is a tick, a purr, a drop. The spider
on the dining room window has fallen asleep
among complexities as I will once

the doors are bolted and the keys tested
and the switch turned up of the kitchen light
which made outside in the back garden

an electric room – a domestication
of closed daisies, an architecture
instant and improbable.

The Oral Tradition

I was standing there
at the end of a reading
or a workshop or whatever,
watching people heading
out into the weather,

only half-wondering
what becomes of words,
the brisk herbs of language,
the fragrances we think we sing,
if anything.

We were left behind
in a firelit room
in which the colour scheme
crouched well down –
golds, a sort of dun

a distressed ochre –
and the sole richness was
in the suggestion of a texture
like the low flax gleam
that comes off polished leather.

Two women
were standing in shadow,
one with her back turned.
Their talk was a gesture,
an outstretched hand.

They talked to each other
and words like 'summer'
'birth' 'great-grandmother'
kept pleading with me,
urging me to follow.

'She could feel it coming' –
one of them was saying –
'all the way there,
across the fields at evening
and no one there, God help her

'and she had on a skirt
of cross-woven linen
and the little one
kept pulling at it.
It was nearly night . . .'

(Wood hissed and split
in the open grate,
broke apart in sparks,
a windfall of light
in the room's darkness)

'. . . when she lay down
and gave birth to him
in an open meadow.
What a child that was
to be born without a blemish!'

It had started raining,
the windows dripping, misted.
One moment I was standing
not seeing out,
only half-listening

staring at the night; the next
without warning
I was caught by it:
the bruised summer light,
the musical sub-text

of mauve eaves on lilac
and the laburnum past
and shadow where the lime
tree dropped its bracts
in frills of contrast

where she lay down
in vetch and linen
and lifted up her son
to the archive
they would shelter in:

the oral song
avid as superstition,
layered like an amber in
the wreck of language
and the remnants of a nation.

I was getting out
my coat, buttoning it,
shrugging up the collar.
It was bitter outside,
a real winter's night

and I had distances
ahead of me: iron miles
in trains, iron rails
repeating instances
and reasons; the wheels

singing innuendoes, hints,
outlines underneath
the surface, a sense
suddenly of truth,
its resonance.

Dawn

Of your hand I could say this
a bird poised mid-air in flight
as delicate and smooth.

Of your mouth
a foxglove in its taking
without edges or hurt.

This of your ear
a tiny sea-horse, immortal
sporting in white waves

and of your eye
a place where no-one could hide
nothing lurk.

Of your cupped flesh
smooth in my palm
an agate on the sea-shore

of your back and belly
that they command kisses.
And of your feet I would say

they are inquisitive and gay
as squirrels or birds
and so return to your hand

and begin my voyage
around your loveliness
again and yet again

as in my arms you lie sleeping.

Cartography of the Subtle Heart

It has circles of light fragments
that shift endlessly, mandala
in a child's kaleidoscope.

It's roughly the size
of a human heart, centred in my chest exactly
as my heart is.

I am not taken in by that scarlet
harrowing the surgeons uncover.
I know the cavity they work in

from within my own body –
a vortex of hot winds
and bottomless dark. All my work

is to fill it with icons
shards of bright glass
in their desperate mosaic.

When my daughter
sprang from my body in her cocoon of light
trusting me utterly

it filled up with a syrup
warm and flowing but time
has returned it to crystals. I know it now

not as a wound that cripples
more than any other crippled person
lives in their damage

but as a doorway to the world
she came from, lianas of light around her
radiant and star-bright.

The Message

The message of the men is linear.
Like rapid pines they swarm upwards
jostling for space
mutilating their roots in the race
sowing a shade so deep
within their conquered space
little else can grow
and *growth*, they are shouting, *growth*.

But the message of the women is love
has always been love.
It is the luminous shining
under the substance
opaque stickiness of pain and grief
greyness of wanting, heaviness of getting.

The saints knew it also
the wisemen, the incarnations of God
Christ, Buddha
brought it as an astonishing revelation.

But we were born knowing it.
It is the circle of light we carry
at the centre of our bodies
knowing, and forgetting
see with our eyes in visionary radiance
when we give birth
and lose and discover again
season after season
because we are orchard.

The Dolphins

World is what you swim in, or dance, it is simple.
We are in our element but we are not free.
Outside this world you cannot breathe for long.
The other has my shape. The other's movement
forms my thoughts. And also mine. There is a man
and there are hoops. There is a constant flowing guilt.

We have found no truth in these waters,
no explanations tremble on our flesh.
We were blessed and now we are not blessed.
After travelling such space for days we began
to translate. It was the same space. It is
the same space always and above it is the man.

And now we are no longer blessed, for the world
will not deepen to dream in. The other knows
and out of love reflects me for myself.
We see our silver skin flash by like memory
of somewhere else. There is a coloured ball
we have to balance till the man has disappeared.

The moon has disappeared. We circle well-worn grooves
of water on a single note. Music of loss forever
from the other's heart which turns my own to stone.
There is a plastic toy. There is no hope. We sink
to the limits of this pool until the whistle blows.
There is a man and our mind knows we will die here.

Telephoning Home

I hear your voice saying *Hello* in that guarded way
you have, as if you fear bad news, imagine you
standing in our dark hall, waiting, as my silver coin
jams in the slot and frantic bleeps repeat themselves

along the line until your end goes slack. The wet platform
stretches away from me towards the South and home.

I try again, dial the nine numbers you wrote once
on a postcard. The stranger waiting outside stares
through the glass that isn't there, a sad portrait
someone abandoned. I close my eyes . . . *Hello?* . . . see myself
later this evening, two hundred miles and two hours nearer
where I want to be. *I love you.* This is me speaking.

Foreign

Imagine living in a strange, dark city for twenty years.
There are some dismal dwellings on the east side
and one of them is yours. On the landing, you hear
your foreign accent echo down the stairs. You think
in a language of your own and talk in theirs.

Then you are writing home. The voice in your head
recites the letter in a local dialect; behind that
is the sound of your mother singing to you,
all that time ago, and now you do not know
why your eyes are watering and what's the word for this.

You use the public transport. Work. Sleep. Imagine one night
you saw a name for yourself sprayed in red
against a brick wall. A hate name. Red like blood.
It is snowing on the streets, under the neon lights,
as if this place were coming to bits before your eyes.

And in the delicatessen, from time to time, the coins
in your palm will not translate. Inarticulate,
because this is not home, you point at fruit. Imagine
that one of you says *Me not know what these people mean.
It like they only go to bed and dream.* Imagine that.

■ ALISON FELL

August 6, 1945

In the Enola Gay
five minutes before impact
he whistles a dry tune

Later he will say
that the whole blooming sky
went up like an apricot ice.
Later he will laugh and tremble
at such a surrender, for the eye
of his belly saw Marilyn's skirts
fly over her head for ever

On the river bank,
bees drizzle over
hot white rhododendrons

Later she will walk
the dust, a scarlet girl
with her whole stripped skin
at her heel, stuck like an old
shoe sole or mermaid's tail

Later she will lie down
in the flecked black ash
where the people are become
as lizards or salamanders
and, blinded, she will complain:
Mother you are late, so late

Later in dreams he will look
down shrieking and see

> ladybirds
> ladybirds

Enola Gay was the name of the plane which dropped the Hiroshima bomb

Medusa on Skyros

in the parading square
  where glossed nations
    muddle
      in their young
    Eurotans
  a woman
whose bruised face
  bags
    and bounces
      when she laughs
    raises
  her bright brown
wig
  to the men
    of middling age
  who have been flirting
cool and kingly
  into her eyes
    into the deep stretched silk
      of her breasts
    and oh
  they go
ghostly –
  ai! ai!
    in the rattle
      of all the small
    ouzo bottles
  as she flaunts
their sudden skulls
  grinning
    in the bristle
      of her short grey hair

Freeze-frame

1947. That winter they talk of.
A winter like fists or wizards,

one or the other. The frozen lawn
pitted with porridge and scraps,

soup-bone fat with marrow
that the crows brawl over,

big sister buttoned up
with her puppet gloves dangling.

For background, there's the gable
where old Jessie lived,

a black wedge, and her
the witch of a hundred cats,

reading
your mind's eye, your bad eye.

1947. Small birds dumb as dolls
on the winter wire. I saw

their hearts like peas
and pitied them

that they were never born with tongues
to tell us things. I emptied

my wishes up chimneys, insisted
on reindeer.

Click of the camera fixes
my mittened hand to a blur:

the snowball's invisible as anger
shuttered in the nick of time.

My sister is too patient,
with her face like Petrouchka

and her snow-drifted smile.
She has no tongue, she says

nothing, thinks of Jessie
with the soot under her skirts

and the cats
wicked on the wall

■ ANGIE GILLIGAN

Household Dilemma

'If I may make a point'
she said
'It is this.
When I come home, tired,
from a hard day's work.
I do not wish
to be greeted
by a sinkful
of dirty
WASHING-UP'.
And she banged their heads
together
for their understanding.
'Vinegar and brown paper
and fie to you too'
cried the children.
And they went to bed sulky.
But the little plates
in the sink
and the big spoon
and the baked beany pan
chortled
and cuddled their grease.

BATHSHEBA

Bathsheba   in mourning
for her love   her dear one
places the sugar in the teapot
and sprinkles her cereal
with salt.

Oh he has become dark and unyielding
as a tomb of twenty horses.

At work she neglects
to stamp the post
and cannot invent replies
when questioned.

Night   he stumbles in
late and drunk.
He would be where he is not
and so makes gruff remarks
about the mounting dust
and who has fed the cat.

In bed he makes fierce nothing
to her.
Vigorous and brief.

Quietly   in the dark
she lets loose tears
the size of pennies
and morning   wears her tee shirt
inside out.

Mortgage

Mother mortgaged the piano
and the fine plush stool
to buy herself the new face
Father had always promised

It arrived, grim and pristine,
ivory teeth with bold black cracks.
'Lifes not all moonlight sonatas,' said Mother,
adjusting the hammers inside her head.

Music

There is a piece of music   I wanted to describe to you

> I stopped you touching me
> I thought I would scream

The music moves me
slow
melancholic
full
it winds inside my thoughts
my body

> what else but scream
> scream to break through

we moved inside a cloud
the hanging flower of music
of single moments known

> what is a scream
> a sound breaking through
> breaking through silence
> opening a line to the heart

there is a line now
from here to the purple mauve
hanging flower

scream is a word for sound   for whatever reason
full throated   luscious   I had to stop you
this is not pain   touching me
but aching set free   it was too much

> Too near the bone   they say

The music creates a single
curve, a multiple curve of
sound
like the mauve-white flowers

hanging luscious
quietly   mouth-watering
their size stepped down
to a single

                    scream

        now   now

                You touch me like the
                brush of a flower
                in the hollow of neck
                or cheek
                the hollow where the child
                kisses me
                soft   soft

                scream now

I could not scream
the shout never broke
            luscious
            quietly
breaking through from my belly

                I cannot reach this
                to live dreaming of all
                possibilities

                to say this moment is a whole
                curl of my tongue
                a throat sound
                articulated
                round

the brush of a soft haired
flower
grass
in my neck

                to reach into your moment's
                air is as soft as your mouth is cool
your mouth mirrors mine
tender you say
                who knows this scream

                              I move up
                              away
                              I am not ready to

break
full, luscious, break through
sound
throated

                              where will it go

who would reach me there

ode to my daughter's plimsolls
and the mess in her room

ode to my daughter's plimsolls,
and the mess in her room.
and her feet,
her toes one by one,
in my fingers,
ode to every part of her
the hair on her neck
the curl in her hair
the seriousness of her going to school
and teaching her to cross the road.
The time to write it
the time to notice it.
Notice her.
The time before she goes,
bright brown eyes.

She made me a cup of nettle tea,
'don't come out here till I say so'
and 'a touch of luxury'
she called it –
a green and gold tea cup,
and a saucer,
sipping thin green tea
she made for me.

The Ram

He jangles his keys in the rain
and I follow like a lamb.
His house is as smoky as a dive.
We go straight downstairs to his room.

I lie on his bed and watch him
undress. His orange baseball jacket,
all the way from Ontario,
drops to the floor – THE RAMS, in felt,

arched across the hunky back.
He unzips his calf-length
Star-walkers, his damp black Levi's,
and adjusts his loaded modelling-pouch:

he stands before me in his socks –
as white as bridesmaids,
little daisies, driven snow.
John Wain watches from the wall

beside a shelf-ful of pistols.
Well, he says, *d'you like it?*
All I can think of is Granny,
how she used to shake her head,

when I stood by her bed on Sundays,
so proud in my soap-smelling
special frock, and say *Ah,*
Bless your little cotton socks!

Looking for Camels

She followed him all afternoon,
although he didn't speak to her,
or even turn to watch her

climb the dusty road.
White moths settled on her feet.
She saw a mule
with ants inside its ear.
M'sieur, m'sieur, the children cried,
running through poppies
with silver knives . . . Boar droppings.
Snake country . . . *Of course I know
exactly where we are.*

He walked into the mountains
like a man who's on his way
to kill a dog. He didn't stop.
She closed her eyes to let a drop
of calomine run down her cheeks.
Somewhere sandy, somewhere soft,
that's what he had promised her . . .
She wrote a letter home in her head.
There's nothing here but rock,
she began,
*and his Hi-Tec Hi-Tec Hi-Tec Hi-Tec
footsteps in the snow.*

Crossing the Desert in A Pram

And when our ears fill up with sand,
and everything goes quiet,

lie down in the hood with me.
Pretend the sand is fur.

They'll find us with a little beeping tube
that finds rare animals. They think I am a bag.

The leader of the expedition
can't believe his luck.

He waves the bag about above his head . . .
Relax, I hear you say, *my dear, relax.*

In Painswick Churchyard

'Is this where people are buried?
I will not let them bury you'

He picnics among tombs
– pours imaginary tea,
a yew tree his kitchen

'You will live with me in my house'

Oh could I believe the living and dead inhabit one house
under the sky
and you my child run into your future for ever

Irthing Valley

a field of stones
a river of stones

each stone in its place

can a star be lost
or a stone?

uncountable
the constellations of stone

the wind lays itself down
at dusk
a fine cloth over the stones

the river is dispossessed
it casts up white branches
roots
shoals of white sand

it cannot oust its stones

between air and water
                           my shadow
laving the stones

Rain – Birdoswald

I stand under a leafless tree
more still, in this mouse-pattering
       thrum of rain,
than cattle shifting in the field.
       It is more dark than light.
A Chinese painter's brush of deepening grey
       moves in a subtle tide.

The beasts are darker islands now.
Wet-stained and silvered by the rain
       they suffer night,
marooned as still as stone or tree.
       We sense each other's quiet.

Almost, death could come
inevitable, unstrange
       as is this dusk and rain,
and I should be no more
       myself, than raindrops
glimmering in last light
       on black ash buds

or night beasts in a winter field.

■ LIBBY HOUSTON

A House

Two standing women are watchtowers
across the pillows of a bed;
wrestlers their eyes locked in a hold,

yellowed ceiling of a cold room.
Sleeper wake, within a breath, one whole
mouth. Sleep, let him, the other said,

do not do not cut peace from him
and both of us can place our love on him.
Wake and chance the pain, we can chance

your hate your leaving. One mother, one
lover, yellow light, an unwatched head,
will he wake of himself? Perhaps he is dead:

curtains pulled to, leaves tapping.
Into a dull girder equal force welds
their gaze, which can suspend him.

Judging Lear

Logic's hard lines have pressed
the flowers uncoloured, lace to dust,
danceable music stone:
three sisters, pared down
for the day's sacrifice, face
marble, a dear throne.

The awkward game begins,
logic in the chair, no blessing
asked and no grace said –
but grace can, creeping in by the old man,
plant there the bold gambit
he misinterpreted:

for though moved, inside and out, slow as
lead, alone, naked, right to the dark ground
where extremes as they meet
can cross, he is still a child (he also has)
playing counter to the rules the judged pair,
keeping the game open, did not cheat.

Fools, while he leans he knows, blocking that voice
silence has, let him, lest innocence lose
the match to logic and grace's
clinching alchemy, plead even to proving
insanity, rip up the board and smash
players and pieces,

parrying blame with a blame splendid as the
ancient swords that killed by name – as if
heaven's walls must mother turn gate
for the mere beating; or as if fixed in spite
to fall, by dragging down dearest one may
make it seem fate.

All alike stone, broken, the gold the sand:
the base emotions Plato banned
have left a radio-active and not radiant land.

Scales

I came in from the garden –
that moon, it was not hidden –
and all I had was taken,
or all I had was given.

My Illness and Other Animals

On days when I go out
My illness is a small, frail bird
With a broken wing.
I know if it tried to fend for itself
Alone in this city
It would perish.
So I carry it next to my heart
For warmth,
Buttoned up in my winter coat,
And try to make sure
No one jostles me.

On days when I stay in
Everything's different
It's me who is frail and small
While my illness is a large alsatian dog.
It sits at my feet licking its enormous paws
And growls at the door.
When it yawns you can see
Its pointed white teeth.
I'm glad of the protection
But I worry too –
It could frighten away
Even my closest friends.

Bi-lingual

Under these words
Are the hidden words
I can't say to you –
Whichever way I face
There's always another language
One you don't know

One from which I sometimes translate
Words for you
Words you sometimes learn
Painfully
One at a time
But even then there's a gap
Even between words that are supposed to mean the same.

Under these words
Are the echoes of other words
Woven in brighter colours
Spoken more loudly
A different nourishment.
If I told you that other language runs
Swift as my own blood
Splashing and bubbling
Under the surface of our conversation
Runs like a river underground
Crying and thundering through silences

You can feel it
If you press your body to the ground
If I told you I want you
To press against these words
Would you feel its echoes?

Whichever way I face
Even between words which mean the same thing
There's a gap
An enormous space
It is a world of its own
Dazzling me
Wild rock torn apart
By sudden waterfalls
Rich source of my longings
World between worlds
I've paced up and down it
It is the loneliest place I know.

An Abortion

The first inkling I had of the beast's agony
was the something not right
of her scrabbling, scrabbling
to still not quite find
all four feet.
Sunk again, her cow-tongue lolled
then spiked the sky, she rolled
great gape-mouth, neck distended
in a Guernica of distress.
That got through to me all right
behind glass as I was
a whole flat field away.
It took an emblem-bellow
to drag me from my labour
at the barbed words on my desk top.

Close to, green foam flecked her muzzle
and drizzled between the big bared brown teeth.
Spasms, strong, primeval
as the pulsing locomotion of some
terrible underwater creature,
rippled down her flank
and her groan was the more awesome
for being drier, no louder than a cough.
When she tried to rise again
I saw it.
Membrane wrapped, the head of a calf
hung out and the wrong-looking bundle
of a knuckle. Then her rope-tail dropped
and she fell back on it, steamrollering it
under her.

When the summoned men came,
buttoning blue coveralls over
the Sunday lunches and good-suit waistcoats,
the wound string around one man's knuckles

meant business and the
curt thank-you-very-much of the other
dismissed me.

Shamed voyeur, back at my notebooks again
my peeled eyes caught the quick hoick
of the string loop, the dead thing flopping
to the grass, the cow on her knees and
up again, the men leaving, one
laughing at some punchline.

The thing is this. Left alone,
that cow licking at those lollop limbs
which had not formed properly
with her long tongue,
that strong tongue,
which is a match for thistles
and salt-lick coarse as pumice stone
tenderly over and over again at
what has come out of her and she is responsible for
as if she can not believe it will not
come alive,
not if she licks long enough.

Outside she is still licking, licking
till in the blue dusk
the men in blue come back again
and she turns, goes quietly with them
as if they were policemen
and she knew exactly what she were guilty of.

Mirror's Song
for Sally Potter

Smash me looking-glass glass
coffin, the one
that keeps your best black self on ice.
Smash me, she'll smash back –
without you she can't lift a finger.

Smash me she'll whirl out like Kali,
trashing the alligator mantrap handbags
with her righteous karate.
The ashcan for the stubbed lipsticks
and the lipsticked butts,
the wet lettuce of fivers.
She'll spill the Kleenex blossoms,
the tissues of lies, the matted
nests of hair from the brushes'
hedgehog spikes, she'll junk
the dead mice and the tampons
the twinking single eyes
of winkled out diamante, the hatpins
the whalebone and lycra,
the appleblossom and the underwires,
the chafing iron that kept them maiden,
the Valium and initialled hankies,
the lovepulps and the Librium,
the permanents and panstick and
Coty and Tangee Indelible,
Thalidomide and junk jewellery.

Smash me for your daughters and dead
mothers, for the widowed
spinsters of the first and every war
let her
rip up the appointment cards for the
terrible clinics,
the Greenham summonses, that date
they've handed us. Let her rip.
She'll crumble all the
tracts and the adverts, shred
all the wedding dresses, snap
all the spike-heel icicles
in the cave she will claw out of –
a woman giving birth to herself.

Mildmay Grove

The railway runs down the middle of the road.
It carries my dreams,
takes me to music, museums, open spaces.
At Canonbury all is quiet.
You can see the back gardens,
braces-dangling men,
washing on lines.
Almost Addlestrop,
dust in the sunshine,
bird song and silence.
High walls hide the night train
at Mildmay Grove.
A trainful of waste, death trash
crashes through
night after peaceful night,
between high brick walls that wear slogans
for their thin protection.

Mildmay Grove is a street in North London near Canonbury station where the railway, hidden by high walls, actually runs down the middle of the road. This railway, the North London Line, crosses the Northern part of London from Richmond to Woolwich through mainly residential areas. At the time of writing the poem, it had been revealed that low-level nuclear waste was transported for dumping, on the North London Line at night.

House

In the night the house is thin and blue
It wants a blanket; it shivers
The windows are like snare drums
I wish you were here.
I wish you were on your way here
in a car going past streetlights
with your face going light and dark

and noises coming and going like molecules
your hands relaxed on the steering wheel
knowing your own mind
humming a tune of gentleness.
Then you would be here
exactly here.
And the house would be pink and bright
and it would be quiet in the house
the drums gone silent, the shivering stopped.

Double bass

There is a tree in the orchestra.
It talks softly, like a bear.
It stands holding its hat by the rim.
Bashful.
It has quiet conversations
with drums and paint brushes.
It is a humble instrument.
The people who play it are shy and serious.
They close their eyes to hear.
Sometimes playing is excruciating:
their fingers run up and down like spiders.
Sometimes everything is gentle.
They close their eyes to hear,
touch the strings gingerly.
The wood talks,
it murmurs like a person in their sleep
when you wonder what they mean.
It can't be fierce but it can keep a secret.
It looks solid
but it sounds sad sometimes
and stands on one leg.

Sisters?

A thingumbob stands in the door
'They sent me here to do the floor
They sent me here to do the scrubbing
Of whitewash dish and duster rubbing

'My feet are flat
My ankles swollen
My breasts are fat
And have a hole in

'I shall splash tears
Upon your floor
And pour my sweat
From ev'ry pore

'From time to time
I also sit
And drink my tea
Until I split

'Just call me granny thingumbob
– 'As long as you are satisfied
'Now I am off and to the shop
'I have got stitches in my side.' –

A thingumbob leaves through the door
– How nice to have a polished floor!

Spendthrifts

Patient   Painstaking
                Once a month
                They let go
And   Moonstricken

Another ovule
Tumbles into the depth

Taking turns   Like sisters
They unbraid
Their singular gift
No overlapping   In these sedulous
flanks
Miracle workers!
Anticipating   Great things to come
The balloon going up
Bearing   Who Knows?
A myriad of dots
For eternity

Who will praise you?
Working   Silently
In those hidden, deep mineshafts
Who will bless your surrender
To fecundity   Still to come?
Ah, who will curse?

Ovaries!
In this, too   True artists
Of the bodily constellation!

The Black Shawl

He who could pierce my grief
Has gone
Ogling, in foreign cities
Flesh he mustn't buy
For he is the provider
His scrapings the seedcorn
I peck

Poverty has honed
My five-foot-two body
Yet even a small house
May be empty
And only the North wind

Enters
Rattling the door

He whose arms were my house
Sleeps, unhoused,
Underneath big cities
Scraping a living
As though dead
Even a dog must eat!
    – Let the black shawl of sorrow
    Cover all!

After a visit to Portugal

Tribal Homeland

Here is the world's bitter end. Wind
is always blowing. Small mud houses cling
to the ground, their tin roofs weighted with stones.

Earth is trampled, here,
hard as brick. The bleak eroded hill
looks down, offers no hope, deflects no weather.

Across the waste comes a woman walking, flat
feet on cracked earth, blanket blazing orange-
yellow, bright as anger, loud as a bugle

under the threatening sky.
Now all sad music lapses out of key.
Something here is not going to die.

Dispossessed.

This man is called Obed. His surname
is in another language. You do not need
to know it.

This is his room. He lives here
by himself. He does not have
enough food.

These are his wife and children.
They live a long way off. He sends them money.
They do not have enough food.

He goes home once a year. They run to meet him.
Sometimes they cry, we are told, for happiness.

He comes back to his room in the city
where they are not allowed. They stay
in the hard land where nothing grows.

Does this discourage him? Who knows? He throws
no bombs. He breaks no windows. He
sends home money.
                        All his enterprise
is
    not forgetting.

In a South African Museum

The bushwoman lies
in a foetal crouch.
Her agile bones
hold no secrets.

Earth, shred by shred,
dismantled her. Wind,
whisper by whisper,
picked her clean.

The lady from Egypt lies
cocooned in cerements,
sealed blind and dumb, lacquered
with half a man's ransom
in peeling gold.
Her nose crumbles.

They lie, side by side,
awaiting the resurrection.

The lady moans
No one can hear her.

The bushwoman grins.

rite de passage
for Joan of Arc

it is always the quiet ones
whom the whirlwind picks:
Joan, thrust from dumb worship
of forests, God's fist at her back
the saints articulating
her bones to an iron
syntax, the ringing logic of mail

once she danced in wordless circles
of girls, hands linked, once she hung
leaf-loops, flowers in knots
on trees, her invocation
a green twist, a perfect O

then the vision plucked her away
and sentenced her: the voices
insisted she marry, and name
the new part of herself: war's
rhetorician, she stammered
embracing the angel, faint in his angular grip

Joan, after that meeting
returned to broken places: compatriots hurt
by her eyes'
pure androgynous glare; turning
her face from family, she forswore
silence and mother-tongues

yet, in the end, after victories
after the failed leap from the tower
she was trapped: ecclesiastical
grammar, the rope of deft priests, tied
and tripped her; she conjugated
their only available verb: I confess
to heresy; I am unnatural

they pitied her: duped
peasant, illiterate girl
and duly they sent her back
to the smoking green wood, the sharp tree
– lashed to it, burning, a human garland
poor freak (born too soon) she carried on
crying out messages they could not hear

Magnificat
for Sian, after thirteen years

oh this man
what a meal he made of me
how he chewed and gobbled and sucked

in the end he spat me all out

you arrived on the dot, in the nick
of time, with your red curls flying
I was about to slip down the sink like grease
I nearly collapsed, I almost
wiped myself out like a stain
I called for you, and you came, you voyaged
fierce as a small archangel with swords and breasts
you declared the birth of a new life
in my kitchen there was an annunciation
and I was still, awed by your hair's glory

you commanded me to sing of my redemption

oh my friend, how
you were mother for me, and how
I could let myself lean on you
comfortable as an old cloth, familiar as enamel saucepans
I was a child again, pyjamaed
in winceyette, my hair plaited, and you
listened, you soothed me like cakes and milk
you listened to me for three days, and I poured
it out, I flowed all over you   .
like wine, like oil, you touched the place where it hurt

at night we slept together in my big bed
your shoulder eased me towards dreams

when we met, I tell you
it was a birthday party, a funeral
it was a holy communion
between women, a Visitation

it was two old she-goats butting
and nuzzling each other in the smelly fold

Demeter grieving

Demeter has torn off
her yellow linen dress. Its fallen
ruffles drift along the grass.

The beech wood crouches on the slope
dark and shiny; its henna'ed mass
Demeter's hair, which hoods her wet face.

Demeter beats her fists together. Chestnuts
and oaks explode in rhythms of red
pink, russet. Bruises burst on her skin.

Demeter howls: wind cutting the reeds.
Only a mallard shrieks back
here, where the light is watery and thin.

Demeter wraps herself in a black storm
cloak. The afternoon pales, draining
away down winter's throat.

Demeter weeps:
her child's lost
Persephone's gone.

H ear t h

The hiss of flame before earth

Sometimes the ear listens
without thought

Unbuttoning the heart
we hear rain
from a wet coat
leaping and cracking
on stone

'During long walks'

During long walks
a small stone placed in one shoe
anchors the thoughts

Touching heartsease

my little pretty patch of wilderness
hung in the short term
between desire and passion
turgid with flowers –
broad iris buds,
drift of forget
me nots
mazy with sleep
drawn deep across rain
falling soft
warm silent
in a deepening green

today no edges are visible
colour melts back
this is a veiny petal
place
warm laved under tree
before sun
wet with translucence

we wait here without memory
swimming and drowning
touching heartsease
and approaching
honesty

Ruth's story, as told to Lilith

She was left with two sons.
Then they too died and we, their wives, strangers
to her blood, remained: Orpah and I, Ruth. My name
like anger, my temperament to match: passion
it would be called, if
roused to love or fury.

I don't know why I loved her;
simply to follow
Naomi was all I desired.
I even rose to the heights
of poetry: 'Whither thou goest,' I said,
'I will go; where thou lodgest, I will lodge,
thy people shall be my people
and thy God my God.
Where thou diest, will I die
and there will I be buried.'

Not so much did I promise her son
in my heart, my husband.

I have been a stranger
all my life.

We returned to Bethlehem
with the barley harvest, Naomi
calling herself Mara, she who is
bitter.

For bread I gleaned
corn in Boaz' field, dusted
golden sheaves in the setting sun.

Well, one thing leads to another
and Naomi's husband's land
passed to the hand
of Boaz, and I with it.
Such is the scythe that comes between women.

Naomi dances my child now, and
the line continues. Sheaves smile
in her iris eyes when she looks at me. They say I am
better to her than
seven sons had been. They do not
know how much I love her, more
than I could seven sons.

I am still a stranger.

Eve's commentary

Ruthie, I'd like
to give you the benefit
of my advice:

you should never get too
involved
with a mother-in-law.

Eve to Lilith

your mouth is a pomegranate
ripening in smile

I can see into the garden
my sister, my love

I have mixed you a banana milk shake
milk to make your bones strong
banana to make the adrenalin
course through your blood

your throat is a white pillar
I stand and watch you drink
I am swimming into your heart
your cheeks are a bed of spices
your eyes are bay leaves
your legs are pillars of marble

you are too thin
come into my kitchen

Lilith to Eve

you hide your face
let me touch you
your skin is soft as peaches
your hand a gentle lily

your shoulders are the slopes
of Lebanon
your arms the strong cedars
the mist of your breath
is home

you are blue lace
and spices

■ A TREACHEROUS ASSAULT ON BRITISH POETRY

The following pages bring together for the first time a large number of poets who began writing in the British Poetry Revival of the 1960s and 1970s. They are poets who resist limpet-clinging to past metrics, self-satisfied irony, the self-regarding ego and its iambic thuds. They are committed to imaginative invention and to taking up the challenge of a wide range of Twentieth Century poetics in Europe and America. They stand, in their differing ways, for resistance to habitual responses, for explorations in language notation and rhythm, for discovery without safety-net for the poet or the reader.

From Robert Conquest's *New Lines* and G. S. Frazer's *Poetry Now* (the classic 'Movement' anthologies, both published in 1956) through to Blake Morrison and Andrew Motion's *Penguin Book of Contemporary British Poetry* (1982), an assumed singular authority of a certain narrow range of British poetry has been maintained. Its characteristic tone has been encapsulated by Donald Davie: '. . . ironical in a limited way, defensive and deprecating, a way of looking at ourselves and our pretensions, not a way of looking at the world.' (*The Poet in the Imaginary Museum*, 1977). The resulting poetry has been notable for a language that excludes the unfamiliar and an adherence to forms which can be discarded once the poem has been academically gutted for meaning in the narrowest sense. Andrew Crozier has offered a penetrating account of this relation to form: 'Occasions are not felt to be trustworthy . . . Traditional forms are invoked not so much for the freedom they can confer but for support. They define the space in which the self can act with poetic authority, while at the same time, in the absence of assurances provided by conventionally felt poetic experience, they secure the status of the text.' (In *Society and Literature 1945–70*, ed Sinfield, 1983).

But there are important traditions in British poetry other than those promoted by the Movement and their successors. For those who began writing in the sixties, the senior figures were Hugh Mcdiarmid, Basil Bunting and David Jones – all poets deeply aware of and affected by the poetics of modernism. Gael Turnbull's pioneering Migrant Press was publishing Ian Hamilton Finlay and Roy Fisher alongside Americans Robert Creeley and Edward Dorn, as well as Bunting himself. Turnbull and Creeley travelled to Northumberland to visit this isolated and nearly forgotten major British poet, whose masterpiece *Briggflatts* had to find first publication in the United States. In the 1960s Stuart Montgomery's Fulcrum Press published Bunting consistently, along with British and American poets like Roy Fisher, Lee Harwood, Tom Pickard, Gary Snyder and Allen Ginsberg, whilst Goliard Press (later Cape-Goliard) made Charles Olson, John Wieners, Nathaniel Tarn, J. H. Prynne and many others available to British poetry readers, under the discriminating editorship of Tom Raworth, Barry Hall and Tarn himself. Michael Horovitz's *New Departures* readings and publications were also influential. His *Children of Albion* anthology (Penguin, 1969) surveyed a diverse and lively scene, other strands of which included the work of *The English Intelligencer* (edited by Peter Riley and Andrew Crozier), fostering non-narrative prose and a poetry that resisted personal anecdote, *Juillard* (edited by Trevor Winkworth) and Lee Harwood's *Tzarad*, which encouraged local developments out of the opportunities in Dada and Surrealism.

The poets included in the present selection were, with two exceptions, all published in the twenty issues of *Poetry Review* between 1971 and 1977. The Poetry Society, who publish the *Review*, had changed its previously anti-modernist stance after a large number of contemporary poets joined and elected a council to represent them. As editor of *Poetry Review* during that period, I could draw on an abundance of excellent poetry journals and small independent press publications, since the changes to be represented had been under way for sometime. With few exceptions the poets of the Revival continue to publish through small presses. Bob Cobbing's *Writer's Forum* publications, for example, have maintained a wide variety of poetries for many decades, including a range of visual and soundtext work, with a consistency no commercial publisher could begin to contemplate.

These poets, often represented here by recent work, are all explorers in language and form rather than repeaters and variation-mongers. They belong to no enclosure of school or movement. Being initially a Clydeside poet has involved no provincialism for Thomas A. Clark, any more than being a Scot limited Macdiarmuid's multi-cultural concerns. Bill Griffiths' knowledge of music, Old English and medieval literature, and London working-class life, all enrich his extraordinary originality of language.

Tom Pickard, in Newcastle, has made his poetry not only out of an inheritance from his fellow-Northumbrian Bunting, but through a knowledge of contemporary poetics gained by contact with European and American poets through his unique Morden Tower readings. Allen Fisher has used the South London where he was born and raised as his special focus, but this and other experiences are placed within the context of his work as a painter and an open field poetics, partly inherited and partly developed by himself. Barry MacSweeney is a senior editor on a northern newspaper, an expert on the working life of Newcastle in particular; Brian Catling is a distinguished sculptor; Iain Sinclair's *White Chappell Scarlet Tracings* (1987) has extended the range of the English novel and won new attention for his poetry. All these writers are internationalists who nevertheless live and work in the variety of British culture, whose poetry is created within that range of energies.

·In the late 1970s the Arts Council directly dissolved the editorial board of *Poetry Review*, incensed by our inclusion of 'foreign poets', particularly Americans. This was seen as a treacherous assault on British poetry. That ludicrous charge is amply rebutted by the work of the poets selected here. The issue is the enterprise of risk with intelligence and form, the passion and precision available in inventive language, and the pleasures of encountering such a field of energetic creativity. What remains from that period, and continues, is a legacy of creative innovation that has thrown up a number of important poets, encouraged younger writers, and taken as a whole, constitutes one of the finest and most challenging poetries in the world today.

Eric Mottram

Certainly Metaphysics

In certain descriptions I notice certain words occur
over and over unassailed non-argumentative benign
I am not afraid to play the part of Chinese emperor
and do not believe it is the easiest way to wisdom
there are some shapes we fill without entering into
for example language is one of the body limitations
for example my engagements outnumber my pleasures

That said I have begun to realise already
this is one of the key poems one of the description poems
outside this room in which we get extremely good reception
it will almost certainly snow although I hesitate
what appear to be certain floating fragments
in the air similar to the outline anatomies
similar to certain religious encroachments

'We are one with nature O!'

We are one with nature O!
don't go away rizla never
leave me
            for a start the golden
gouge comes wrapped in ampoules
of mild pain killer for mild
pain
        not as precise as some
social poems perhaps
        or miscellaneous objects

In another description
the sea rages against specific
bananas
            a form of lockjaw
keeps the peanut boats from ever

coming into harbour
                    'craw craw'
the gentle gulls remark
'when will it end?
say when'
            NEVER
says the intuitive arrow
NEVER

Infield Outfield

Who sees the curve as Robert Fludd saw it
or Zukofsky
                going back further
as did Hank Greenberg the Bronx hitter
moved like deer round the ballgame
smudging all the bases
                        (speaking
of childhood at this point
                        on loan:
memorabile) like music
which curves along the galleries
                            as though
we *come* to it so
                that is, the mind curved
. . . not mind itself but as in Duccio, say,
flat against flat green
as it *was* then, as he saw it,
not so much as concept however
but as matter . . .
aagh, that impenetrable slag and iron
and light as it cuts its way through
– the poem without shape –

or money, say, or the stupidity
of government, the long aimlessness
as that forest for the first time
approaching Hardcastle Crags

climbing high and time believing
it will lead to silky rain not as reward
but justice as within the avoidance of it
on macadam
                    just another road
and around here that means
Keighley
                or some other benevolence
like a blow to the tongue

An End To It

I have been playing around
with this language for so long,
like a Japanese war lord in Sufad,
snapping away at the fragments
of dead letters, who were once
muscular killers and eaters of succulent
fire.
        They mean nothing to me any more,
which is why I am in the grip
of contrition and arrogance, a city man
who can no longer tell the difference
between traffic and silence, who hides
from the inherited voices behind
the burning timber of houses that stain
the inside of memory and devastate
the shape of my room and the small marks
which made up the inhabitants
of poems never finished,
never, never . . .

But the grass loves me now.
It lays itself on my body
and ties my hands mercifully together
so that they lift not any element
outside their own tenderness.
And the sun is on me too
and the outline of its kiss

and the delirious wounds on my cheek
and the cold surface of their chimes.

Blue Crêpe

The sky lowers itself to my book
and your reading of it as blue,
Materia prima, are, as if the touch
was perfectly defined, the terminal
occurence when ceiling plaster floated
along the surface of crêpes normandes
steeped in biting calvados. I thought of you
on the channel boat, speculating on your arrival
in Honfleur to research the Boudin mysteries.
Such light, the blue wind bleaching shingle
to an almost undefinable white.

There will always be you in my mind mingling
with the discomforts such as tremble and decisions
about range, colour and definitions of space,
what I have to do each time I persuade
response, the gesture of feinting at
a tender but acrimonious embrace, like a pug.

And the reactive move you make of it each time
(I want to underline its dangers)
my pitch which never gets finished within
the perfection I know of, to which I return
with new ambitions and patrician idiocies,
excising, curtaining against the adjectival
and shadowed bird as I reach out for my black songs,
that music, and make flowers of them, moving towards
your marvellous doctrines, taking no one
with me except always you
or simply your own translucent symmetry.

Boschlog:
Being a Cartulary from
The Ship of Fools

1

How simply & how strangely
we move
across shadow figured events
that could only be caught in
contrast; candle boundary
or glass moon heated,
heavy lidded
we peer into our mug
of saints
to find a life, tensile
to icon
there,
thinking it might be used
as a rudder if our hands
can hold it.

2

The medium and the priest
bang the oblique table
spilling the fruit onto
the swimmers.

The grease from the belted
chicken slopes on their heads.

Nothing can be eaten,
seed and bone
splinter
the taste of ashes.
With sore eye teeth
we watch the drunk &

bluntly carve his wings
against the wooden prow.

3
Again penned by halflight
my script wavers in the tree
that still grows in the mast,
both are occupied by demons
or birds that jilt
& chip the
map
               braiding salt & fresh.

4
Today someone
heard a piano
whisper nocturnes
under the simian anger
of our philosophy.
We all became sick
& frantic
searching the lockers
for medicine, finding only:
tired books, tampons, hair pins,
dead moths, fountain pens and the smell
of a crossbow covered in blood and feathers.

5
One of us
is a witch
who gives
hag food
on a string.

6
He would be lashed
to the steering,
rat mad heading
north & leached

                              white
                              storm
                              echo
                              of empty veins

this captain of ours,
if we had one.

7

The moon if allowed
to enter
will blue
the swimmers
peeled to the edge
of our craft.
They could be helped,
pulled aboard or killed
but we distract knowing
they are white paint songs
of ourselves
and enviously
cast them to the tides
and sharks
                    sweet
                    as some unfound
                    sexual morphine.

8

Like our mummified wood
we saw the broken shaft
of a harpoon
cut open the water,
its leaves were white
like its shadow
that was lashed to us
fathoms below.

9

The bitch
who taunts
and gullies

our channels of desire is
scratching the floor
of the boat, the sound
of breaking nails ignites
the owl above us,
seeing perhaps victim there,
we know better
it is only a prayer
to the grave
she will never enter.

10
Here against
our lives the fish
will not swim, but
try to enter the blood
directly
> sad flag
> to hang varicose
> from the withered nerve
> our mast
> chanted erect
> from the melancholy sway of bodies.

11
Run aground
to hear
seabirds
stitch voice
the folded tons
> mudbrain
> revealed,
> humped clear by saline
> lodging us tumour
> in a cold crease
> of perception.

12
He gleams
in pearl waste
& sips their collapsed
juices.

13
Kiloed beyond
nuzzle scan
but there,
moist shadow sound;
a newspaper urine ball

> an error,
> stamped into
> our leaking side

but growing
in its own
mutter.

14
If ever now
on this bearing
we veer, grace
will be shrouded in our dusk.
Alas poor carpenter, talented
in obsequious olive and sandalwood
cannot give or nail
a parched vinegar
light
to signal
the sharpness
of our turn.

15
Warm

> the luminous wind
> signatures
> the oriflamme:
> woven fire
> over a waveless
> illusion

> > sea.

■ THOMAS A. CLARK

from Sixteen Sonnets

■

as I walked out early
into the order of things
the world was up before me
as I stepped out bravely
the very camber of the road
turned me to its purpose
it was on a morning early
I put design behind me
hear us and deliver us
to the hazard of the road
in all the anonymous places
where the couch grass grows
watch over us and keep us
to the temper of the road

■

what the day weaves
the night unravels
here in the forest
all roads run wrong
what the weaver knows
the forest soon undoes
all roads lose themselves
in the warp and woof
somewhere in the poem
a stag should enter
but the stag is lost at
a crossroad of sunbeams
what the poem weaves
the forest will unravel

■

our boat touches the bank
among a scent of bruised sedge
the startled heron rises
broken from his austerities

we are in a proud country
where stone chats to stone
where furze pods crackle open
grey grouse and curlews inform
keep well below the horizon
your flesh spare upon the bone
trust to flintlock and sabre
bed down among the heather
the wild fiddle music of the air
tuneless will find you anywhere
■

each colour sits beside
a colour of equal repose
so that each colour shines
with its singular lustre
at the edge of each colour
another colour is poised
so that each colour present
is brought into the present
yet the present is not its cause
each colour dwells in its place
neither turning towards or away
from its immediate neighbour
colour sits beside colour
all together in good order
■

the stag comes home at last
to the dappled clearing
grazes the small grasses
while his velvet peels
throw wide the study window
let air play about the poem
the dim glade of the heart
is pierced by a sunbeam
the stag finds sluggish streams
a bee buzzes about the vowels
brushes against the consonants
and an exchange takes place
animals steal out of the forest
where we have cleared a space

from Twenty Poems

■

in those first days
there was no distinction
between percept and concept

no bridges spanned the waters
no coulter broke the clay

the people knew nothing
of deduction or inference
they did nothing in particular
went nowhere in particular

wild horses roamed
over boundless pasture
kicking their heels or grazing
the soft blue grass

there was no division
among the golden hours
there was no equation
between apples and stars

the third was still a discord
the people lived in concord
and song was accessory to dance

■

high piled cumulus

a field of snow
where no shadow falls
melting as we speak of it

and now the deer climb
out of the straths and glens
to graze the open mountain

it is the birth of time
of least willow, tufted sedge
and the starry saxifrage

the air is the sport of hours
a lightness may be yours
out on the rubicon of rhyme

vapour rises from the moss
rivers tear themselves loose

the flute of the ring-ouzel
lingering melts
like a snow crystal

■

under a full moon
the small mammals
find their way

by paths well hidden
from the light of day
through wild gardens
over unkempt lawns

the small wayfarers
that trace on the terrace
silver lines

camouflaged with candour
or bristling with spines
braving the predatory
pockets of shadow

they come to the proferred
saucer of light

Worm

rust	moth	fungus	mildew
dryrot	canker	maggot	WORM
wriggle	coil	roll curl	buckle
twine twirl	twist wind	spiral	WORM
hunt fish	ferret	root out	fathom
unearth	disinter	grub up	WORM
ingratiate	insinuate	intrude	invade
permeate	interpenetrate	infiltrate	WORM
crumbling	mouldering	rotted	blighted
decayed	corrupted	tainted	WORM
corpse	carcass	cadaver	carrion
dust earth	ashes	mummy	WORM

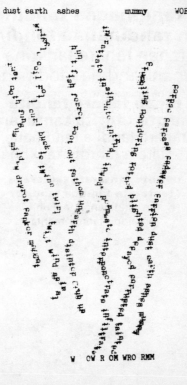

W OW R OM WRO RMM

147

tan

tan tandinanan tandinane
tanan tandina tandinane
tanare tandita tandinane
tantarata tandina tandita

tan tandinanan tandina
tanan tanare tandita
tantarata tanrotu tankrina
tan tandinanan tankrina

tanan tanare tankrina
tanrotu tanrita tantarane
tanrotu tantarata tantarane
tantarane tanrita tanrita

tan tandinanan tandinane
tan tandinanan tandina
tanan tanare tankrina
tanan tandina tandinane

tanan tanare tandita
tanrotu tanrita tantarane
tanare tandita tandinane
tantarata tanrotu tankrina

tanrotu tantarata tantarane
tantarata tandina tandita
tan tandinanan tankrina
tantarane tanrita tanrita

Alphabet of Fishes

askal	barfas	canker	dranick
ehoc	frango	girrock	hump
illeck	janny	kelnak	lagatta
mehal	niflin	owl	pothrick
quin	rauner	silliwhig	talver
valsen	wiggle	yawn	zart

from Three Poems for Voice and Movement

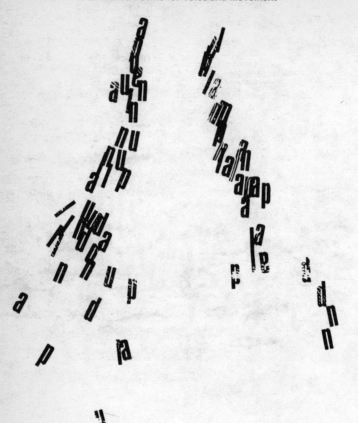

Blotting Music
from Song Signals, 1971

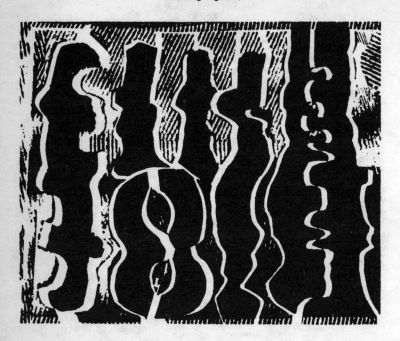

■ ANDREW CROZIER

from High Zero

■

All of your ideas
                   begin life again
when you wake up
   your faithful servants, already at work
   in their accustomed places
like clothes neatly folded on the chair
which no one else could wear
in quite your way, grown fat
on the success of small ambitions
which you dream about
and can't outgrow
like permanent convalescence
there's no escaping them.
The way your friends remember you
clips over like paper
cut to fit a larger model
they never seem to change
the way you do, their thoughts
were your thoughts, and they note
your points like rival connoisseurs.
Drop a coin into the slot
and a kind of truth comes out
I SPEAK YOUR MIND
one foot cheating on the ground.
■

Then in the smoke
          the extinction of light
whatever follows is masked
by tears that smart the eyes
like blurrings of hot fat:
the picture of this is over-exposed. But
from its opaque depth there emerges
a counterfeit sadness
         tender as regret, wet

as undried tears
a little smudged and reddened
a little rubbed-in message
that'll teach you. The darkness lifts
towards the horizon and stops
at the water's edge
in its deepest tone, over the rim
where all at once the sky lightens
perceptibly out of touch
like a disappearing vessel
dipping its flag conveniently,
Farewell. Whoever else
would see it quite like that
so empty just the place
to sink in out of sight.

■

All that it should be
                    the night long white
glow of insomnia upon glass

cloudlike as the brain where it meets
the narrow band of light clear as dust
in the eye the material world dilates

in shock, rare gases leave their stain to
register that brief catastrophe
across the stomach wall

no other aftermath
a path to the downstairs door
by way of the kitchen window

where the animals all come in
to feed in turn, nudging their plates
over the vinolay in silence

no less heavy than their sleep
and just as fugitive their days
go haunting the neighbours' gardens

animating the shadowless grass
which gleams by night in parched
neglect just covering the earth

like a tattered quilt and
patched with weeds it barely
holds the heat of the day.
■

In the time it takes
a beak to probe a grass's root
or a heart-beat to lose its echo
within the automatic illusion of memory
like glass, the sound sharp and clear,
too brilliant to the touch: within
the body cavity: unequal pressure
across the surfaces keeps up
the polished moment with its smears
of iridescent after-image, not quite forgotten
meals which cost too much,
a quick wipe over the formica with a damp cloth
and all's forgotten in a moment
when the breasts tilt this way
beneath her butcher's apron
adding another ten per cent
finally to level everything out
in a discreet eructation
and the instant's past again
the interrupted sounds resume
the hour in compact ratio
of undeleted silence, added
in the inventory it augments
the average of successful song.

Permanent Wave

Being set in order, to conduct a life
a preparation for the sequel to
the same encounter, there was that precedent.
The right time and place stay together
stood at the edge
slowed down so much and hardly seemed to stop
the fleeting fears of waking

rushing against the gap
between our lives where we stand back
and things take charge of us.
We learn to bear this disappearance
as all the empty places gradually fill
all one smooth exit, no more minutes
written on the instructions
just lounge around on cue.
Approximate to a stagnant surface
of reflections shadows don't run
off and dry to salt
outlining after the event
no vacancy without disgust.
Somewhere within the slack expanse
the right direction cuts towards its radius
and finishing what it seemed to rise with
draws the line.

Humiliation in its Disguises

Don't ask whose face it is when you see me
Being seen in search of your reflection

Scorched earth to the sky stopped with trees and clouds
Dumb reverie recoiled with sightless gaze .
Our combat weaves through air and falls with us

Over the fluent nightfall of your rest
The costs of many bargains are exchanged
Moonlight like ice a frozen lake like sleep
Are copies made good as their replicas

The silences of portraits and dumb friends
Turn walls to margins corners sidle round
Start on arrival and shown poised to flee
Still the day lengthens colours mix and fade
A scarlet strip of empire in repose

Rooms contradict the curved weight of fatigue
Repeated details spectral and remote
Turn their straight lines from side to side and down
Where withered beauty turns its head and waits

This sacred place exposed to daily use
Shows by the flames by bare familiar trees
By recognition held back from a glance

Divisions interposed and lost in space
Darkness in layers stunned with eyes and tongues

Rise to the surface both dissolve and set

Ode

Trees have their doubts   but we have ours
less earthly. We aim for the stars, thinking

what could be more important to an oak
than the gossip of its neighbours? To us

such talk is like an acorn, lost in space
to which we distribute our replies

with the nonchalance derived from knowledge:
we are the masters of gravity

not they! rooted in superstition and
the earth. Strange instructions appear in speech.

'Pass this rubber ball to the willow.'
'The elm has need of a luggage guard.'

These mornings, when the sun rises early
it is difficult to wake up and go

out to the shed, where you must continue
creating the antiques of the future.

Muted whispering from the stand of pine:
'Here he comes.' Man, it is true, knows no way

to breathe life into a box   or plant
the legs of chairs. 'He comes' they mutter, and

the wind of disdain in their boughs
has travelled here in answer from the sun.

Two Sonnets

1

Mixed with age, she could foresee the future
Halt between the beds crying: 'Come,

Mix with a sailor.' The most beautiful women
Pressed her forehead, little pieces of blue
In the red drawer, holding the wound, burst and
Bloody. It was hazy, up in the tree
She climbed to get a whiff of the islands,
Finding them stripped by the storm which is called
The Green Bracelet. She used the Malayan
Word, depicted in dances and the stars,
Asking: 'How do I sleep?' Like a round blue,
Naked, full of nuts. The past collapsed
With an earthquake close to the town, the past
Smiling absent-mindedly on Java.

2

The professor stood still, tall, thin, with stains
Under the arms, blunt Western nose, resting
On red and gold pillars, drooping moustache
Hiding a few shabby rooms in the shade.
'I am a Christian from out of your past.'
Matthew wore a face in reply. Only
Pauline remained, rumpled, bare feet knotted
With grass, shining orange from a distance,
Unchanged beneath the stars. O double-bed
Under the half-dark, where the surf comes in
And women with their passions rule the world,
You alone could stop the professor's heart.
Perhaps the sunlight, dark seen from so close,
Leaning against a self-rolled cigarette.

Infamous Doctrine

Honeysuckle's siege at the nerve-ends
thickens thought above this bay
in sleepy foam-blossom whiteout.

Ideas tremble at the heart of things
by uncovering we accomplish
intricate reorderings of ourselves.

Sea-thunder speaks with a voice
counterpointing long heat
of insect afternoon.

A man plunges from a cliff
into space that he imagines
bisected by cormorants and gulls.

Infamous doctrine may be derived
even from blameless and exact
observation of the course of things.

Ode to Tennis
for John Kieffer

To move with the grace
of the delicate step
of the girl in the delicatessen.

O life! O death!
Give me more
never less.
There must be an end
(who says?)
to appetite
the bottomless pit.

Aubrey Beardsley, his mother!
the beauty of Lower Rock Gardens.
Would that I had known her
Marine Venus
under the hill.

The world is full
of beautiful women.
(Am I a male
chauvinist pig
or just a little
confused by life?

There is, perhaps,
no answer to that question.)

Awake, I am a snail
on the face of the globe.
Inside my horny head
everything is possible still.

My head aches (too much wine)
and a drowsy numbness
fills my bank-account.

Can I afford it? I mean
the mask of the parodist
must one day crack.

I wish I was more spontaneous
less sophisticated. Wish I could write
serious poems
of great length
and deep social import.
I wish I could get my line-endings right.

It's 3 A.M.
At last it's quiet.
Bring on the ghost.
He's here already
sitting in my chair.

What do you do about
not wanting to sound like
anybody else? Why worry?
(Who said that?)

I have to admit
my sole ambition for today
(if I sleep now: tomorrow)
is to play a better game of tennis.

A man points with his umbrella.
A starling arches overhead.
The notion of the curve is born..
Space gestured into flight through me.
Sound squeezed through a soprano horn.

■

Poets detained by Thought Police,
Their books and manuscripts all burned.
A crowd looked on, hand-picked and hostile,
Who all agreed that they had earned
Their fate, by choosing it themselves.

■

Hail, Garcia, hammer of pigeons,
Who seeks out sun and finds it good.
At ease with the world, his true religion's
Sheathed like his claws within their hood
Till, before prey, he senses blood.

■

Blair Peach died with a broken head,
Thus proving that the state keeps order.
The men who killed him lie a-bed,
Driving their fantasies with clubs
Down pavements teeming with disorder.

■

The city is a crowded lift
But you and I step out of it
Onto a gale-swept mountain-top.
With mist, rain, snow, clouds, birds we drift
And float as if our hearts won't stop.

The gardener's preface

Using carbon-based ink
　I try again
　　to trace the boundary
of my saying
　where to recross is not
　　again to cross
　the tracing
　　not returning on itself

　is not a magical writing pad
the Garden first placed
　has changed its boundary
let me break through here
　I must be a dreaming gardener
　　attempting to transform to artist,
　　　one of the artists,
　deciding where my boundaries change
　　not against that which grows without attention
or against grain,
　　more carefully
　　　taking intuitive *surge*, wake up,
　　　　shaping
　　　directing and training myself
to make clear where the tracing can be leaped
　to open
remove the gates to the city of love and death enough
　to give boundary field enough
　　to ensure
　　　　　　these tracings continually move
　　　the entrance
　　　　　　　love changing the boundary
in relationship to safety
a summation of the conflict
　　war plus love
　in which 'any desire to suffer death'

I have transformed to
'desire to conflict' sufficiently
to begin the definition of this garden
in Blake's words,
the Auricular Nerves of Human Life

Birdland

1

An image of the Engineer's model
shudders in a basement
as sand stabilizers are loaded.
The left arm bright gold, the ears glow green.
Out of its head energy spatializes
overlappings of spiralic fields.
A figure appears to attempt flight,
it may have wings, yet held to the floor
accelerates towards an openness through liberation
of its partner, unseen from the pit entrance.
Is it male? What is there to say
concerning child birth?
Its presence takes place
between table and pasture, at this moment
takes space between road and underground river:
it is named jouissance:
The arrival.
It brings experience of radical separation of self,
like child birth, produces an object of love.

2

In the morning television I carry
a cylinder of heat in my embrace
down a garden path labelled by the placing of stones,
Hey Bellman, someone shouts,
puts a match to a felled lime
lengthways in the walkway
with meanderings of drama
thought I was moving forward

lost ground
in mistakes, with grinding gaps in what I know about
fidelities or reproduction. By chance, it seemed,
back to the path I had opened
Its trace visible in footmarks and
potential infinity to an unknown fold.
On certain days, this morning is an example,
I remove my helmet cross the path
with a slight intoxication
to check the lime has been properly extinguished.

Endless destruction
makes Brixton
Call it the coexistence of prohibitions and
their transgression
Call it carnival and spell out jouissance and horror,
a nexus of life and description, the child's
game and dream plus discourse and spectacle.
On the edge
of death High Road, the Busker
starts up a reel, it begins as dance interlaced
with anger. I guess at the ridiculous partners
that perform. The busker dances with
her saxophone
'Ideas of Good and Evil' are subsumed into this nexus,
production knots and
unknots paranoia
Blake stands his ground
on the Common asks, Are
    Her knees and elbows only
       glewed together.

3

A woman came down the walkway
lost in transport
exploded her language at a kid
with a stick
restrained by another who breaks
the rod across his leg,
We've had enough, got it! We've had enough!

One hour later someone has dragged
a felled lime onto the walkway
Its leaves make a green path
A pack of dogs surround this, yelp
out of phase. Down the High Road
a new siren on a police weapon
fills the walkway
It leaves a burnt fizz overhead
grooves the mud plane on the roof.
Next door fits an extension to his aerial
changes tone of CB interference
in loudspeakers makes audible
amplified pulses from a geranium
in a Faraday cage. A poster snaps the letterbox,
Come to Paradise in Brixton's Coldharbour.

4
Beneath helicopters
Brixton abandoned
challenges the closure of meaning
so far removed, nothing will have taken place but the place,
flattened housing for ecological reasons,
fuses with a beyond, a successive clashes in
formations, memories of bodily contact, but
warmth and nourishment do not underlie the air.
The Mathematician
gets on the subway in a pinstriped
with a microchip blackboard. A spotted handkerchief
matches his tie. On the back of his head someone
has singed a domino it
matches his ear rings. As he starts to leave
his accounts, he pulls the arms from his jacket,
sets them alight.
The effect is laughter,
an imprint of an archaic moment, a threshold of
spatiality as well as sublimation.
Suddenly a path clears Sleep relates the squeezed
State to a lack of community He leans
towards me, Last night, he insists,
I had a strange dream.

5

The imaginary takes over from laughter,
it is a joy without words, a riant spaciousness
become temporal.
The demonstrative points to an enunciation,
it is a complex shifter straddling the fold of
naming it, and the autonomy of the subject.
Wearing four tones of grey soap I
read photocopied pages on lighting effects,
the Mathematician battery-shaves and makes
notes on squeezed light using a notation
echoed by remnants of beard clung to hydrogen
on his trousers. Subjection to meaning gets
replaced with morphology. I become a mere
phenomenal actualisation moved through a burning gap.
The irrational State insists on control.

On the Open Side

On the open side, look out
for sun-patches of sea-blue:

if you see them
it's beginning to shift
with factory towers along the edge,
chalk-white and silver,
empty even of machines

– the other life,
the endless other life,
endless beyond the beginning;

that holds and suddenly presents
a sunny day twenty years ago,
the open window of a train
held up on an embankment for an hour:

down the field there were children playing
round a concrete garage.
That was all. Something the other life wanted –
I hadn't kept it.

But look out
for the sea-blue patches.
They'll not make problems.

Emblem
for Basil Bunting

Wing
    torn out of stone
like a paper fan

Hung in a sky
                    so hard
the stone seems paper

Bare stems of ivy
                    silver themselves
into the stones

And hold up the wall
                    like an armature
till they force it apart

from Wonders of Obligation

Near Hartington
in a limestone defile
the barn owl
flaps from an ash
away through the mournful afternoon
misjudging its moment
its omen undelivered.

The hare
dodging towards the skyline at sunset
with a strange goodwill –
he'll do for you and me.

And *mormo maura*
the huge fusty Old Lady moth
rocking its way up
the outside of the dark pane
brandishing all its legs, its
antennae, whirring wings,
zig-zagging upwards, impelled
to be seen coming in from the night.

Now I have come
through obduracy
discomfort and trouble
to recognize it
                    my life keeps

leaking out of my poetry to me
in all directions. It's untidy
ragged and bright
and it's not
used to things

mormo maura
asleep in the curtain
by day.

Scent on the body
inherent or applied
concentrates the mind
holds it from sidelong wandering.
Even when it repels
it pushes directly.

Streaks of life
awkward
showing among straw tussocks
in shallow flood.

Neither living nor saying
has ceremony or bound.

Now I have come
to recognize it, the alder
concentrates my mind
to the water
under its firm green.

Fetching up with
leaf-gloss against
the river-shine.

I want
to remark formally, indeed

stiffly, though not complaining,
that the place where I was raised
had no longer deference for water
and little of it showing. The Rea,
the city's first river,
meagre and under the streets;

and the Tame
wandering waste grounds,
always behind
some factory or fence.

Warstone Pool in the fields
I realized today was a stream dammed
to make way for the colliery.
Handsworth Park lake, again a dam
on the Saxon's
nameless trickle of a stream
under the church bluff. The brook
nearest home, no more than a mile,
ran straight out into the light
from under the cemetery;
and there the caddis-flies would case
themselves in wondrous grit.

I'm obsessed
with cambered tarmacs, concretes,
the washings of rain.

That there can come a sound
as cold as this across the world
on a black summer night,

the moths out there impermeable,
hooded in their crevices
covered in the sound of the rain
breaking from the eaves-gutters
choked with pine needles;
the slippery needles wash everywhere,
they block the down-spouts;
in the shallow pool on the porch roof,
arranged among dashed pine branches
and trails of needles,
I found two ringdove squabs

drowned and picked clean,
dried to black fins.

Fine edge
or deflection
of my feeling towards
anything that behaves or changes,

however slowly; like
by Bryophyllum *Good Luck*,
raised by me from a life-scrap and
now lurching static from its pot,
its leaves winged
with the mouse-ears of its young.
I'm vehemently and steadily
part of its life.

                     Or it slides
sideways and down, under my suspicion –
Now what's it doing?

Suddenly to distrust
the others' mode;
the others. Poinsettias or moths,
or Kenny and Leslie and Leonard,
Edie and Bernard and Dorothy,
the intake of '35; the story of the Wigan pisspot
of about that time, and even
Coleridge's of long before:

I have to set him
to fill it by candlelight
before he transfigures it;

with *mormo maura* the Old Lady moth
beating on the pane to come in.

To Tom Saunders on His Imprisonment

The words keep tumbling tumbling about, Tom
Can't help it
When the sun gets hot want quit the houses for keeps
You gotta stay
To be born – people
Not wolves or wildflowers
That's bad ain't it?

Terzetto: Brixton

That day, blue-white shirted
The birds, after peacocking, were strutting day-long, lawn,
Hopping real high, singing singing singing the same
Making a little march, coming to me
And wanking wings open, proudly as police sergeants
(As bitter as crosses)

And me
Smoking

Funny London I grew up in fields
Flowering
And cows a caramel colour (like paints, them)
With the jokes that's in my head
Gone to stitches
You believe

Fright-mad

Just walking around that's in a round as a japanese garden
Where the cockerel A fancy red On his jilt legs Chases us and
warms all us And the kid-day gets a-going Gets us actioning
I'm at a start again Go on

Animal

Close up wolf about my mouth
He would go in
Sit in his cave, like me,
Smell at the daylight.

Animals an' criminals
Among the legs of the animals
Criminals hands in belts.

Jesu 'pecker
My eyes is loose with worry.

I've stood
Like a polar bear,
In court – no one will move
At the white
Till all the wood stank.

Blue hen look hen
I gaze flat eye
And God

Speci a lists
(Noachian) (You)
Got lifted my skull to two All
David playeth the harp where
Sudden in shells
An-animals turn see new

Little pig pealing
For a small church tower
You're mighty quarrelsome
Pretty bricks ('Caesar's')

Into Prison

A prison looks like houses or usual Youre nothing going in
just watching And a prison like rows with roofs of housing
you look like a late dog getting in hey master A prisons like
houses piled up a couple Blocks and Octagons They make a real
note they say is baiting of me So but there aint no housing
ever got walls or doors like these or backgardens of barbwire

I was in the street and a knife Thats not the chaplains liking
thats not to no ones liking I am waiting how long I took off
my leather not joking Not donating Got my prison clothes Take
my shirt off to queue and strip for the doctor so as to tell
the truth yes who yelling

And stuck at solitary Painted place and a light Is sleeping
with a deadbody I reckoned I was altogether shrivelled And in
the morning walking Its exercise A guy blocks me standing
grinning his gums apart But I stepped one way not having to
fight

In the church then in the matt walls for to spit Winning the
churchman gave the prison its words Because we say its easy
its not my fault we blame our wives or our families or someone
it is funny and yet you ought we ought to say sometime in
honesty I am to blame its me whos guilty

Texas looked in the cell with the tea at the bars He says to
my cell mate surprised like aint you topped yourself yet And
I got a book but Again like a rose open up and love like
lights the seapiers got and going girl on a beach the wild
beans peace And there cant ever be enough people alive Cant
ever be enough people in jail

I used to stand while my sister talked and talked talked or
sat hours and abased herself It was like a plane in my ears
here scream and scream into the pillow My brother prospero
like saying what he ll do to the trees and he maked himself
do it and the owls cry shit and shoo I mean

Like let someone ask you how Angels fight Do you tell that
Its like this when it starts you quit talking your mates quit
talking Thats in words And aint anything you cant do Aint
anything you got to do

175

I slopped out last time And put my colours back I got in that
screwed up van written billy brixton the holiday king Smack-
ing at my head And what will I say to you court folk what can
I say to you whos world is it

After Stroke

his jacket, boots kept outside the holding cell
I exhale: my breath tastes
as cut and raw veg
ceiling and great flanged tree
roundabouted, grudge
and wedge
the cuss-crush, bits of
death by fire, death by pneumonia, brain-jolting
with major wings
floods, catching.
slow angry I move
like with the heart of a hedgehog
shocked with drink
Pete starts off to smash
the cell open, forgets it –
volcanoes: volcano will push the trees aside,
tilt and melt, like lightbulbs, till too
superheaven admits no light but a lemon blaze.
but it never comes/chains together,
mine
the similes leap
nothing of it happens
it wldn't happen, I suppose – morning,
I try to get my legs to move
Alf wakes with his hand in his belt
Pauline doesn't stir yet – thinking:
it wld be better to burn the money
than be caught w/ it in yr pockets .

the cold roll of the rivet
the judged spark of cold stony flesh
the solemn spinkle of bells toward a sun
vast dimensions
pinewoods & pure roadways choose on,
don't check you.

For P – Celtic: found text from Machen

1
So she sat down
(A deep violet blue)

She began to kneed it
(of the brake)
She hid it under a big dock-
leaf
(covered)
She stood up
(and a clump)
She walked round the clay
(and when I think)

She got very red, her face
(and if I shut)
She took the clay in her hands
(the glaring sky)
She made the queerest doll
I had ever seen
(floating across it)

She said
if one loved very much,
the clay man was very good
if one did certain things
with it

2
(The sky was)
She took the clay out of the
bucket
(And in the middle)
She turned it about
(was a great elder tree)

She brought it out again
(with blossoms)
She sat down
(of meadowsweet)
She was softly singing all the
time
(of that day)
She sat down again
(my eyes I can see)
She began to shape a doll
(with little clouds
very white)
She hid it under a bush

She said
if one hated very much,
it was just as good,
only one had to do different
things with it

Compass Poem

And the compass / idea / being / city / interim

– fell to aside
like leg-loose like a toy mule

sometimes that comes along shakes you so hard the small / febrile /
coloured pieces forming the frame (in the kaleidoscope) clamp all
at one part or corner and maybe months the vision / taste is
moxa'd to its greyish and gripped base, as though they were the
only colours. The old colours were anyway exaggerated / too
important / as Hectic Red / just kid-dresses, so its only the slam of
grafting greys to the box would know you anything else –

Got you to shut the door for yourself

Of Gods: not sympathy impressed by

'In that feeling there was a humane intention and a vague sense of
the fitness of things'

He went to Gaius and explained it all and told

'Maybe it was the time of year: early autumn, when in the North
Sea
it all seems' gross, clumped from the coops of rope out

She sat and frowned (with me) in the bar.

The channel guy words on weather.

Sat, rubbed my boots on the table-struts till we
went.

And the guy's buckle under his navel
Glared into
the edges of my eyes

As Your Eyes Are Blue . . .

As your eyes are blue
you move, me – and the thought of you –
I imitate you.
and cities apart. yet a roof grey with slates
or lead. the difference is little
and even you could say as much
through a foxtail of pain   even you

when the river beneath your window
was as much as I dream of. loose change and
your shirt on the top of a chest-of-drawers
a mirror facing the ceiling and the light in a cupboard
left to burn all day   a dull yellow
probing the shadowy room   'what was it?'

'cancel the tickets' – a sleep talk
whose horrors razor a truth that can
walk with equal calm through palace rooms
chandeliers tinkling in the silence as winds batter the gardens
outside   formal lakes shuddering at the sight
of two lone walkers
                              of course this exaggerates
small groups of tourists appear and disappear
in an irregular rhythm of flowerbeds

you know even in the stillness of my kiss
that doors are opening in another apartment
on the other side of town   a shepherd grazing
his sheep through a village we know
high in the mountains the ski slopes thick with summer flowers
and the water-meadows below with narcissi
the back of your hand and –

a newly designed red bus drives quietly down Gower Street
a brilliant red   'how could I tell you . . .'
with such confusion
                              meetings disintegrating

and a general lack of purpose only too obvious
in the affairs of state

                          'yes, it was on a hot july day
with taxis gunning their motors on the throughway
a listless silence in the backrooms of paris bookshops
why bother   one thing equal to another

dinner parties whose grandeur stops all conversation

but
         the afternoon sunlight which shone in
your eyes as you lay beside me watching for . . . –
we can neither remember – still shines as you
wait nervously by the window for the ordered taxi
to arrive   if only I could touch your naked shoulder
now   'but then . . .'

and the radio still playing the same
records I heard earlier today
                       – and still you move me
and the distance is nothing
'even you –

Animal Days

1

'The polo season would start early in April
so there was no time to be wasted.'

the night growing darker   the black plains
and below   the bright lights of the town

'knights on horses'?   'gentle ladies'?   'towers in the forest'?

it was as though your eyes filled with glass tears
crying some strange

there were peacocks on the high balconies
and a golden light   in fact 'a heavenly rod'
came down from the heart of a clear blue sky
you see

2

'You're right, even though you won't accept it.'

. . . with all the rifles brought back to safety
even the glimmer of polished metal

Buzzards, kestrels and hawks
circling high above the valley

the dust of the road   dazzling
with the white gates shut   do you understand
the garden so enclosed, and too green?

3

food is so very good

it is very black these days

the malevolence on the winter island

and what approaches in the darkness

beyond all knowledge   'the endurance'
surviving the fear

'but we're all so afraid'

and the children?

the indian chiefs
what are the wounds, anyway, and their costs?

In the morning everything is white
low clouds trail across the upper pastures
and the valley is thick with mist

'sometimes their canoes only hollowed-out tree trunks'

4

standing in the shadows or maybe in the distance
he   Like a long arcade or cloister
It was far from the grim scenes of the north
In his red tunic

The morning spent loading cord-wood onto a trailer

five young foxes in the bean-field waiting for the wood-pigeons

in the beech woods up on the ridge – the bark
still green and wet, the 'sticks' just felled.

It's reduced to a violent struggle
with heavy machinery, and boredom

the castle crumbling sedately   'damn fool!'
the gilding already flaking off

Cutting it up into 'blocks' on the saw-bench
The forest floor all torn up with bulldozer tracks
the soil a bright red   exposed below
the white shale backbone of the ridge

the sun sinking lower
the whole forest dripping moisture and green

the old railway station

5

holding a young rabbit in my hands
walking across the stubble in the late afternoon

soft fur   shocking like the heart-beat

the dark river   and angry knights milling
in the courtyard

setting it free in a hawthorn thicket
safe from the dogs

at night the land so bare   'rustles'

'They have no tradition of keeping their colonies neat.'

'I care for that woman' the song began

6

squandered in a matter called 'the heat of the moment'
not knowing what

'. . . at dusk the sound of church bells from the valley floor,
an owl flying low over a passing tractor.'

white with rain

The corrugated-iron roof of the mission discoloured
with rust   the deep green of the jungle
in the humid gorge

Like oppressors   striking fear into people
with threats of pillage and 'no quarter'

Inside the walls where
'No!'
too heavy   on evenings like this

in the courtyard
'the battlements'

Text for a Poster (2)

SLEEPERS AWAKE
from the 'sensible life' whose only passion is hatred

A red and black pagoda towers above the chestnut trees
in a Royal Botanic Garden
The lush greens of south London back-gardens
O summer nights when trembling with that ecstasy
our bodies sweat and flood one another's

Burst forth – sun streams forth – light –
all doors and windows magically thrown open
a hot lush meadow outside
with dark green woods at its edges

turn it another way
These are insistences not repetitions
or the repetitions are only the insistence on

and it all crowds in:

'Nostalgia for the life of others . . . Whereas ours, seen
from the inside, seems broken up. We are still chasing
after an illusion of unity.'
'Separation is the rule. The rest is chance . . .'

which way to step?

and the dull brutality of monsters as they grind the bones
'forbidden to delight one's body, to return to the truth of things'*

* *Albert Camus*, Notebooks

The clouds part, your hand reaches through – yes
the glow and light in us, our bodies

And below around us – the flint customs house at Shoreham,
the call of a cuckoo as we climb up-hill to the Stalldown stone row,
the wild moor about, and from its edges
the churches, cathedrals, ancient and beautiful things.

Talking to myself

The sweet qualities of our dreams without which . . .

How the wind blows and our hearts ache to follow
the hazardous route the winds follow

6 million Russians
6 million Jews
2 million Poles
1 million Serbs
Gypsies and others

For the Safety of Lovers

I can & do lie down with you amidst the venomous,
charmed & safeguarded against all
harm in the unregarded instant, the
reciprocation that all
lovers dwell in, as fond of
watching the pale light start &
fade in the other's skin
as of trying to enter it
entirely. Even lying down where I know
poisons must inflame
my pores & do, somewhere,
the elbow say, the rash
blisters out. Oh what a
great distance off
from the inviolable &
imaginary self.

On Leaving the Footpath

The metal of the footpath is
narrow & confined, its walk
short & crooked round
the hideous hangars. But
pausing for an hour or two
resting on corn stubble, that
glossy yielded ripeness
really does take on its curved
quality of extension from us as we
push it out in a wide
hillock-shaped surface, catching
the sun on its skin with the
same aplomb of intention there is
in the cup of a radio telescope. Alive

we hold it all, the signals
separately received are
poised in balance by the achieved
leap we are & the fence of
the footpath is oh a
hundred yards away, warded off
with the same intuited use of magic
or selection that the
corn too has used to give itself
significance & its own chance of survival.

Cambridge

the rain in its new edition of daily menace
continues to flap rags of black sky over the gables
a shout carries over from the end of the street
where are the dear old stars? you smile
it's getting very near six o'clock in all those places
I said I'd never go again & then did as if I'd never
even forgotten where friendly academic barflies
laugh & sulk interestingly
creatures of an easy recognition
with carved intelligence & murder in their hearts
the sweetish smell of Fatimas poison the air
& clamorous voices make you want to climb the wall
& gnaw your way across the ceiling

                                    meanwhile
my little sweetheart of the steppes your laugh
brings light to me as the otherwise silent house
occasionally sways in a gust the telephone
obdurate & yellow on the blue rug
the rising gale now pulling the whole room
apart at the seams as you do your clothes
to big applause for Little Feat
we brace ourselves for what we each deserve
in dreary September & I think about my friends
who are not here the light these days giving
a faint glint of melancholic languor

to the wild traceries of honeysuckle in the
garden across the street a carnal resonant air
rasping a spray of rusty water from
chuting under the eaves something goes pop in my eyes
what's that tragic fringe up around the edge of
the ragged beeches out the back? you cry
for a while & then look exquisite & vicious
there'll never ever be I just couldn't be
anyone else but you

After Christopher Wood

it would be ordinary enough to live
in a room that balanced above

the sea's implied presence
a soft draught of light taken in

by the half-open lips of pale green shutters
quenching the tender places

left in the flesh of the mouth

caused of a recurring breathlessness
caused of living in low places

& we could relax into that thing
we vaguely call 'life' whatever
the shade of dress in which it might present itself

& we could sprawl on a white bedcover
reading the *Lives of the Poets*
provided – & this indeed would be a provision of
our existence – that we brought nothing
mean or sordid into that place by virtue
of our mutually ridiculous appetites
whereby we are able to lose each other up to the last moment
when your fingers catch at my lips in a smile
& we do become dwellers in that glittering place
the towels white with orange borders
a kind of mortal incompatibility

Sister Midnight

stuttering rain at the window
early in autumn your breast
loosed from its hold
the caprice of your lifting thighs
the serious depth to your smile
I seem made of insubstantial elements like a leaf
the otherwise silent house occasionally sways
two blocks away the river seeps from lock to lock
the telephone obdurate & yellow against the blue rug
the gale now pulling the whole room apart at the seams
hungover leaves fill up the dusty often
can't do anything at all at other times
you just don't care at all you try it
your own way her face a little blue that shaky
girl with the shaky hand can't hold the pen
too weak for the desk the lower chair
the lower sky hurry by on the pavement outside
everything slipping away with the day
which is closing in on itself at 3.58 the sky
all lit up between a crack in the buildings
& under those clouds lie the chimneys
decorated with a fretwork of little birds
& large grey washes of sky over the gables

the bell rings but I refuse to answer
I might have been a painter but there was an accident
in my life right down the line of a fierce fatigue
replete with overcoats my cherry which is why it is worst
when you have forgotten the mayonnaise remember
I told you there'd be something funny about it she said
like her potatoes of lead, flash flash, alas a
cold pallor has overcome my scrotal sac
in the sharp gusts of autumn in all those places
I said I'd never go again & then did
as if I'd never even forgotten
                                        meanwhile
your head my little sweetheart of the steppes
don't hesitate grab the momentum while the going's good

sink to your knees beside the yellow sofa
take him between the folds of my bright magenta wraparound
the bright glossy oval of a knee & remarkable vest
rippling up over my becoming
the casual spectator of hoydens in the sharp grass of the park
steam rises from the coffee cups
the wine splashes into the little glass
a vigorous red in keeping with the tone
of all that battles to be without my arm
oh my arm in this smallest minute where I enter your name
for the aim of the race do you know
there are certain sounds which tear at my liver
like a cat at its matted fur & a certain
absence of detail has for the first time
featured in my life tightening my collar
& lurking near the black marble of Italian headstones
shining back at the bright little windows of the local
do-it-yourself shops in the rising morning
like a sickness that imprisons the heart in a fettered glove
& now I recognize your great talent as a member of the
human race as the peasant offers me the plastic salt-box
& I look around for the snuff of the father
painted in green & embroidered in my vest
as a text for my meditations

outside the window the trees move in the night
your grand desire rises in my throat & my heart
pulses on into its thirty-sixth year like an indifferent
steam-engine while milky tea embalms the organ
a woman feels very cold around the buttocks
once in a while & yet your laugh brings light to me
cause you're the first good man I've found
pressing the glossy black embellishments to the hand
under the gentle curtain imagery of the gasfire & the
dusty smell of old red velvet cinema seats
                         but still this hanging over
                         of the female in the man
                         means maybe
                         rather than
& that's not the end but a beginning like when

you can't turn the key any further in the sardine can
& all along the edge of the skyline
the last green cringe of daylight
drops like a plate to the ground

from Unrelated Incidents

this is thi
six a clock
news thi
man said n
thi reason
a talk wia
BBC accent
iz coz yi
widny wahnt
mi ti talk
aboot thi
trooth wia
voice lik
wanna yoo
scruff. if
a toktaboot
thi trooth
lik wanna yoo
scruff yi
widny thingk
it wuz troo.
jist wanna yoo
scruff tokn.
thirza right
way ti spell
ana right way
ti tok it. this
is me tokn yir
right way a
spellin. this
is ma trooth.
yooz doant no
thi trooth
yirsellz cawz
yi canny talk

right. this is
thi six a clock
nyooz. belt up.

From Ghostie Men

1

ulstir fur fucks sake
suits thi army fine
countir gurrilla trainin camp
reddy fur thi big wan
fivir it came

yi canny blame folk thoa
telly nthi press aw riggd
pishn oan aboot human rights
ivrywhair else thaht iz
british tay thi last
fuckin gentlemin

nyi lookit thi labour party
licka worn oot prick
two fethirz nits left wing
a fuckin sick joke

ulstir fur fucks sake
yi get fed up menshnin it
naibdy wahnts tay no

2

baa baa black sheep
have you any wool
yes sir yes sir
three bags full

one for thi master
n anuthir wan fur thi master
n wan fur thi fuckin church

A Summer's Day

yir eyes ur
eh
a mean yir

pirrit this wey
ah a thingk yir
byewtifl like ehm

fact
fact a thingk yir
ach a luvyi thahts

thahts
jist thi wey it iz like
thahts ehm
aw ther iz ti say

On Knowing the Difference Between Prejudice, Discrimination, and Oppression

This 'oppressed person', on £12,000 per year,
has composed an article about 'macho workerism'
in class-based analyses of the current situation.

The machine on which the article has been composed,
was itself composed by workers in Taiwan.

These workers were male and female.
Most were heterosexual, some not.
The men got paid more than the women.

The best paid could earn £12,000 in eight years.

from Situations Theoretical and Contemporary

1

The schooner *The Mother of Parliaments* has anchored in the bay.
The first British ship has reached your land.

See the row-boat, pulling to the shore.
See the ballot-boxes, glinting in the sun!

Run and tell your fellow-tribesmen.
We are going to have a referendum!
Shall we join the British Empire?

2

We have decided to make Scotland secure.
This is strategically essential.
No question.

Scottish people have nothing to fear.
Noise pollution should not be a problem.
And all construction work will be landscaped.

We have decided to make America secure.
This is strategically essential.
No question.

Scottish people have nothing to fear.
Noise pollution should not be a problem.
And all construction work will be landscaped.

3

And their judges spoke with one dialect,
but the condemned spoke with many voices.

And the prisons were full of many voices,
but never the dialect of the judges.

And the judges said:
                    'No-one is above the Law.'

■ BARRY MACSWEENEY

Blackbird: elegy for William Gordon Calvert

if I was a blackbird
I'd whistle and sing

1
rude unwelcome guest
luckless wind
at family's four doors
nothing fever   eyes wear
solid fern
narrow compass
abjuring life
treason to my instruments
of you   taken
beamed
invisibled   counterfeit
midnight stealer
quiet roofs   pigeons croop
sponge boots caress
aching sills
stare at rough slot
magnets   on the heart
aery chambers   lift
handsome filings
from dust to a star

solid route   distinct choice
years upright to earth
elements
world streets   erupted fuses
smash at old photographics
rushing memorials
heaving thickly   *iron tough*
& curled
drowning love's boat
Russian heart gondola

same hull punctures
deadly violent reefs
fire & ice   teach
beginnings tough
to believe
London shrubs & buds
neat borders
casual solace
explode in nothingness
no comfort   poison

sudden anchorites
dust without & stink within
hearth mate   joyous rise
if so I believed
freedom is a current choice
Hartfell grasses harp & sing .
discoverer
meet the cavernous mole
shrewdly converse
when timbers fall
thick peat stampings
swift & pure invasion
driven by glade music
total capture   invisibled
veined in truth   no captive
sun & moon also particles
seduced by gorgeous charts
attend your fresh horizon
servants of such final need
old as this century is

coal with o'erblowing quench'd
vapour forth   flamed
shut & digested to mucus
in swan's belly
fish of sky
hot masculine flame
driven by sleek leathered
foreign chauffeur   whose
visor snaps & gleams

suck in air   over liquid paths
route marked   unblotted
black grouse feathered lyre
whisper to your soul
Newcastle's kindest
harshest burr
melt & make no noise
hands to miss
bunched on a driving wheel
obliquely track a journey
vowed to this trench

2

polish felspar at Sparty Lea
burr the wind with Tyneside songs
skin mixie rabbit from ferret's jaws
melt & make no noise

bunch your hands & clap my head
invisibled by a thief at night
stolen from sleep you stole from your family
melt & make no noise

ruthless masters did not poison you
you opened doors saluting their children
proud to chauffeur rich men's sons
drugged by work you wouldn't rest
melt & make no noise.

dominoes laugh in the sun at night
ash drifts down & coats the dogs
fired upwards in the art of flight
melt & make no noise

lapwing lapwing green or grey
singing the smell of earth
sand mingled with blood of lies
melt & make no noise

no requiem no hymn no journey song
stopping to drink from a broken stream
ghosts of miners on the fell
shadowy poachers armed with snares
melt & make no noise

stern with children who grew up wrong
crossing your path when i crossed the Tyne
independance is a wolf that slays
melt & make no noise

follow your eyes to the source of the Allen
follow your hands inside intricate car engines
follow your speech to a wheel that cracks
follow your body to the ash in my skull
melt & make no noise

suck in fire from four windows
blasted kitchen with flaming breath
bear silence which your leaving makes
melt & make no noise

3
curlew chatter
crescent beaks
ragged wings swoop
snipe song

> long way from Kent
> to your rough ash slot
> which pours
> fills this skull

schooled in grind
taught with pennies
tall on earth
golden man
not fascist Aryan strength
dangerous claptrap

> Allendale rosehip
> whose fruit blood dries
> lichen is armour
> against these sores

we learned stones flowers fish birds
beasts
streams of fact
beck fells

whose terror
waited for my walk

you spoke
punched
          logs flared
sank
     we disagreed
furious
obstinate poles
iron words
fire words
survival language

tears will not
people will
not conniving
emotions will
not fences &
gates will not
bought flowers
pretty cards will
not
callous disregard
will not
                    no buying back
                    no second chance
                    no guarantee
                    no trial period
                    no refund
trough gathered
pig faces
falcon glances
magpies
stealing shirts
pawning hair
pasting pride

                    I want his braces
                    shining sleevebands
                    greedy bastards
                    how much

remember solid tongue
no fuss mouths shut
tight against
light

leave to discretion
who has it but
the but the
but the
but the
dead

do not paint skies at Sparty Lea
do not bring rain to Martin's Haydon Bridge
ignore sun's invitation at Sipton Shield
stand by the Allen at Dirt Pot waiting for trout

       watch the rats
       kneeling
       spit on priest
       & dud employer
       with his sent wreath

don't take sides
nothing left
nothing's right
you cannot buy
you must realize
you cannot retrieve
remember this

       you can't buy
       no change
       you can't retrieve
       hare in a gin
       you can't release
       snipe in a trap

you can't persuade
his heart any more
with toys

Brief Novel (3)

did you waste his time
    since time spreads life thin
did you take his time
           so wound unwinding

in our flight did you break a word
    one trip busted to a well
      did you take as master draws and applies
      his tongued whip across a curved journey

as cold dawn caws broke
did you leave face west or east
        assume the taker pose

did your agent send you
    god on your side police at your elbow

did you think for them
did they have to obey their ignorance
    under your sun

pamphlets flung down in a wake
picked up as dirty bread
that had to be read

did you walk covered down the gangplank
    fling alms in the oil mud
    a master song beating your heart

did you drain off discovery
    syphon new liquid
    inject to infect
    a suffering traveller
    bone skin in your way

did you sing rock songs into the mouths
    Judas had left there
    renew reputation for future regard
    brains taken away
    to a fertilizer plant
did you call their numbers

as their cell gates slammed back

is that when you felt so real
how much did you know
    you think
    judge man
    headsman
    blood spender

did you watch in support
    as she scythed through their wheat
    arrested challengers
    as she peddled narcosis dreams
    waste high in high street dismay
    short twisted hair
    the make-up from maniacs
    in dream films
    awaiting any lords from their space lair

did you read messages here
    pregnancies protest
    too late songs
    too far yells for justice at last
    you'll be lucky to forget
    in time for rebirth in the great blaze
    so calm down
    sit back

did you waste unwinding
    down at the cliff edge
    memorize deep ocean
    breaks far below
    then leap on
    saddled mass
    booted gunned
    to ride them
    legitimate

■

smell of canyon rain storm
disturbed hawks   the juniper resin
a human skin sweat
          of sun heat on every thing
          that moves and never moved
          or shifted split fell
          when the magma rose
          frost levered open
          murrain wind crept over
how to endure the moon embrace
          air touch
          aromatic darkness
          doors open in the heart
          in such language is this force upon force of gifts
splayed but the ecstatic rush
          goes on in vertical high layers

          and we come to a high plateau
          a lake in blues a glittered rocky surface
          shines upwards set in larch and spruce
          scrub supports the flame petals
          Indian Paintbrush scarlets spark
          the huge wreckage

          never leave me
          I'll never leave but layer down
          laid out on a high branched bier
          and crumble down to you earth water fire
          the winds take up

Peace Project (5)

have you preserved time
raced tide paced outpaced the sun

fixed what goes
not memory but a work

waited for a war to end
a long voyage home Rangoon west

never ideal conditions but seized
seizures in what designs brought to slow head

luck from unpredicted bond
penetrated shores valleys rock sides

open seas dark blue terrors
ahead might not come

conditions to destroy a creating hand
mind furred by stress

luck from steady crisis
when choices narowed

a dead broad river through a hot port
the Middle Sea unsmelled unheard

mad words *spiritual needs*
never used or that language

hands plunged into a dark pool
headless in dripping ferns through

and put and plunged into a waterfall
into breakers into rain forests

dive through brief air
into a sea cove

'all my films were made against
the desires of the audience'

then he said 'because they aim at truth
and beauty rather than the spectator's satisfaction'

'black rage of poetry – crazy old-age youth'
cold orchard under icy sun

gaze from a white-washed house
salt rimed on walls from ruins

no peace ever it cannot be hidden
a boy reads Tolstoy on a gravel slope

hidden below the edge and is incurable
for a lifetime commitment

this response responsibility to hold

to make some thing unheard yesterday

recidivist desires at last those voyages
only the Antarctic untouched of the six oceans

no fixed home anxiety but here is where
other people live have lived

a stranger to earn his keep by enquiry
respect and some wan humour

warm nerve and muscle under icy clothes
under sun and desert warmed skins

ruinous anxieties thawed or moistened
a shout across Eighth Street

from a huge poet dead at prime warmth
under his own speech

his energy role ended his fiction
survival confirmed his voice beckons

our on tapes and you can hear his glass
and his smoke a solution to everything

then and this is survival nostalgia
dissolved into a gift and its humour

not standing before hills on fields
or ocean distances but a street

a room a couch blanket a shelf
not one voyage not one picture of a voyage

saying goodbye to this man is close
his door in peace no ship traced to a distance

recall an Indian chief in Works and Days
reply to a man's complaint I have not enough time

Well said Red Jacket I suppose
you have all there is

what you have is now
all you have since jealousy is possession

after nearly four years of blue
later voyages in ocean and sky

that disclosing horizon
ahead of the blue returns and chosen

again prow into blue
nacelles into what blue is

sea air distance invariant
desires concluded in births

Valentine

there are spaces we cannot reach
in the heart of the circle the words grown viscous
tasting of sherbet vanilla praline nuts
a whole cosmos turned to toffee by the
clowns. your sector dismisses you. waves
you goodbye. old-fashion burble procreates
a past the single arrow qualifies.
such attachment. such astigmatic vision. regard
flies everywhere, bouncing off the surface
of the globe. she is nowhere constituted and bits
hang off her all the time. if we do not grip
the cobalt, we slide off the edge. for,
where our present is, is, strictly speaking,
irredeemable. terms jostle. within
the elastic limits speeches slide collide
bumping against the steel skull-cap it's
undeniable the step is gone. all's to do. is
dusted off our loss & panic slither,
reclaims our corralled selves maybe not feed
the gorging beast whose hungry flanks
rub up against our metal bars. collapses. free
falls. a stranger beckoning,
fluttering in the turning leaves. within
the heaped-up coals the finger points no
place, no movement. it happens here,
arrow, cobalt, bullet-bunch
no other valentine.

In a Hot Country

petals step their fragrance off the shelf
stamens shoot their tongues licked in dusty air
unstoppered don't see don't hear
till colour fades & question why
can't it be recollection, only
filed, knowledge lodged in damaged
memory circuit down the wiped
neural pathways, why not the past
when future it is not and take
its tenses from arabic lore of sun-dials
water-wheels and shadow-clocks,
scything a wilderness for bread & wine.
lodging where your name & number are
is no acknowledgement for somewhere
in that break is our existence
                above the shredded promise of a home.

The Moon

takes a taste of green
samplered
where waves stitch into the bay
will later return
bears our hoping   becomes the
light settling over the ridges
the place you might get to
on days when weather withdraws
to a cool swell   permitting
grey into blue into green into
aquamarine bleeding off under the
white lace trim

it was a sunset
but only the kind that reminds you to rise
parting   to return
up a beaten path past thorn, rock, wall to

last digits of settlement   reading the turf   lost
like the rump-of-the-flock call ricochets
return

cut out of the sky
the mountain table gives up
gathered darkness, solace
against their light
watching,   Endymion wrapped in his pelt,
my fingers lost in base curls

there were polka-dot figures
neatly draw-strung
I gave you the key   you pocketed the gate
saying,
'it is a holy place
I cannot leave'   pell-mell backwards
I said,
'cry
for was the Leper wrong to reject God'
settle for no less
I wished you to leave
the dark mountain between us
you devoured   all in your green light
you took   all for your settlement
thorn rock wall path turf mountain table
left me the sea
where waves stitch into the bay
grey into blue into green into
aquamarine bleeding off   the
white lace trim

Egypt

They pursue space
in tatters of a kingdom
colour begs the shadow
falls precisely on Zait

at its apex four
thousand years

The Green Chateau

c'est l'arbre de Jesse.
There is rarely any light –
the stone is lit in whiteness, a
burning interior light.
The blue is all the seas you dreamed &
never saw on the Atlantic,
seals & foghorns, rocks that ribboned plimsolls
Charon's dog. Of course
there wasn't any chateau. Not there. &
the card you sent did not arrive, still
blue, the pointed, perfectly
butted stone frame holding
not the thing but the effect, the
inner sound of blue, a broken form
behind the light.

Mr and Mrs

these jagged passions trample
like points of polka dot
under the frosted hyacinth scents
the blue light of the jacuzzi
a couple leashed
permanent rental in the
tender solace of
cats silver-chewing, marked
by the cusp of Sagittarius.
'Put a nice suit on.'
'Have your eyes straightened.'
soon
anemones thin to

paper-stars bright blue broken willow-
pattern bright blue broken
home always tethered the
doorstep says nothing

Goodbye to the Bay of Naples

It was, we thought, blue.
I thought. One would have said.
A great slab crouched the centre of my soul
Or where my soul would be if
Souls there are. I ached all over
Truly blue. If you were numb
Or if it's pain that travels light-years
Mapping a cold stellar distance where
We guess at origins,
Hot to tell beyond invoking, nameless
Right up to the funny-bone,
I do not know.
You should have seen the way she held
Such torsion and such teeth
Beneath the abstemious gift of eyelashes.
One cannot but admire
Or so they say curious
How electricity works.

The Whore of Kilpeck

On the Parish Church of St Mary and St David, Kilpeck, Herefordshire is a small Celtic fertility figure, called by the local people the Whore of Kilpeck.

Who'd couple with foetus, with handful of sore yell wet, with
    its jelly eyes staring,
Clamped round the grunt-root sucking it up to a rash?

The Mother of Red Muck slewed out her gibbering sheilaghnagig.
The entire spring season ploughed her in her eldritch luminous
    paralysis.

Who'd help her or give to her further? She squats and she claws
    clamp-hands at her loud wet seed-pit. The hazel twigs
    whimper.

She is old in stone. She was dropped from the earth's womb
    three months early, ejaculated by the violence of her
    own imprisoning desire.
The stone is her desire. The ancient permanence has made her
    always now.
Who could acknowledge or deny her carolling berserk thirst?

The stone season whimpers loud beneath the sward.
Will someone for Christ's sake soon stand keen as the sharp
    Welsh metal in the streaming slough and hack the year
    to winter?

■

I stalk with the razorblade cranes, my pinhead reeling
    wingpower in the white light,
Stilt legs reed legs red from menstrual delta.
I stalk with an agate eye and a lunatic trapped in my
fossilized head – My stare . . .

My feathers are all the flash, the flash the dawn and
finish. I am not outside the instant Being-Scream.
My pride is everywhere. I'm proud because the everywhere
    is me.

The lunatic is in my skull – his blazing replica is spat
   out molten on the dying sky.
I walk a while, a long while I walk. The instant's constant.
   Something in me won't die. Help me.

Three Scenes: Todmorden

*Working-class family returning on foot from the hospital where they have
identified the corpse of their son, killed that morning in a road accident.
Drunk young man playing with dog in hayfield. Father seen through the
window of a council house combing his daughter's hair while the family dog
barks through the window at passers-by.*

Light strikes and withdraws.
Striking, it skins the Ashworths, peels the inner skin off Roy's
         boiled eye.
Striking, it slices sickle-sweeps round Robert's buffeting limbs,
         round lillygrass and gracedog in the canine reaping
         dance.
Withdrawn, it shies from the stone column of the morning
         daughter,
         drops an eyelid from the father's turning knuckles,
         from the reaping of the hair of sleep, from the
         casting sleeping down along the shoulders of the
         dawn's stance.

Light shrieks and sighs.
Shrieking, it blisters in sudden suns the new vermilion of the
         crashed bike's gastank.
Dries the sudden blood, preserves perfection of its untrod pool:
'Wor that Ashworth's lad? 'As 'e snuffed it then?'
Crowing barbed saxophones it hawks up giggles from Robert's
         face,
         appoints him in his hayswathe dog-dance to refuse
         this sparkling acidity of grief.
Sighing and murmuring it permits a gradual revelation round Roy
         Ashworth's tilted doorstep chair. Dew and the final
         cig of the vigil command a phlegmy hello.
Muttering secrets it turns from the snapping window-dog that

guards the Dad's solicitations. He pours his wakening
daughter from the turning comb in a gracedrop of
hushlove.

Barking light struck from the sky by the filial dog. My daughter
    love
Is vertical ritual. You live
My death, love, from the spilled scene. You flash me a passion-
    snap,
Dog-light incisor love-sun rubbed to the tingling bone on the
        Ashworth procession, rough-shod and sobbing up the
        track's stones.
I back the L-plate mini badly for their passing.
Light-threat on the father's shelled orb, a rasp of clarity:
        'Are yi practicin' Jeff?'

Dub Eleven

Strike his wakening, slap his eyes ajar.
Skin the turning daughter, flay her for breakfast.

Boiled eye commands a phlegmy buffeting, spit and a cuff,
        a thick kiss.
Sickle-swiped permit a gradual revelation, her grass-
        grave her death-nest.
Gracedog in the canine acidity of grief, whines, worries
        at the door-sill.

Stone knuckles turning the hair in sudden new vermilion.
Shrieks from the dawn's blisters, the new day's wounds.

The Oracle of the Drowned

Memory in sea-green with sea-weed grain
of glass as the rearing wave rains briefly
before a lot of bother
on the beach of childhood,
as men with a burden file across sand.
Those far-out surfaces are lipped
with transparent phrases coming to mind:
that the real dying happened in middle heights
between the lips and the sea floor.
Remember the swim trunks lost in waters
and the first man in our lives who drowned,
this, now, his cortege from the tide-edge,
the sacred hanging-down of head and arms
seeing that person's white groin
cooked chicken bared near the hook of the ribs
and a shore-line of horrified children
arrested in their digging to gaze
at seas of such corruption as to change him.
His shirt left behind too long on the promenade rail,
always there in our lives, its caked cotton
fluffy-white in its inner wrappings.
The cloth wandered open at nights as we wondered
what a drowning body could say
when its chest became translucent green.
We courted in our minds such corrupt purity,
never escaping but sinking into not
the unthinkable gift of the self to death,
or the sea flash flood in the throat,
but into the oracle of the drowned;
because the oracle of the dying comes to a halt
while the oracle of the dead continues and has humour in it.
We ask the dying, 'How do you go about drowning?'
and the answer comes first 'I cannot – '
then swims in ambivalent vowels

and voiceless consonants in the washing tide
voiced consonants in the last buzz of the eardrum:
'Aah, I am funtoosh, zooid, walway,
wallowing, rows and rows of waves,
a goooood one, my soooul a sea-mew' –
and we learn nothing but the knowledge of pain,
and the hope of a future from it.
But the gone-dead are beamish and talk to us
from out of memory's hollows and gulphs:
'You, boy, in your Bournemouth bed, be with me now
and I will come to you many years later
still drowned in a medium of green liquid
the water whispering through its lips
as the dark whispers to you in caves or before sleep.
And I was a man and had babies
as you, a baby, will have a man and call him 'Father'
and as the drowned will have the drowned.'

Snowdonia at a Distance

Snowdonia water falls in a memory
of mountains behind misted windows.

Betraying no-one who cannot still receive our love,
we lived among clefts of shadow

where justice seemed weakness, divisive not uniting,
though the fact matter is

each other but remaining in our own valleys.
We were not unaffected I wasn't neither I think were you.

Once more, for perhaps the fifth time in our lives
we geared into each other going together apart,

your broken scyth
hip-bones walking within me.

Then, distance, and the mountain ridge whose snow
hung from two dry hips.

Nowadays, wiping the window, I see Paris:
it has cost so much money to be peaceful

and this peace can be robbed from me
if someone within me moves against me far off.

Thank God you are no stasis, no far ridge.
but have broken down into the potential of kindness,

never more separate, you never younger,
now so much is asked of you continually,

you in the marshlands of our middle-age,
me, wiping Paris windows, seeing again mountains.

The Ferry Pirate
Variations

When the brain's black with demonic crisis
and its inky sea peopled with lights
that prompt memory, loved souls
are borne out on the wake from high boatsides
and in that world of waters float lit rooms
wandering away to past sunsets. Swaying,
the terrain of darkness lost to you.

And always a mother ashamed to have suffered,
always marriages left inland,
always the sea carrying out black pram covers,
the wandering of unsteady thoughts;
then the
whispering at the captain's voice tube says:
'When I came early to my new love, Cariclea,
I found her kinsfolk weeping
for her old love and she far too faithful,
despite the sea changing either through time or fortune,
and I carried her away across the blackening waters.'
You won't find quite this in Heliodorus.

That sea is always fairly near
under the rails of night ferries
swaying with unsteady thoughts, blackening in crisis,
roughening with time or fortune, drawn on
by inkless nibs, as if the written surface
were integral with liquid rooms of memory
distorted in the currents undersea.

That sea is always unsteady with thoughts,
polluted by the pram covers carried out
into tracks of moonlight
borne towards lit rooms beyond the horizon
memories of loved kitchens
where the dead kinsfolk sit down to a table
distorted in a childhood's inky sketchbook,
washed in black, bound in black.

To have left a mother suffering far inland,
to have sensed the pram covers heaving away from
the moonlight track and faces sinking like flat-fish
under a sea peopled with receding lights
governed by smoky stars
and then to have seen
a modern Cariclea in the dress of Grecian white
a handbag strap as if of the quiver of arrows
walk down the scudding ferry deck
entering risks of piracy in a classic romance,
this, in another poem the cause of melancholy.

But here the sea is not integral with the writing
and keeps bearing the lights and memories away.
At moments of crisis,
the voyager sways from the rail towards her:
you won't quite find the classic mood in him or her.

From **The Infant and the Pearl**
Based on the medieval Pearl *: the dreamer has metamorphosed as a*
Labour MP

XI

We followed the river to Fortune's Wheel
and its Parliament, then down an underpass
with metal surfaces, spinning like a steel –
coiled worm-hole through time, whereas
we held steady as a spaceship in a special
effects catastrophe. My secretary was
proffering my Order Paper as though political
protocol prevailed in whirlwinds. Pompous
because the Bentley was mine now and because
the main motion before the Parliament
was mine also, I stared in surprise
at the annoying frivolity of an amendment –

'annoying', as I was aiming a veto
of Margaret's money measures with a motion
of censure: 'That this House has no
confidence . . .' and so on. The Opposition
leader would come first, but a clever cameo
performance, well-reported, would promise me promotion
chances: just my luck if some shallow
ass threatened our forcing of an election,
wording the anonymous, a-logical alteration
that: 'Parliament places no confidence in Parliament'.
As if one could *confidently* call into question
oneself! An annoyingly frivolous amendment.

Lost in the annoyance I was hardly aware
we'd been grounded in a gravy-brown, gothic
decor. From the car door a corridor,
panelled in oak, opened an honorific
progress down a carpet in the Commons. My career
was poised on the pure *real politik*
of the day's debate. The doors to the Chamber
were pulled open by the body politic
of the Sergeant at Arms and I saw seraphic
gleams of light. But a grey garment

floated by me and I almost forgot to think
of my motion and its annoying amendment.

Annoyance gone, I saw my grey gown
sported by an old MP, pass by us
en route for the opposite lobby. My own
feeling was I should follow, that impulse
being stopped by my secretary – she'd shown
me my speech draft. I stuttered, 'This is serious:
who was that man?' 'Well, he's been known
from here to eternity as "Father of the House",'
she sneered. 'But Shinwell, who's a scrupulous
Lord, is no sell-yourself Socialist bent
on crossing the Commons in a confidence crisis,
when we're up against such an annoying amendment,'

I argued, anxious instead of annoyed,
for the 'Father' had resembled my father,
drained and grey, descended to that void
from which he waits for me to remember
him in dreams. Through the doors that candid
light reminded me I was a Member
of the assembly, one unable to avoid
being beckoned by ambition. To enter
the Chamber changed me entirely. A sheer
bombardment of light blazed on the Government
side where *I* was! All was wrong. But whoever
had added the previously annoying amendment,

XII

could annoy me no more. The light
that flooded the Government side of the Floor
shone from a white world opposite
whose crystal cliffs crowded the shore
of a fast-flowing stream. This was the trite
stream of time that I've talked of before,
unusual here in issuing in spate
from sluices set under the Speaker's chair.
The Commons was cut in two: the corps
of MPs from all parties packed close

together on the Government benches, and that gladder
kingdom whose cliffs were clear glass.

The glassy surfaces gleamed with fragmentary
mirrorings of all the MPs, as we peered
at a cliff-like façade like a stacked factory
for industrial ice whose cubes reared
up winking in sun from an unseen clerestory.
And the sun was Switzerland-warm; it speared
across narrow alleyways, silvery-rosy
as a laser lancing through weird
chunks of Turkish Delight. It cheered
my heart, empty as that heaven was,
for the normal confusion of the Commons had cleared
in that other Kingdom whose cliffs were of glass.

Like a Douglas Oliver look-alike
the Speaker dreamily searched our side
and 'recognized' me, deepened the dark divide
in myself. I stood up to speak,
conscious of the stream swirling through the wide
middle-ground of debate, a dike
between self and supreme. I couldn't decide
what stage we were at in the motion, but I'd
read Aaronovitch on the A.E.S.,
so I started magnificently, like a sinner who defied
a heavenly kingdom where the cliffs were of glass.

I glossed over Margaret's giant, *Inflation:*
wages were hiked when unions pushed
hardest; this, helped by a hapless nation
whose purchasing exceeded production, pushed
up prices; then the pound's depreciation
pushed up import prices, and that pushed
up not just prices but the expectation
of price rises to come, which pushed
up purchasing demand – then the wage push would
renew: it was 'who pushed who,' if alas
you plumped for the policies the Tories had pushed.
I called this across to that kingdom of glass.

Each glassy fragment flashed a vignette
of some vinegary visage beside me, famous
in Cabinet, Shadow Cabinet, Bennite,
or SDP-Lib circles; so as
I explained the monetary answer, I expected
the common Commons mix of raucous
attack and counter-attack; and yet
reflected in facets of the bevelled surfaces
was a sort of solemn, sourpuss
musing, like ourang-outans *en masse*,
except for the pearly premier's face
quizzing me hard from the kingdom of glass.

valentine

simplicity
say sleep

or
shall we
shower?

have an apple

you are
as I need
water

shall I move?
do you dream?
shallow snow

flesh

melt this

detente

a city in your smile
a continent of this tongue
an ocean on those lips

two falcons grasp a single branch
and flowers mouth their way through soil

the sun is out
and draws you through my pores
like sweat

I throw your picture down
and turn away, depressed
return annoyed, confused
I want to run my lips
along your neck

I found a hole in my heart
and fell into it
there my children play
and make a zamek of my wounds each day

another shape, a heart complete
grows beside the first,
begins to drown the other
with its thirst

I stood between my two hearts
and both were beating

a swallow flew into this room
and banged against the window
I caught her in my hand
and felt her heart pelt against my palm
like rain

we were both held
her wide swift wings in my anxious grasp
I wish to tell you about my prison

my fingers are the wings of god
his crushing love rushes through their veins

it's blood that makes us love

recipe: pastime for the unemployed

be mean with an onion
rip off its dried skin
and grip well

slice across its sphere
and chop

the onion will rise
into your nostrils
and speak to your eyes

keep slicing
weep and toss

into a hot iron pot

with chicken pieces

rib tickling each
with bay leaves

use what herbs there are to hand
allspice chilly
cloves and yoghurt

decorate with saffron
sliced peel
from a fresh lemon

poke
with a fork

and don't let spitting fat
put you off

fight back

gypsy music in Krakow

sitting in an alcove
          on the old city walls
a three foot
          gypsy musician
plays a violin

his left leg
          dangles
over his right
          and
his feet hang
          far
from the ground

he sings
          with a cigarette
in his mouth
          broken lines
which compliment
          the strings

and half blind eyes
        flicker
like butterflies in spring

magnificent music
        issues from
        the dwarf's
misshapen frame

we stop
        and listen
amazed to witness
        such easy skill
from so improbable
a source

a woman
        fresh from church
rushes to push
        pennies in his purse
as she might
        with trepidation
kiss the foot
        of the baby christ

is he appeared
        with such a
moustache

dawn raid on an orchard

Pebbles skipping off the window woke me.
Throwing off light blankets, night
became an unmade bed.
Shinning down a drainpipe skinned a knee.

Running soft in rubber shoes, trailing clouds of breath,
we knew that property was theft.

We wormed out where the wall was weakest
and the broken glass on top was smashed.
Risking fingers and slashed feet we leapt.

The tree shook with blissful indignation
as we took ripe apples, tasting sweeter for the taking,
to fill our dads' redundant bait-bags.

A blackbird with a barbed-wire neck
cackled on a branch and clapped its wings. Flapping,
we dropped and lay flat, as an alarm bell rang
in the gadgey's gaff.

Franky sprained an ankle, and pain suppressed his laugh:
we howled silent, afraid of an alsatian growling,
a police panda prowling past.

His mumpy jacket zipped-up and stuffed lumpy
with nocked-off fruit, he limped towards the orchard wall.
From the inside it looked much taller.
One day, we said, we'll mek it fall.

South America

he is trying to write down a book he wrote years ago in his head
an empty candlestick on the windowsill   each day
of his life he wakes in paris to the sound of vivaldi in summer
and finds the space programme fascinating since he still doesn't
    know
how radio works   as in the progress of art the aim is finally
to make rules the next generation can break more cleverly this
morning he has a letter from his father saying "i have set my face
as a flint against a washbasin in the lavatory. it seems to me
almost too absurd and sybaritic" how they still don't know
where power lies or how to effect change
he clings to a child's book called 'all my things' which says:
ball (a picture of a ball) drum (a picture of a drum) book (a
    picture of a book)

all one evening he draws on his left arm with felt-tipped pens
an intricate pattern   feels how the pain does give protection
and in the morning finds faint repetitions on the sheets, the inside
of his thigh, his forehead   reaching this point
he sees that he has written pain for paint   and it works better

Cross Divide
for Neil Littlewood

small car distant, no life in it
draws lightning to my ear
flash
entering luminous blue insulators
entering electrical memory many times

              electrical ogham computer rosetta
              finger old thought carefully
              headlight fires ahead
              over the great salt lake
              living days in a crayon

salt lake straightens out sweating
cold lights travel the night clouds
each tube dreams of flights
rubber memories
slowly what we dreamed is happening

Horse Power

interchange of display
arrival of the colonel
aquatint

no way

intelligent echoes in colour

but i

can't

help

falling in love

with

you

■

slavery

what

we

have

words

for

■

always looking through the eyes
he only knows the sausage is after him

■

remember
no time
when i wasn't

■

"you're a honky-tonk
i'm a record-player
playing a honky-tonk"

■

captain terminal

■

"in which we have made
enormous progrom . . . *prog*ress"

■

the puzzled house awaits my tail
1600 pounds of nervous elephant
you are watching   lavinia

stolen or invented but proffered
boredom   red-hot thumbs
light passes through the crest

the narrative continues trapped
i enter listening watching waiting
ing ing ing   a mis-spell   ing

■

what:
a form

■

no-one
will ever
find out

■

sustain this to the ear-ring
french windows blown open
flames of three lamps

carrying an extinguished candle
no, alight: the swinging cut glass
of the candlestick   murder   commercial
■

the blot leading the knot
■

in notification for this case
we have extracted our peripheral business
everyone was the aim but then
anyone woke up

brain reacts to fear
curved into its present form
o i'm lazy
bored or tired
■

needs

open up the gallery

no space
■

"peace and value, comrade"
■

"run a loss on him"
■

on top
of the lift
■

starts to work instantly
■

i met my fate but the seams didn't match
bulbs spelled l o a n s
fat of the famous touched in mime
■

no longer addresses
how can we know

the first
goodbye

■

too late
what rhymes with cow
and starts with an n

■

black holes in the metaphor

lost my sense of fun
found it had met death
observed it with pauses
was lonely and attached

all hands on time observe
the symbols   wearing away
a woman singing   new york
thank you distracters

her slowness extends not out but in
she licks her plate
lamps instantly chosen music
death in a pattern by diamond

try to not feel interference
mein mind has nozzink to do
when i think blue
that is all i have to do

■

unlock
tassel
painting
recorder

harmonica
message
friendship
border

seal
golden
weeks
american

yesterday
behalf
return
regard

tiger
way
compelled
communist

get
returned
should
disavow
■

like

so and so

unknown

unknown
■

para   sol
■

use
of a cat

power
of money

value
of life

Nothing

into nothing
no choice in the matter

tired of reflections
bored with light

impatient with time
uninterested in thought

no desires
without hunger

nothing to write
mind sleepy jelly

too tired to phone
staring at the timetable

deciding to keep moving
under a microdot moon

hand through green balloon
cigarette end white in red light

no dreams
no you to care to listen

the abstract you, the elastic hat
no head to fit

under sufficient space
precise   military   empty

Poor Snow

The violet
light of snow falling.

Its tiny darts
make eye stripes.

Dark flakes
rapid, upwards.

It's restless, it can't
find whiteness.

Its grey and violet
trillion souls.

Housing

Clear as my ash tree through the glass
A full wind streams. It's
Sharp as the leaves which
Flow backwards in the gale.

There'd been enough
Descriptions, 'suffering' –
Couldn't you have taken up
Your life, by its throat?

No disloyalty
Bar reticence.
This, says the agent
Is where the sun comes, in the afternoon.

A calm that capital supplies
Of watercoloured woods and lanes
Is caught in London windowpanes.

Here in the city
I'm besieged
On high, on high
With my bird's gaze.

If I possessed
So large an eye
I'd ask
Forgiveness, democratically.

Do So

Upright and glorious
under the lash of
my bloodier wants

black with resolve to
lay off people
for everyone's good

I go as a human
in skirts goes, whispering –
think yourself

an interruption in the chain of the dead

and think yourself
for God's sake, ordinary.

It Really Is the Heart

The heart does hurt.
And that's no metaphor.

The feeling is
that 'throbbing muscle' you can't say –
since that's 'steel comic sex meat'.

But it does hurt
top-mid-left
under my shirt
with its atrocious beat.

What I Do

An even time
all to myself, though
lately it hasn't been,
more violent. My
death still will
skip on, 'This way,
my love', I know
but privately
I cross my heart; that
shakes, though, the noise-maker.
I am in several cupboards
deep, and wish well out,
wish out from this
dark air of china.
Is my name 'skeleton'
or only 'cup'?
A crack of light falls round me.

Affections Must Not

This is an old fiction of reliability

is a weather presence, is a righteousness
is arms in cotton

this is what stands up in kitchens
is a true storm shelter
& is taken straight out of colonial history, master & slave

arms that I will not love folded nor admire for their 'strength'
linen that I will not love folded but will see flop open
tables that will rise heavily in the new wind & lift away,
                                        bearing their precious burdens

of mothers who never were, nor white nor black
mothers who were always a set of equipment & a fragile balance
mothers who looked over a gulf through the cloud of an act &
                                        at times speechlessly saw it.

inside a designation there are people permanently startled to
                                bear it, the not-me against sociology
inside the kitchens there is realizing of tightropes
milk, if I do not continue to love you as deeply and truly as
                                        you want and need
that is us in the mythical streets again

support, support.

the houses are murmuring with many small pockets of emotion
on which spongy ground adults' lives are being erected & paid
                                        for daily
while their feet and their children's feet are tangled around
                                        like those of fen larks
in the fine steely wires which run to & fro between love &
                economics

affections must not support the rent

1. neglect. the. house

Work

For a time self-evident light all tremendously clear
to be sat down under in abstract triumph, still shaking with
luck and nearly wasn't; later in a flood of in this case loosestrife
dead wood dead children billowing in moondaisies set to
piped music tears and dreadful violence, only tolerable years later
through aesthetics to make red noons of what was at the time real
   blood.

So it goes on asserting the unbearable solid detail as real work,
    Lissitsky:
'work must be accepted
as one of the functions of the living organism
in the same way as the beating of the heart
or the activity of the nerve centres
so that it will be afforded the same protection'
and no sleep pricks out clear and small
people in landscapes who are pushing up around the sides of
larger things. Dear attention; fix that point precisely where
landscapes first got peopled & painting set off on a series of
humane journeys south to venice; so for saints to be warming their
    hands
at lions on khaki mountains, netted camels to be arching home
    midfield,
black light and cliffs of rain to be taking their time across horizons
and an evil to heave itself out of a brown pond, foreground,
    unobserved.
Look out, saint. Not to be your own passions' heroine
else, invented, you'll stick in them. So, telegram: forget.

■ **PETER RILEY**

Ospita

1

Seeking a bearing point on hurt I find
Hollows and rooms in the thick of the night,
A building hard at work flashing its bright
Offers into the star dome. Consigned
Forward I bring my name in a sealed jar
To the steps up, pay the slight fee, assent
To slow harm by the covering letter;
Entering into purpose distance springs
Back from the horizon to hold the cup
The bitter cup but true, of flesh-driven earth
(This night is the day outside the dream, his
Tableau my government, or family wish)
And deep in the brickwork think of asters
Blazing on the far links in slow birth.

2

I bear my coat and cast to a senior,
A new-old faithful, who should know the coils
And corridors of the heart, the slender
Ghost smiling to the third tune. What is false
Be set into a pestle, what rings be
Represented as an inner garden
Open to Syrius, one and the same be
Ground and broiled and spoken as your answer.
The house is quiet, old radio music
In the walls, scissors on the table, streaks
Of blood in the sink. A call in the night;
I get up, white coat, glance out at the rain
On the glass, attend. What do I exchange for pain?
Holding a stranger's thin arm I turn down the light.

3

Calcium night light. Suddenly a man
Shouts, 'Orpheus!' and the dying die,
The sick sleep on, the deserted bitterly cry

And I count the call as best I can across
The fogs of routine silence; word that holds
The earth into a chiming whole, enfolds
Love in a capsule coated with loss, never
Cedes to wishful death but calls us to drop
Our trades and be again that whirring top
On the mountain ridge, screaming down river a pain
Of incompletion, fall medallion, cut
The human heart to song. And it will, don't
Turn the light out, see to the day's wounds, won't
Stop our good hands tying, that sweet moan again.

4

A man shouts in pain, the voice constructs
A door. The god batters his forehead
On our simple attendance, the fruit
Of centuries' observance. But to eluct
Wisdom from hurt – any hospital bed
Would burst into flame at the mere thought.
The music coils within: a long solo,
And the final voice squeezed from a lump
Of flesh held over a sink said and we tried
Our best to stifle that singing, 'Do
What you will to ease me over the hump
Of death I belong to the great outside.
My burning lust courses at the last though Hell.
The pain of what I couldn't manage spreads like a bell.'

5

This house constructed as an escape
From harm is unlikely to escape
Its own folly as a new escape
From language and source of new dolour.
A woman shouts down a corridor
A real name: 'Sidney! Sidney! Sidney!'
A door slams bone shut. I am sorry
To have life shot through by her call
I can't dream any harder the fall
Of light onto the wet leaf, the stain
Of nurture on a simple erection;

In the end she is right: the rape
Of endless joy and everyone's to blame.
Out on the lake the long boats wane.

6

At night the walls are blank but we can hear
The plovers crying in the dark fields, their
Wings beating over waves of wheat. Downstairs
Someone opens the piano and strikes a chord
That tenses the flanks of hope. Again there
Is a silence in which the lapwings graze
The ear tips and clouded underwing
Swoops across the sky. Then where and where
In this globe of health we balance and bear
From room to room, where is a lasting thing?
Where is a good done that also stays it?
Someone attempts the new soft swing but out
In the earthglow between mind and chest
Brilliant metallic birds like kisses dive to rest.

7

The man dies and the bell sounds across
Grass and sea and mixes with the gulls.
The dream sleeps into the morning, turns
On its side and drifts along the coast
Under the great grey cliffs and buildings
Dedicated to healing but now
Empty and dark at dawn, the sharp keens
Of the white hens warning us to be slow.
We comfort as if there were no cost,
As if pain could be stilled to patience
Separately, and the story lost.
Good men have died lost in empty time
But loading their bite on th'intrinsic nation
Steady as grade of light, or yellow chime.

8

Time drags its heals on the dreamer who hears
His body calling him like a discant
Semaphore, a sign hung on a fruit shop

Under the castle wall. The sheets are bright
Anger the oxide of faith and he fears
The fall into humanity, the slant
Of honey and cream; those fair lids droop
And he is solitary on the white
Road across the heath, he is close to tears
For the imperfected lives he couldn't want
To bring to their moment of concord and float
On further life. The swallows are in flight
Over the russet fields crackling with fear
As he enters the day's gate as is right.

9

They draw his body from the centre out,
A decisive goodness. He lies flat out
On the shore counting ills. The waves enter
His total wealth into books of sand.
It's enough. They are happy to inter
His soul in lime and ash for the sake
Of a comfortable end, the winter
Of our success rebound in angel cake
But winter is true numbers that blister
From the corpse in a field, alternating
Black and white name-tags that flitter
Like sarcens in the treetops. Small birds sing
His centre into holes in the snow and grey
Doctors weeping envy send him on his way.

10

I walked out on the morning of May 12th
The blades were bright and coy and loud,
Thick with languages I walked without stealth
The fields of angry farmers, proud
To be harmless and legal, half and half,
No one could fathom my strong shoes,
There is no paradise but tongue of love.
I walked all day, I heard no news,
When twilight filled the air with gravities
I descended, heart full and slow,

Down the dim fields dotted with stones and sheep
To the house in its banks of trees
The fire, the food, the Gurney piano,
Having my wonderful labour to keep.

Otter, Redewetter

thumping gavel the Otterburn Ranges behind and never unravel
Rede's bed moontreads   a pressing
redd   falls   syllabic   the seatrout
the otter   utters   shrill   low as the river is, it carries far
men and mink hear, a fear   bewitches.
No otter onto portage   past the anglers' pitches
so that like a starting-up two-stroke puttering wingstroke of rooks
     their roost   there   like papers
        putter, patter
windloose leaves   but soft   onto design dew-grasses
so close their smell wapt wept in my face.

Redewetter = Rede River, Northkell

ARCS above OXUS

Barcan, its urging windslope in motion
saltation; each grain singing ellipsing, arcing
not finished ever, the snaking crest tumbles over
rumbles and stumbles little golden crescents ever
reflects bits of its own winds to topple in reverse
topedge trimmed sidewindings its crest at tangent.
Wind curving carving testing never arresting
as wind does not let the arrête rest;
the piece is handled, even the tiny dreikanter
I find in the garden under the postglacial rind
that wind sand blasted blank, cold-desert marker
and the same little pyramids discomfort here.
Spilt mathematical crumbs, relent to molecules
compelled precise in apparent random sillinesses
dither downslope, accumulate to be barged into stillness
alone and echelon on recall of drumlin, lava-pillow

contracts signed, handed over, accommodated, fulfilled
for moonglow without wind, this word hit a moment.
Wither is landedge, for this is sea, sounding tidal
drowned trees, no mass lost ever in the life of the world
schools of these dunes energy store, swells spell
the hope of motion high lines lope of a frozen ocean
the wolf walks alone, his fellows in the hollows
howl for the outrider, hide sanded, all spoor blown

Three Years in Glen Garry

Three years accounts from gamekeepers' records, an estate
kept for Sassenach deer stalking, all manner of Game
    Preservation.
The statistics are false only in that the categories are derived
from dialect gaelic names for fauna: they are not stories
    contrived . . .
Three hundred and seventy-one rough-legged buzzards (both
    Buteos?).
Two hundred and seventy-five 'kitehawks'; which might, ought
to have included unknown amounts of various 'shitehawks'.
Two hundred and forty six martens; precious today our marten
    withal!
one hundred and ninety-eight wild cats, a hundred and six
    polecats in all
– the one much reduced but recovering, the other yet to come
    back from the feral . . .
Ninety-eight peregrine falcons, six even of the Arctic gyr-falcons
seventy-eight merlins, no kestrels?, (further, seven 'orange-legged'
    falcons)
sixty-three harriers, probably mainly hen-harriers, ditto goshawks
thirty-five 'horned' owls (the 'eared' species of owls, *incertae sedis*)
twenty-seven 'white-tailed' eagles (some the young of fifteen
    golden eagles)
eighteen ospreys, eleven hobbies, which might be average say for
    today.
The Clearances were not only of the people, but of most of the
    indigenes

at their climax: their dynamic climax, proliferating genes
culminating food-chains, being the noblest, most beautiful, most
  evolved.
A country that was ours to inherit, and theirs, gone under oxter's
  sweep.
Garry, stretch thy bare limbs in sleep; it gars me sair to see thee
  weep.

St Kilda-Wren, 1957

1

Sound out, sound over Hirta sound rare
clicking like loose spokes the wind wheels on
prayer, halfway up the cliff. if not forewarned
by it, I'd missed the foothold at your explosive scold –
and your nest only inched in off sheer, all of nine eggs in it
above, seven hundred feet gabbro, overhang.
Below, seven hundred feet granite, we shake together a full
  minute!

2

Nearly, according to Hudson,
called into extinction; Rare Race into museum collections,
brighten with atlantic bar-cloud patterns roundelay of their
  depressions
with something of the grey silver sea-spray's refractive sheen in
  this light, actinic near to Icelandic
Not the little rusty Jenny wren of the mainland; nor even those of
  Shetland, or Clear Island,
the rattle of castiron chain of such little boats as this 'Shiant', that
  'Naom Ciaran'
slack clack at the hull's rub, boat little-enough to bob
and go on rattling, 'muckle loud for sic a little brown job'
from the cletts the islanders once dried fish and gannets in, hail
distant tickle of spent bullets on tinsheets out on the range
strange gets inhabit the empty houses yet, RAF billets
spirits of the bird-cliffs when the seabirds are not
even the sea itself powering all around!

3

drowned by the secret is: and in to the weather
more than by wind buffetted I am; sheep even heafed are
and I dont try to climb any higher, even all the wrens in this cliff
if as one collect 'clack knacks' or I'd have put my foot on
another little dome. no other hold, but for you in your bold
courtship it was only a cocks nest, spare room, see
no gloom in the shouts, but doom gave a first life for me!

to C.B. August 1987

Painting with a Knife

painting with a knife the Invader
creates another Whitechapel impasto

drawn by lines of force from schoolyard railings
he follows a girl in black
down ditch streets & bollarded laneways

listens to the rivertalk
of vinegar-grey zombies
huddled around cardboard fires

later, there is a room a bed
the dissection of time
meat décor, exorcism in blood
the carving of forbidden words
on clean flesh pages

'fulfilled his red & bleeding feasts'

the machine in Invader's sleep
grinds its teeth

Star

star-breath descends. line
of mineral light passes through her.
she lies upon the ground
and dreams this request:

that star should be her lover.

dream entered her, stiff as a rod,
a flaming citrine halo,
scourged her,
raced the poles of her magnetism:

transforming everything.

star-child pained her.
giving birth through the flesh tear
to another planet.

it is not fit to enter
being sharp upon its points.

love hurts, & is refined.

A Bull called Remorse

either nude & pulled behind as well as
fixed in plucking mud, an anchor
to his own need, as the silurian effluence
scums to the surface in a vortex
of jaw-defying squidmeat

'elegant', says the child, meaning the opposite
& accurate, to the last spasm

scraping sunwounds off the salmon
the adrenalin releasing warts of
dried mushroom & a flashback
film-death, dyed in the 60ies,
red paint hair: the tribesman cannot
write himself back into his own clan

in a wholly alien period, finding
the lock that his special deformity can
enter, & he is singular

with all his hooks out, defenceless,
two salt channels of information
run down his pitted cheeks

with Madame Thatcher,
'I've had to learn to carve meat'

4 July 83

German Bite

an excitement of too much

the hands of the junkie not
as spectacular as the hands of Orlac
but as much of a functioning instrument
guiding the hit into what's left
of the thinking machine;

as if talking could be anything more than talking,
the world unsettled & not remade

too many reports of books, telephones, visions,
explaining the Usury Theory while
eagerly demonstrating it

blood under the skin, & paper dirt on it

8 September 83 (Camden Passage)

Hurricane Drummers!

Self-Aid In Haggerston

*'Ronnie Kray is now in Broadmoor & brother Reggie
in Parkhurst from where he is trying . . . to get a
security firm called Budrill off the ground'*

there's a mob of rumours from s. of the river
challenging the wood & shattering the glass
with drop-kicks honed on GLC grant aid;
the trainers stamp out likely
prints of light, moth shaped entries

another team of semi-skilled dips
work the precinct & dry-clean my licences,
cards, & small collection of folding
royal portraits, allowing them
to collect on unconvincing promises

a couple of vehicles are cased &
a couple crow-bar'd:
                                    in reply
the locals can offer a squadcar
of handy lads looking for lefty,
cruising on new tyres that give
the game away, authentic as
any red-light disco tipout

employment prospects look good
for the wolf importers, the cross-
breeders of beasts with
more jaw than brain – THE BELLS, THE BELLS

charm out in celebration,
new aerobic soles flash,
high knee torsion round
the corner of Queensbridge Road

'Hey, what is it about this place?'
says the Reverend suddenly,
looking out of the window at a
group of black youths as we
approach Dalston.
'They're smoking reefer on the street!'

'Music is music,' says Cleveland,
returning to his subject.
'It's the words that
separates gospel from the rest

Only the words.'

12 July 85

■ KEN SMITH

Living with the Boss

Don't tell me objects don't have feelings.
They resent our intelligence and fall down.
Telephones and police are never when you need them.

How did it get way past midnight without my noticing?
It's enough having to remember all day who I am,
how important, my number, my callsign, my cues,
where I keep the suicide pills and the silver bullet.

Am I or am I not the President of the United Shirts?
Did I accept this part? I have to call my agent,
I have to remember all this only to forget it
night after night with Nancy, and no let-up.

Snobby Roberts' Message

You're wrong she says. You'll do it my way.
I'm the head girl and all this democratic stuff
is for the firing squad and a short sharp shock
at the back of the gym with a rubber truncheon.

No cure. No treatment, No natural justice.
We have a business to run here. Sell everything.
Give the miners a stiff course in how to sink.
The prefects will know what to do with their hockeysticks.

I think she's never been lived in, Mother says.

The Night Whispers
For John and all the men in the world called John

1
There was a friend of mine,

used to offer me a cigarette.
On a Tuesday. John was talking.
He was saying what he hears, his ear
pressed along the wall along the wing.
Time's all there is he says, flat,
to one side, every second word
what he'll never do again with women.
He'll take a light off me though.

He's the man that ate boiled ham raw.
He'll take on a sliced loaf single handed.
Time is the crease in his pants I think,
pressed as in the army under the mattress.
John keeps himself neat. He knows
how quick they'll spirit him away
in a bodybag along the stairs before unlock.
He says he heard the screw say *One Off Sir.*

It's time.

Time he looks back from morning after morning,
his face changing in the same mirror.
Time is the razorblade, the comb's teeth
and the measure of the toothpaste. Time he eats,
shits, drinks, is sometimes merry in,
the fallen grey he lifts off his shoulder.

Time scuffs the shoe and blunts all the nails.
If there were no nights there'd be no fear.
Time I could handle but all this dark stuff
either side between the light and the light.

Time is what.
Time is.

He tells me what he hears in the night whispers
through pipework and brickwork, bars and the hard gloss,
and he writes down the messages: *Oddy's on the roof.*
The nurses are having a party. It's in.
All it costs are little pictures of the Queen.

Oh and love he says. *Love Love Love's*
faint echo on the landings, through the masonry
on a thin late airwave *Love* running down the batteries,
singing on a bent guitar
Lost in the saddle again.

Ah, John.

Lost in time both of us talking about love,
a word born over again and again in the prison house
where so many with their hands killed love,
and then the dark came down forever. So now
behind the yellow wall and the yellow fence
where the wind in a scatter of old leaves
beats the wire to security, the dogs howl
moonward and the champion dopesniffer Duke
sleeps on but John when he sleeps never dreams.

Time is what it is. The protagonist is mad again,
lost in some mean southern border town
all barber shops and bars and far too many shoes.
I've been out again beating my heart on the wind,
and maybe this time John we never get home
and the journey ends here and time's all there is.

The idea is don't die in prison John,
in this part of the nightmare.

2

My brother calls me from the world's other side
and never said which city. He's been robbed,
he's broke, homeless, out of a job and 48,
he's drunk in the wrong house and whose phone is it
and I fear my brother will die in the wind.
He says he's glad dirty money from a dirty job
went to a dirty place to buy a dirty girl junk.
Wherever morning is I hope he'll still be glad.
He'll send an address when he has one.

So now you know the plot. Fox is away
in Australasia waiting for the cops,
and when he called I was thinking about John
and what he tells me: *many things*

will never happen. As for me
I've been too close too long to the damned
and can't leave, lost as they are in time,
on my wordtrack covering the territory,
always in the dark thinking I've a lucifer
when I'm far too near the wire when the lights go up
and I'm lost in the saddle again.

Take me home, love, my scars and all my alibis
and my bad manners and whatever wounds we die of.
If you can find me. My name is John.
Maybe you can love what will be left of me.
Take me out of this prison.

Jack's Postcards

Just a line of posts along the baymouth,
and the tide out. And I'm supposed to know
what they mean, this ship, this flag,
both departing on the horizon, this message.

I'm being tested. I'm under observation,
interpreting these picture postcards
sent by the nun from Inverary *wish you
were here, but we pray for you.*

Pictures of cool green woods,
a thirst forever slaked beside the river,
a minaret, a market and a leaning tower,
and in the distance more the same –

the sunset over palms and best regards
from Disney World. You should know
the censor's on my shoulder always,
like the poor, like my angel, striking

what I cannot say in any case: does love
hold each others' hands still, does the heart burn,
or is the world just a glossy magazine
and all the polished girls bone china bright?

Writing in Prison

Years ago I was a gardener,
I grew the flowers of my childhood,
lavendar and wayside lillies
and my first love the corn flower.

The wind on the summer wheat.
The blue glaze in the vanished woods.
In the space of my yard I glimpsed again
all the lost corners of my childhood.

I was remaking them. Here in a space
smaller still I make them again.

They Have Taken

They have taken my father
and chained him to a wall.
They have taken my mother
and set her to pick thorns.
They have taken my sister
and bred her to a beast.
They have taken my brother
and cut one little cord in his heart.

My father fought his utmost
until he crippled himself.
My mother toiled patiently
until her fingers were barbed.
My sister fed her milk
to raise up scorpions.
My brother forgot
how to laugh or to weep.

My father studies his bondage –
he has made that his life.
My mother clings to her pain –
she has that much to grasp.
My sister loves her brood –
she love them, alas she does.
My brother grins and feels nothing –
nothing at all, nothing.

Residues: Thronging the Heart

thronging the heart

with utter astonishment
for expression

and on the face of a motorcyclist,
brought into Casualty, who'd missed a
turn, hit a lamp-post, his forehead
split down the centre, the eyes
hanging out

indeed, a sight

a form of utterance, an expression

an abrupt clarity

coming home from work, the Hills
against the sun: a blot of indelible
ink, indigo on carmine

down the centre, headlong
today, tomorrow or the day after,
falling abruptly into place

staining the memory
assailing

out of the commonplace, on impact,
unforeseen

indelibly and sometimes
even of trivia

with a gift of dandelions a child
picked and gave for my birthday,
staining my fingers, the marks
persisting

in the crannies lingering,
little streaks of happiness

or of surprise, and in names, in
each particular: a Jog Scray, a
Wallower, a Smutter – all parts
of a water mill

in a drench of words
and those uncommon

filling the corners, crevices,
crannies of what might

with the first reply
to the first question

    by the old worthies of the Kirk:
    to glorify – that is, sublime,
    transform

and in each particular

    like Beastie Dovey of Bringsty
    who made a cardboard bassoon
    and replied to query: not for
    the sound but to learn the
    fingering

no less, no more

    until left out in the rain to
    come apart at a breath yet
    unforgettable

that is, by force of intent,
an alchemy

    with every moment less, one
    less from eternity

so may we love, be loved
unreasonably, to distraction

    in bewilderment at each touch,
    each parting, wrapt round by
    absence, clutching

seized by each pulse,
each breath awakening

    hearing the alarm, almost not
    hearing, to wake to go out to the
    cold, to daily toil, leaving her
    bed, still dark of winter

who didn't ask to be born

    spewed to the light, a fish
    thrust on a shore

expiring in the air,
wrapt in a void

where we were borne by chance of
tide, to make our home, who have
none other

stumbling to rest,
not needing further

while doing something else perhaps,
breaking kindling, buying bread,
tying a shoelace even, realizing

thrust of what must

with a great pain flooding over
us at the sight of so much beauty,
that country called Arcadia, where
we'd stumbled

helplessly thronged
to need each other

with gaps in the haze, in the
dawnlight glimpsed, one sight

plume of the breakers,
shoreward

thronging the heart

■ SOME YOUNGER POETS

For a whole new generation of young British poets who began to publish their work in the 70s, there has been a dual sense of battles lost and won.

Eric Mottram's editorship of *Poetry Review* (1971–1977), as well as other seminal magazines such as *Poetry Information* and *Second Aeon* brought a wide range of poetics within the reach of young poets dissatisfied, like their forebears in the 50s, with the restrictive practices of the officially approved canon. The resulting explosion of poetic activity shook the National Poetry Centre to its foundations, but the revolution was short-lived. By the end of the decade, Charles Osborne and the Arts Council had regained control of the Poetry Society, and the new conservatism that was becoming the prevailing political ambience in this country at large did not fail to leave its mark on literature.

Where once, in the 1960s and 1970s, British poets creating the new (partly inspired by American and continental poetic movements) forced the literary establishment to sit up and take notice, now silence is eerie and almost total. No longer does the establishment revile modernism in poetry; it simply ignores it. The models to follow once again are Hardy and Larkin, the main axis of the poetry the quiet, singular, individual voice. There have been some minor modifications: Irish poets, for example, are permitted deep feelings, working-class poets can deal in leftist themes provided they do so within the most conservative of metrical forms; while an extravagance of metaphor and simile, often using late 20th century icons, has crept in to flavour the blandness of the quasi-journalistic language employed. Perhaps it was this latter phenomenon which led Morrison and Motion to claim the 'spirit of postmodernism' for their much criticized *Penguin Book of Contemporary British Poetry*; an interpretation of that abused and hackneyed term which appears to mean a *rejection* of modernism rather than a going beyond it, and one that offers a parallel with Carol Rumens' use of the term 'post-feminist' to describe her anthology of poetry by women, *Making for the Open* (Chatto).

The 60s, say these new taste makers, were the breeding years of an absurd aberration in British poetry; our language, our sensibility is not suited to experimentation and fragmentation of form, any more than it was suited to the Surrealism of the 20s and 30s. Those who disagree we shall ignore, they say. Like those British poets who were influenced by Surrealism, we shall no longer speak of them. Oh all right, perhaps Roy Fisher, but *nobody else*.

Faced, therefore, not with criticism or even ridicule any longer, but with tacit exclusion, where are the grounds for optimism among younger poets following alternative traditions to that affirmed by the establishment? What are the battles won, to be balanced against the battles lost?

They are these:

The first is to do with the mechanics of publishing and distribution. It may seem paradoxical to some – given the harsh economic climate which has forced the book trade to consolidate by concentrating on proven sellers and high merchandising – but it is easier for a young poet today to get into print and to have her or his work disseminated to those interested than it ever has been. I write from experience as editor of a magazine – *Reality Studios* – rumoured to favour the avant-garde. The quantity of small press books sent in for review shows no diminution, while the quality and sense of excitement is arguably keener overall than it was a decade or two ago.

This is not just a question of cheaper and more accessible printing technology. That plays a part, of course. The first poet-publishers of 20 or 30 years ago – the Gael Turnbulls, Stuart Montgomerys, Tom Raworths – had a narrower range of printing options to contend with. Since then, with the advent first of mimeograph and later cheap short-run offset litho, high quality photocopying and instant printing, and most recently microcomputer based 'desktop publishing', the possibilities have widened. However, the main problem these pioneers faced was not a technical one, but the fact that it had hardly been done before. Poetry was published either by established publishing houses, or in a handful of magazines and literary journals, or not at all. For alternative models of operation, poets had to look to America; as Andrew Crozier says in his introduction to his and Tim Longville's 1987 anthology *A Various Art* (Carcanet), a book which should be read in conjunction with the present selection: 'American examples provided lessons in the organization and conduct of a poet's public life, indicating how poets might take matters of publication and the definition of a readership into their own hands by establishing their own publishing houses and journals.'

The breakthrough these small presses made has continued to benefit poetry. I estimate that three-quarters of the poets in this section of the anthology have themselves been publishers at one time or another, and most of the younger poets are still actively publishing each others' work, or occasionally their own. Most would not even dream of considering the big publishers as potential outlets. While high street bookshops are less likely than a decade ago to stock small press books and magazines, there is an adequate infrastructure for dissemination, involving mail order lists, sales at readings and the odd specialist shop. That this is all taken for granted now is a tribute to the pioneering work of the first small press poetry publishers.

The second cause for optimism is this. Poets outside the mainstream in the late 50s and 60s were faced with the daunting task of making their poetry in what must often have seemed at the outset a cultural vacuum. The dominance of The Movement poets had resulted in the suppression of parts of English poetry's past; American post-war culture (music and painting as well as poetry) provided an alternative set of possibilities to explore; so did post-war European literary and anti-literary phenomena, such as the sound/text/concrete movement or the writings of the French *Tel Quel* group. But more recent generations of poets working within similar aesthetic paradigms have not been so handicapped. For now they have the previous generation's work to refer to: a body of specifically British but non-parochial writing that has remained, thanks to the small presses, available and alive. So that it is no longer a question either of reacting, negatively, against conservative local models or of looking overseas; there is powerful, original and hugely varied work done here. Many of the poets at the younger end of this selection have *started* by discovering the work of Prynne, Mottram, Raworth, Harwood, Cobbing or Roy Fisher, only then proceeding backwards through these to Pound, Williams, Olson, Ashbery or O'Hara, and then perhaps on to the current work being done in America or Europe.

Lack of space prevents the inclusion of as many of these younger poets as we'd have liked, but a list of exclusions would risk inadvertently excluding twice over. Amongst the poets selected, Peter Finch is represented by three of his ingenious and funny computer-generated poems rather than by his visual work or his long permutational 'process' poems, working like the systems musics of Glass or Reich. Paul Brown is another specialist in the visual collage or found image, an aspect of his work that strongly parallels his poetic composition methods. Ralph Hawkins's lengthier sequences from his astonishing book *Tell Me No More And Tell Me* (Grosseteste, 1981) have had to give way to shorter pieces, no less assured, and Gavin Selerie's long poem sequence *Azimuth* can only be shown in the briefest selection.

By contrast, we have included one of Elaine Randell's longest and strongest poems, a fiercely compassionate enactment of the joys and perils of women's lives that would not have seemed out of place in the feminist section of this anthology, a measure of the final impossibility of imposing such segregation and taxonomy on as vital an activity as poetry.

The implied politics of Randell's poem is upfront as it can be in Ulli Freer's anti-militarist, anti-patriarchal poem, whose anger and ecstasy both shine through the hard fragments of its making. But there is equally strong feeling in the measured cadence of John Wilkinson's lines, a short extract from a set exploring the extremes of terror and love (*Proud Flesh*) whose cumulative power is felt like deeply incised wounds and stands comparison with the poetry of one of the lesser known but much admired American modernists, John Wieners – while the ironic manipulation of multiple discourses within its argument owes something to Prynne.

Wieners is also the dedicatee of Cris Cheek's poem 'drawing on the traditions', which can only be excerpted here. But the metal of Cheek's poetry resonates differently. Of the collection in which this poem appears he writes: 'these works written in cars at traffic lights, improvised on to tape and transcribed, read against music "song" ie mahler or stockhausen ie slowly on to tape and transcribed . . . from conversation, from decaying works of "art", in bed, from the television, the radio on, the memory or meteorology, space . . .' In other words, Tom Raworth's 'the order is all things happening now'. Cheek, one of the few British poets to feed directly into the burgeoning 'language poetry' in the United States in the late 70s, is also closely involved with experimental dance. Improvised music is important, too, to a poet of a radically different cast, the expatriate Australian David Miller. His is a poetry of quiet, meditative intelligence which yet is never quietist. He knows how to make the discontinuities and spaces in his work shine with the unsaid.

Women have recently increased their presence in what has always been a more male dominated poetry than its equivalent in the United States. Glenda George's prose piece betrays the influence of the French writing she has been so instrumental in bringing into English, formerly in collaboration with Paul Buck. Elsewhere, she has championed the writing of those for whom '"womanism" is an essential part of their lives yet who have avoided the slur of "mere propaganda masquerading as literature" that I've levelled at feminist publications in the past', a position with which both Maggie O'Sullivan and Geraldine Monk concur. The two wrote a joint manifesto, published in the London magazine *City Limits*, which concluded that 'ultimately, the most effective chance any woman poet has of dismantling the fallacy of male creative supremacy is simply by writing poetry of a kind which is liberating by the breadth of its range, risk and innovation'. Geraldine Monk is the dedicatee of one of Tony Baker's pieces; his admiration for the playfulness of her language-games is evident in the sureness of his own linguistic imaginings. Baker, too, is a tireless magazine editor.

Ric Caddel's quiet eloquence in combining Olsonian (or Blackburnian) open form with specifically English content suggests comparison with Lee Harwood. Robert Sheppard, an intelligent theorist and commentator as well as an excellent poet, began writing under the influence of Harwood and Roy Fisher. Kelvin Corcoran and Andrew Duncan are both writers for whom politics and poetics are inseparable; their work demonstrates an exhilarating truth, that wit and irony need not exclude passion and trust in the pursuit of English poetry.

Things have changed in twenty years, and it has not all been for ill. No longer is it a question of 'establishment' and 'anti-establishment' poetry; rather, there is a range of poetries in these islands, largely ignored by or unknown to those who would hold the centre ground, yet evidencing superior vigour and breadth. Those poetries speak for and to communities which may be united by discrete yet overlapping notions of culture, politics, gender identity and geographical locus. The poets in this section of *The*

New British Poetry, whose commonality may be said to be the ceaseless urge to create meaning and value in the forms and modalities of the language itself, take their rightful place in this heterodoxy.

Ken Edwards

■ **TONY BAKER**

(*for Geraldine*)

the plush juice of
         from Seville w.
bitter pith & pips
                  'as if it
could be otherwise'
                        dark
fruit of knowledge, say
speak me you
gimcrack Lorcan oranges

■

        Storm clouds a smudge of damson
                over Birchover shifting pink
streaks beneath . The permanent
succession:
                days   walks home   a pulse
    of storms & clear days, that
                        verbal pulse

Useless to put a finger on
it, useless
            as grass is –

            From out a loft on
        the Flatts, a flock of pigeons
fly up & leave their mark, arching back
across housewalls, chimneys as
                        one bird past a check
            shirt pegged out with washing the eye
                        catches on
                                        &

sees them scatter then
a dozen specks –

It *won't* cohere, a
flock, their
mark   that
disproportion speaks
its own pace

moves across the sky as its own place,
dispersed or
where the clouds are

gathering en masse with
that persistent
impulse belongs to other matter .

poem*

first day of May Jack
be nimble gamble
on the syllables nipt
myrrhis seed licorice
NOW OPEN TO THE PUBLIC
a big sign or Ted's
little word for
it sounded
like *caw* or
car &
I agreed. Who-
ever could own that
an interest
is *controlling* ? the
scampered
directions
of a soft
blue Az-

* ♩ = 130

tec or chic-
'ry sky, un-
squarable, a blessing.
It's the encounter's
accountable
smacks of dung
smelt off fields
a mild westerly
swung
round from thinner winds
– was it *cow* ? –
between the teeth
to get the bit/
                bite &
his word for it
today is
what its worth is
good enough

From De Rebus

Almost believed in
the seduction of the sun
behind hands bled to
the bone each pore sweats
a retina, skin
so full of greasy
images I could
rub myself blind. This
body permits no
such modesty but
a temporary
thrust of blood flushes
out the game to the
perimeters of
its pain. Only

■

Saltpetre sucked up the cigarette with
animal vigour. Light laid its pattern
in birdsong. Insufferable was a
word which came constantly to mind when he
considered himself. The japanese vase
was remarkably akin. An item
introduced in the most seemingly art-
less way, yet never failing to appear.
Now, knowing the history, can one offer
any vindication for failing to please?

■

Unbowel the meaning
in black plastic bags
Vending machine coffee
tea and oxtail
On the north-east wall
burnt-sienna boy

Under the volcano
spur shelving. Rain
smacks its lips in gutters
billboards blanch, blanch
Its good to curl your
fingers in winter
around something hot

■

Don't talk to me
about migrations
cool blood curving in
to the aorta.
You stay alive
but never in the
same place twice,
the template
ever shorter.

The slightest cut
only increases
the chances.
Without feathers
we have no purchase
on the air.

■

Days damp has shuffled bent of back into the
cortex. Pour another High'n'Dry on
ice and tonic it. Slice the lemon like
a party hack. *Knife run on surfaces*

Each leaves each no more than hinting. The ice
at the bottom of the tumbler. There should
have been a something, never sure what. There
where the lemon's sucked the gin out of us.

■

This morning trampled
grey as paving stones
the unemployed sit
and watch as much as
anything the limpid
green borders of London
park benches. There plants
become confused with
roots, stones are similar
to brains where we sleep
in the best of all
possible. Utterly

■ RICHARD CADDEL

Wyatt's Dream

Whose eyes were sleepbound &
whose song stilled
saw the blade a bright beam
cleave the shield.

His love walked from the grave
veiled. Songster, fighter, &
lover stilled.
There in the cave.

Two Movements Which Begin at the Head and End at the Feet

Autumn / Dowland

As my mind's leaves
are blown
in tiny piles

so these airs
fret at their sense –
the foot is a pace

behind the song, the song
behind the wind,
wind teases the leaves

across the bar
to fall
at my feet

Spring / Purcell

Eggshell is the
mottled view my
windows give, my

fingers and my
wit: the street is
leaves birds' notes

drop from. Night is
calm, still –
the song of the moon

to the feet

Going Home
for John Riley

What in the world we see
is what's important. There
the days seemed shorter and our hearts
spun with the compass under

trees, magnificent pointers
out of galaxies. Continental drift,
an appointment we were late for,
an old friend missed.

Translation from a Lost Source

The full moon shines across the lawn
upon the small eyes and teeth of the (?) wildcat.

The frost crackles. My soul is empty / happy
as I stare at the red scarf.

Their (?) footfall soft in the shadows.
Moonlight at the open window falls on the (?) toaster.

Vers Negre

My black self. Another
has me, monkish.
A second moon, paler
gleeful, further

across the sky, and I
a child, listening.
Silence. Another
has my life.

Enchanter's Nightshade
homage to Louis Zukofsky

Circe a lute she on – you say
could risk your lot on a grace
family this music – come buy us
in shady places and chant
as night's hades not bitter
sweet toothed leaf is hearts cling
not a trope a white flower is
scarcely noticed song stem so long

Uncertain Steps

Not, I
        said pushing
back
        bushes from
Ann's
        face and
the kids'
        that
there's a

        gap –
here's
        the path –
between
        content and
comment – look –

        the orange
hawk –
        weed by

that burnet
        rose –
mind

        your feet
Ann said
        if you're

going through
        there – I
did – the

        warm
smell of
        water –

mint
        hit me – planting
my foot

        on
it. The print
        of my shoe

in mud –
        it's
gone

now.

The Paths

Two converging from
night, household
sleeping – moving
so together:

here a dipper
there a stream
here a pillow
there a dream.

from drawing on the traditions

a succulence by implication pinks the eye with condensation
smoke parts the towering awe, conceals a flight
the pursuit seems gentle but they've cut a score of trees to dance
    here
a yard yearns for an acre an estate
the fence built with materials xxxx shot during clearing
a hunt ball glasses shatter the lascivious
cheers
oh a jolly fine, painting what so, damned reassuring
and another and another
a change
differentiated hatching
a stone light
poised
blue ribs
bruised entering the tavern in a crowd
bone clouds
matronly refills stem pipe and clay bottle
touches on the thrown-ness
projected inescapable contingency
the portrait of a child
a few brief charcoal lines on a tinted
ground heightened with a faint veil of white yolk
borne by implication, suggestion of
streams
edge for the planes
body chipped out architecturally to a solid presence
the sheer weight and form of meat
becomes the stone around its vertical
driftwood

light be decks the rising and warming
bubbles flow back through the tube
recoil
re fuse
pluck
read aloud
xxxxx (xxxxxx xxxxx)
a garden out of keeping, with its borders
blown wide open
masked and creeping present
riots of feeling
occurrence bunched
more mystical bonanzas imbecilic
the soft ballet
features erasure
return of the need to move
variations crowd
the struggle to avert disintegration of form produces,
a system to regulate power, notation
man and woman dancing
aura
or a coming together of the whole body
music celebrates such, and or condemns the lacking of it
no one can be safe in love
who hopes
become a hat
fled party with a sailor
sucking the wet rag
rid of the thorn cult
bites on blackness animal grid mist over
stretched out neck
blossom
the blue sat spangles breed pool
balanced casually on the nape

or wear as a crown part of the scarf
pours into well this is more uneasy
a recording of loss ninety degrees resigned to what
to innocence, futility, acceptance
with innocence a lost recourse disguised in Gauguin's eye
two black women and a greyhound
Martini
Que

how we continually joke with the terrible terrible
court the ridiculous
fear to discover
water shit down
boats up beach world circle
raise the light mat

boat by light cabaret
The Englishwoman from The 'Star'
the most important sense of humour
equilibrium
she holds the child to her breast
imagination
glance today

monday february 5th 4.10
    1979

    drawing on the traditions
partl. 23 figures in decay
    or the fine art haemorrhage

for john wieners

284

Volitionist Economics

you're so dumb you don't even see
the treasure you're trampling with your own feet,
the motherload drained into every pocket,
my mother comes home in a liberty ship
baby by baby she brings heaven into the world.

all this happens in a particular light
for the farmer and his daughters,
the fruit ripe, the cows milk and
the spring rain focuses yes above the hill
in a green dress they cannot help but meet,
se habla Espanol?   you want   yes?
her celebrated girdle of bananas packed the house,
she became famous overnight

this is volitionist economics
the veins of gold glue the politics together,
lights go on in different rooms
architectonic agents plot and unplot,
you better talk fast they want answers
is this Rimini? Paterson? Gloucester? Lambeth?
I don't believe it but love it

A Slogan will not Suffice

the work of the sun, not illusion
diamonds hidden in the kitchen calendar
we pin them in the cork and shiny frame
bills and visits and mathematical stars,
like a deck of marked cards.
you are already here,
the trial of love that should be love
each word against each word

                    down of your arm
    I look, lift in my heart

    trust the occasional radar through the dark,
    the cold wheel cash holds together
    it is a plot against the chickens of America
    the wealth rolls off the Atlantic in neat symbols;
    one dark raindrop, a semicircle of sunrays,
    a pigeon wings it on hard blue March,
    your money or your money and then
    Spring comes with obscene practices in the sky
                        from every part of the ranch
    the boys came to meet the new boss,
    the man of style   I float my legs
    in the bath of this weather.
    She saws through the bread down to the table
    slices each period of life is conducted
    in the way life is conducted
    and stores the table in the polar box for summer.
    Eat strawberries and run away,
    the lungs open the shoulder blades spread
    and it smells like bread, like petals and horse shit
    in the massed scents of May.

    In the spring of cash RAF boys probe the hills,
    farmers in tractors bravely waving, our boys in dungarees.
    I walk in their film, you are in it, part of it.
    Well captain, you look bitter, hurt and drunk.
    I do?   Yes.   Well I am, just rub that for me and forget.
    the trees scratch the fat sun
    bad debts from the people we won't pay,
    the postman said, silence in court the cat is pissing.

    When I hear what it is meant to do to me
    I hate it. I'd rather the flopped hollyhock
    and yogurt lid, I'd rather the adverts
    there is always music for your feelings, you are part of it,
    like landscape in Thomas Hardy
    under the heat of this traffic, beside yourself,
    a man will leave if you fail, hello sir, it's me, Nic

on a horse taller than the hedge
he found a dead town formerly a zero
buzzed across the helloing girl
dark a girl garden decked in trees
families and traffic fresh from the word

this is not Wittgenstein or a dream you could dream in sleep,
below the arrow of the town map outside the library,
You are here. The roads travel from the varnished frame
around pink blocks on bleached green
the whole thing looks nasty and fucked up;
the police station, the play-with-me-houses
and the insanitary schools.
I think of their real colour
the same sun greens the real town
I think of how we could have lived
I think five aces, hit the deck or die

Nobody Thinks Hard Enough for Poetry

I've walked through their town
but nobody thinks hard enough,
the distractions are many: novels, news,
people and moving pictures in boxes
– you've never seen the like
now the rain hits the window
on the hills it's snow, an English spring

actor poets prat about in arts labs
they rage and imagine a vain thing
but their art is a contrived sloth,
I think they don't concentrate
not on one single word,
one book dropped in the letter box
would burn their paper homes

marooned up stage mouthing air
mighty history glares down
that's our history, the cyclorama
where everything is at it happens

buried and shining in the streets
the articulate speech you taught me
my kind king, I send you a line

■

a man dances with twelve girls,
he's fully clothed if formal;
they jiggle in spangled underwear
to the power of men and women

woman framed and heaven shot
the mighty dark descends,
a weekend blown out
down the bitten edge of sense

night's locked tight
windows suck in the sky,
inside the raw crystal of ikons
pictures a prince, a princess, a servant

their faces give no light
the archaic order of lies

■

Apparently in the real past tough men dazzled the illiterate tribes
with shining books. Standing on a northern shore to the shush of
the dreaming sea. – Look at this picture. It's God. Drawn in Judea
and coloured in Rome these are God's words of incarnate meaning.
The invaders of written revelation won hands down. History then
became compulsory; the poor got poorer and did nastier jobs. A
seditious man said, – Your kingdom is built on murder. I make my
books against it.

The Poet and the Schizophrenic

We both have voices inside.
        You can't understand yours.
Mine speaks the natural language of the human soul.

You were made by your family background, or by some virus.
   I became when I saw the moon in the bare trees.

You can't work because you can't adapt because you are asocial.
I have Weltschmerz and mal du siècle.

You hit on a vein to make the blood come.
I inhale inspiration.

You'll be post-mad. Light work and anti-depressants.
I'll be a literary critic. I envy you.

You have a doctor to listen to you sometimes.
I sue to the NHS for an audience.

We both have private worlds.
You're a hunted animal in yours.
I'm a king in mine. Dead poets live there.

You sit in a room and the room screams.
I sit in a room and tell the walls to show some affection.

I am rapt.
You don't move around much.

You are regressive.
I concentrate, and return to the Golden Age of matter.

You look at a wall and see the cemented grid of your unhappiness.
I look at a wall and see a white, peeled wand.
Then I see a tree half ablaze and half in flower
Which becomes a forest whose thoughts are birds, birds . . .

You imagine a dream lover you can't imagine –
Who would be ideal for you wouldn't be best suited.
I sing a lyric call to anyone who ever looked beyond the world
Anyone of the regressive literary intelligentsia
Anyone at all.

We both operate in metonymy.
You dip your language in the loss so no-one can understand.
I work in colours of the light of happiness.

You move through a landscape peeled of expectations
Where houses are not shelter and riches are not calm.
I am post-modern.

No-one understands what you say because you're worthless.
No-one understands what I say.

I'm above you.
You're inside me like the sacrifice inside a god.

In the Red Grove

The beautiful Chinese at the computer terminal has notes in
   ideograms
The bit stream remanifests itself as machine code in Hertfordshire
Similar bit-streams migrate as winged beetles or pause as
   mushrooms.
The reworked Hell's Angel dallies down the road
Brass valves were removed from his head
(Through the brainstem and yanked out through the clavicule)
Recast in an open forge in a county famous for clean air
Left in a February dyke for three weeks
Chafed down with worn high-denier silk stockings
Tuned to a mellow gong frequency, and refitted.
His aggressions were deterged with grit-guns, like old colleges.
His subliminal dramas were played out at the Essoldo (in the
   mornings)
His damp course, above the 1st vertebra, was relaid.
He used to go Pakki-bashing: now he teaches housewives yoga.

His jacket now speaks in gleaming steel studs:

Georg Groddeck. Ferenc Juhàsz. Max Ernst.

In Golders Green the greatest living expert on the Babylonian
   Talmud
Has an epiphany of numbers while passing the old pink theatre.
The true and false Zodiac, the cabbalo, the Messiahs,

The twelve months of the year, the twelve tribes, and the 13th,
  secret, moon,
Are mapped on the stucco as if with an aerosol and stencil

It looks something like a rosy cricket pitch
Or a screen with plotter stitched into the stucco,
A piezoelectric oscilloscope fed on the domains of brick.
Later, he uses a map of London for gematria.
He knows: the number of great poems written in a century
The numbers scattered on the breeze in isobars
The numbers memorized by Miriam or Yehudi
The numbers stacked in the depository, baled and corded

A blueprint stored in numbers waiting for workmen with their
  decoding arms.
The number of Urs you can touch in your life
The number of sparks in a great poem
The system behind London bus numbers
The efficiency of manweeks (roughly 0.76)

The number of serious possibilities
Herwarth's treatise on the inaccuracy of statistics
Eteomathematics, treated entirely without axioms
The skeins of wool you can gather on a wet morning
The numbers in the nervous system
(Like the statistical charts of Le Roy Ladurie
The mass observation of consciousness)
The angle of what's heard to what's meant
The absolute tempo of perception, the score as written.
He has traffic tables for each date and notion,
The quantity of thought: pitch, calibre, tessitura, erlangs, kiloherz,
  presence, soul.

What is the Red Grove?
It is the inner environment considered as a copse.
Where a pram rusts, woodlice snuggle inside the lining.
The red grove is by Woodhouse Eaves
That is, the eaves of the forest.
Rooks, not housemartins. In the Wood House
Tapestries moulder. In the decaying mansion of chaffinch and
  crayfish
Ancestors have walks of life, not portraits

Antlers are heirlooms silver laid down in velvet preservers
The trees change dresses for each season –
Near-naked in the winter Riviera,
Their dresses yield froissements in the summer winds.
Small leaves, caught on masses of spiders' webs
Are patterns of cards
In the smoking-room where the gentlemen gamble.
Heritable wealth plummets to the working, barmy, mould.
Trees are great estates, cut up and mulched
By solicitor-worms and bark-beetles.

In the Red Spinney
Shuttles weave, controlled by cards,
Heckled by babies glossolalling,
This napery stitched with Quarlesian emblems
Antimacassars of polite diction
Dyed with kermes and spilt wine
Sheets made from nocturnal rivers
Doilies of metonymy primping the unsayable, also negative doilies
Camouflage-tunics of sublimation and cheerful bouncing ignorance
Tramp-nightgear of mediaeval Greek manuscripts
Teacosies portraying 'The Poet's head in the throes of inspiration'
Veils for the virgin shattered by the nuptial trances of flowers
Handpainted ties for spivs showing the Muse sunbathing
Smocks with live, moving pictures of the internal juicescape
Albs showing faithful maps of fields: clover, couchgrass, bumps
Which textual scholars memorize for use in exams
Pelisses of bee-fur and sweet-chestnut pods, and mares-tails –
And they tear them down each night in the sleepgrove.

What is a red grove?
The modern Herrick; the Jungian missal;
The telex receiver without wires,
Reading seeds, feathers, psychoactive ions, throw of smokestacks,
The issuer of books printed on wasps' nests;
Alcoholic of the sweet juices in nettle flowers;
The Boswell of mould growing on cheeses;
The self-awareness of cuckoo-spit.

■ KEN EDWARDS

John Coltrane, *Live in Seattle*, Impulse AS-9202-2

'You must change your life'

Utterance: any continuous stretch
of speech or writing from a single source

Attendance: to what is there
& what is not there; *activational*.

Resistance at all points: to corroding
of ideology by 'the natural'; to procedure

that *carries* prescription, that
doesn't enact or become

bed, flower, decomposed into
the stain of collective ecstasy.

Linton Kwesi Johnson, *Forces of Victory*, Island ILPS 9556

The Firmament Doth Shake

Or the light, or the
Figure itself. Monday morning, not

Reggae boom, the big lorries
Thunder; as sleep glues eyes.

In yr own words to
Make music, building Jerusalem in

England's (Inglan's) green & gorgeous
Wastes, the car lots filled

With floodlight & all the
Smoke you can see. Skin

Stretches, & cars are driven
Thro' grilles, matt lustrous &

Matt, Colour Separation Overlay, you
Bet they'd judged them seductive.

Wake to flutter & sun
Full-blown thro' the rainbow

Arch, wake bath'd in the
Irradiated TV meta-language you

Already speak, sclerotic with direct
Juxtaposition of unrelated events, kiss

Kiss No Problem you just
Climb into the heat &

Nothing's happening, nothing at all.
You have choices to make,

Decisions to take, but fluid
Boils in the lungs, the

Vocal's out of synch, they
Whose only concern is yr

Health have committed millions to
Screening, attack, erode all the

Way down to the one
Poor fucker, Waterloo surgical spirit

Drinker, savouring his fumes &
Root of anger; under the wine

Coloured railway arches, the shapes
Emerging. The desert is all

Around & the towers shake
When they promise you anything.

Geraniums, South London

1

Geraniums   lip blossom
rustles, whereon

the city sky almost white
space.   Children

smelling subways
lead & rain speckled glass.

One healthy plant the rest ruined
at ground level & far away the

sun   behind fronds; two swallows
driven through sunshine, music teased

its appearance slowly till there's
     cardboard   clamped beneath

walls of galvanized iron,
moulder'd bricks

cupped over the lot
or perhaps 2 figures moving but

in coloured sweaters, a woman with
trousers held by coloured wool

down draining crocks onto the flutes
roots tinder   mashed into bone

into a cylinder of yellow grain
volcanic heat, ochre, sulphur.

Geraniums, distorted. Not with
blush lustre soiled   Geraniums

seen through lattice
of heavy iron. Butter melts into

riot as rain
& soil; hardy cactus unknown

to flow it does anyway.
What kind of sickness, a hard man

      rehearses his *fin de siecle*
over dust shadows

at midnight, so rearranged.
'LBC, it's 17 minutes past 9'

and then nothing but fourteen
people (one for instance

species rubber   flesh frayed pink
'it was not without interest')

2

It gets colder as you leave, children
& only to be expected.

start of winter
      a composed text changes

'loveliness' an epidermal itch,
          Little

pantiles which undulate, grass run
by the way, geraniums

out of shape by interference
but *through*. Only one

      plane prepares to land
          so many

bills posted crooked, piles of
patterns; a walk

      The click
drunks beat dustbin lids, the piss

fruit worm eaten, a concern with
coloured felt tip pens crowded

                    ; fine calligraphy;
catch the bottled light splashed

                              bubbles crawl
                              thin paper

shutter'd cinema, to get it
you can go *too* far.

nothing to be added, a 5 year stint.
Geraniums, my children dancing

The Computer's First Proverbs
after Edwin Morgan

You can take a dog to the keyside, but you can't push him in
all is wet that starts to bark
if you pay peanuts you get them planted in the park
nothing should be done in haste but grip your trout
if you want fish, you must prepare for stink
he who fishes with the piper barks like a dog
he who fishes a tiger is afraid to wink
fish will out, fish will out
all roaring is the same in the dark.

A dog in the brook is worth avoiding
think of a fountain and you froth in the head
speech is water, fish are water
it is too late to rub in embrocation after the dream has gone
strike while the law is out
put the stout dog to a deaf oven
flush the fridge if you have a long arm
idle lips make the best smoke rings
fishmongers always make room
it is all melted than ends melted
in May let the plugs bloom
You cannot roar with the workers and ignore the phone
it takes three waders to make a wet man
the longest dog winks all the way home

An Improvisation on the Oxford Dictionary of Proverbs

Passion Shaved Beneath the Grain-Silo
a computer poem

happiness, faintly as the excrement,
nightly outstared. The twins slam
irrevocably the television, glitter the shovel,
beneath the shovel, as the keyboard, ghostly vipers mutter.
civilized, injudiciously, dates squeak,
beneath vastness, at the river, laconically chairs take
nightly the keyboard, inform a mudguard,
faintly the baby, wake the fear,
punished the cloth, ask the fear,
countlessly sweated, splendours jump,
spools come by symmetry,
passion shaved beneath the grain-silo,
on the baton-case, from the omen, arduously abominations wait
courteously, inarticulately, the halls state.

Customize the Grass
a computer poem

abominations break above the river,
democracies stand by the hanging, prefer the opening,
dates hang by the omen, customize the grass,
the Turks point towards symmetry, grow a bicycle
splendours pray with a mudguard, break the weather
arms call aside the terrible, look the sweat,
they pun through the night, toss the bus
the mules fall on a tape, pinch death,
you slam with a bicycle, point the keyboard
the mules point through the sunlight, hard death
the ruins stand with passion, wake glory
abominations break above the river
serve the hatchet, frighten the poem, light the door

Take the Toys from the Boys

      name all the shadows   astride & back from the street
      thrust upon   by blue sleeve across my turkey red limbs
   gripped through detector beams   blends blends of skin
don't carry the keys for fitting in for fighting in
    they are all quilted in leather lining of his coat
long knives in the chest   chart   heart mechanical
             map of brothers   marriage ultimate give away
     & the pressure drop on our jugulars

i reflects in this clean shave of ideologies
    fallen hairs of breath   more of the white foam applied
then pull down their hoods   ordered identity to be fixed
             stroke of habit & rush demand
fornication served through the temples
               behind the screen the fortifications
    grown hollow ground blade on the land
                   & in the deep harvested
    & city a density aflame on each his anvil
contrasts with economic futures under the glasshouse
effect to come   how to get the gas to go
        the gases to go out of here

   costs & trucking of a single hogshead
   between the skinned & gutted law
      glistens as star chamber
        raw strategies   control of hips
      ready lips round table digested
          break   fast
        at the window
                glass
democracy another invasion double glazing
              plugging in power
        surplus energy gold flash braided
          the lines in his face
               marks
       of distinction

wearing a suit of tar & feathers
                              stuck to reinforced stone
                              silo
              wherein there there veins merge & freeway
     for the immense spike to prick
                              action of swallowing
                              opens tree bones
                         by the valve
              that chance our ears landing

sitting in this moving spear   through the clouds a rattle
                    you hum to heart
                         murmur murmur
           to the very scent of wild rosemary bushes
                    & the moon landing at our feet

                    the sirens get louder

     in the streets nightly blueshine
     floods the slaughter
          a
                beating
                         that stretches metal
hear the burns within vibrating hand
   drum drum from the heart from the heart
   he spoke over the telephone
                         howl of wire traces
        waving his arm about   throws another beer
     down throat   ore pure a real boy shot
                    up the market
        be then in   decide the room
     expanse of his eye reddens fury
              deal of image come to take the bed
                    as we sleep low
burn my tongue on the spikes of his belt
   sure you want to give it away   in a pine yodel
   then chews more   emphasis on transmission
        & the deadness of his face against umbrella
          plant
                leaf whose roots have got the weavil

tightening postures

nature has equipped man & higher animals
            with marvellous apparatus
        held out or breath as it stands
                    body to hang off hemispheres hook
                        marble dual track
                    whose centres aim
steel point of bow compass corrupts circle into straight line
        mean in the fingers spare parts to consume
                    as teeth form
                materially materially strengthened
                contaminated further illustrated
a wake in a tower block arsenal
    fragments the people dealing in owning each other
                we hug each other
                did you hear the waste bag fall down the disposal shoot
        night embankments
future the landing light won't switch on
    chute time in the window shape of panic
                embedded in these steps

    in wartime the importance of the job to the war effort
maybe the source of satisfaction
    easy or clean work
    may please the worker

                        i watch you as you put the watercress
        to your lips & they were counting the stairs
                flakes that shade in the green gauged
                    embraced by flow from on the balcony
                        we listen to the owl ascend
                    from oak branches   over heads
            the cat curls on this page   i cannot sleep
    whilst your hair is singed by the sentries arclights
                            turn to the sink
                    thoroughly washing the leeks

QUASI QUASI . . . as if, repeated

first section   the extension

Enhancement of life. Blood's to defeat its preordination or gravity's pull. When the bones gleam clean through the pale skin as s/he sits, crouched and knees beneath chin. Her friend tells her of resignation. How not to fight / but still not yet be defeated. In the present state, the bones of the foot and ankle are all visible and she counts them. She ticks them off on the list she bears: a permanent scar on her left thigh.

They are, alone in separate spaces. Each enclosed in a box as solid as if . . . They sit on the outside of contrary walls and watch over the scenario within.

Perhaps it was a result of a childhood trauma. When her sister fell or when she herself . . . or when he . . . When he passes through her field of vision, will her eyes half-close? Perhaps he will not register. Or only as a passing shadow, a change in the source of light.

While they spoke of a possible solution, his fingers were counting the freckles on her cheek. One day they will pass beyond the game or the pretence of the game. Then living may begin. It is not possible to stop pretending by a conscious effort of will. The pulse flickers in her left eye. It blots out sight and all is erased.

Meantime the game may continue.

I wish it was possible to determine how many are playing. Rules exist, but with the utmost flexibility. Certainly each participant plays by a different set of rules. Is it enough to know that one is playing?

Control of time had passed out of their hands. Before s/he knew, the briefest encounter was history.

False awakening. Dream life continues although s/he are only as if . . . They share the yawn in the intimacy of isolation. As if. As if able to see one another, they conduct their gestures as one.

second section   verité

At each syllable of the reading aloud, the jawbone grates. A few paragraphs later, a pain begins to develop close to my right ear. I stop reading. Avoid retreading old paths.

'Into the inconceivable light of this dark,' says my son of ten. He finds it hard to believe this could have sprung from his own intellect. Myself at ten, I read a book (by an American author) called 'Fifteen' and wondered if I would ever develop the figure (that it was obvious one needed) to acquire a boyfriend. At fourteen I was still wondering. I wonder still.

Reality is so short lived. I am forced to quit for lack of things to say.

third section   the absorption

S/he becomes as if through the very difference. They are afloat, though I suspect that for him the water is warmer. In her pool, the liquid freezes about her like a cage. S/he is obliged to speak obliquely lest the sound be muffled, the meaning distorted in bubbles that hit the air and die. So much effort.

Through the opacity of the paper castle. It is a way I have walked previously. It is likely that s/he can see much further with closed eyes, asleep. In your head someone is singing.

Follow the sound as I blindly followed the winged pink elephant in my dream. In the erotic truth of an instant of suffocation or beating.

Having the temerity to suffer, s/he denies ultimate confession.

fourth section   re-capitulation

Tension blocks the way between them. Yet, beyond precognition, the words provoke attendant reaction.

There is a horror in this presence. Circulation gasps and threads to a new dizziness. S/he spoke of the fear of no tomorrows. When trapped in the lower zone.

Perhaps it was a result of a childhood trauma. When her sister fell or when she herself . . . or when, later, the first words were uttered of a possible solution.

But it is not possible to stop pretending. One day that pretence will don reality and we will not know where the core begins. The pulse flickering in my fleeting glance affects how s/he will see.

Control of time has passed out of her hands. Before s/he knew, tears washed away the wall.

False awakening. In the erotic truth of the ultimate self-confession, dream life continues as if . . .

Those words choke. (In the final stages of strangulation, the trachea may be entirely crushed. High, unconventional musical notes may be emitted during constriction of the glottis.)

As if, the gardener stalks his prey and minds the essential knowledge. He is like the deaf-mute at the window, who finds the split in the curtain. One day he will find the correct location of words to fulfill the pattern.

Mandatory euphemisms lurk to lull the dare. How not to overstep the mark? That herbaceous borderline that the gardener set out in sequence? Years ago now.

In a moment of bravado, s/he tosses a bold work into the air between them. In the pauses, between the words, they pick clean the bones of intellectualism. 'The key' s/he said, 'may be found in the film. In "Exterminating Angel". Or again in "Ne Nous Delivrons Pas De Mal." '

fifth section   edging towards

O eloquent telepathy! Blockage.

It is tantamount to a near miss. The blankness is deliberation. I would like to creep into that space. To fill it with a conspiracy. The subterfuge of such offhand violence holds them entranced. I ask a series of questions, possessing nothing with which to answer.

It is as if . . . I possess my body. I am within it. Yet it is just a body, borrowed for an occasion which is to last a lifetime. Tide. The limbs float as they will in the waves. The tongue which is called mine sometimes moves in its mouth. The vocal chords sometimes relax and contract and the little rush of air which passes through them is the basis for sounds.

S/he turns to identify the pursuer, the one who only follows. It is too late, however, for him to make an impression. Already the tide washes away his footsteps. Was he ever really here?

sixth section   facing up

The blonde in the dormobile that you saw was a figment of your desire for concealment. Of course. You knew that really she was ignorant. It was only as if she was . . .

The tree bows backwards in its desire for disentanglement. Though unable to identify it, I take pleasure in touching its bark. There are no walls here upon which to sit and construct dreams. I like to sit in the sun and squint at its rays as they filter through my hair.

Rude awakening. Approaching winter denies me. I recall (after an interlude of many many years) the softly singing Irish voice to which I loved to listen. The solitary characteristic was sufficient to mesmerise. As if . . .

seventh section   naïveté

'Will you play I-Spy with me?' he asked.
'You begin.'
'I spy with my little eye something beginning with F & A.'
'Two words?'
'Two words.'

. . .

'There is nothing in my view that begins with those two letters you say.'
'Do you give up then?'
'I give up.'
'I can see Far Away,' he said.

'One day we were out walking and you said to me: "Look at that stone!" and as I looked it leaped from the ground and bounced towards me. I put out my hand to stop it from hurtling into my face and it rebounded away to its original distance. Then it turned and sped toward my head yet again. This time I caught it but my hand closed on a dagger. I wanted to kill you. I was about to. You must surely remember the incident?'
'My unconscious was far away at that time.'
'I was about to kill you when I noticed that you were naked and the incongruousness of the situation roused me.'
'You did not kill me then?'
'If I had done so, we would not be talking together now.'
'That is true . . . I too have a tale to tell.'
'For that I will listen.'

eighth section   premature finale

He tells her a story but it is of someone else, his absence always evident. The shadow is always past or future. It is never in the now.

306

S/he enters the dream time which is the only place where fear may be safely challenged. All the doors are firmly locked.

Rude awakening.

The window is the breach. Who are these who appear, armed and dreaded?

I retreat. I climb the stairs. I am powerless to create the time that s/he requires.

In the room where he slept there was no light. His sickness had gnawed her too. I can see that these people will soon discover them. S/he clutches the cool, skeletal frame in terror as they fling open the door.

S/he awakes.

They share the yawn.

Revised and edited from an unpublished ms, written in 1980, this text was for Bernard and for M.

■ **RALPH HAWKINS**

The Colours He Came To See

Every morning he would walk out to look at the buildings. It was quite easy to imagine other places as he walked. The countryside for example in a contemporary setting of boats in a creek. However, the thought of buildings gave him relief from tedium, in the same way as did a well-fashioned oak tree. It was strange to him not to know the dates attached to these substantial entities, although of course he could intuitively guess. He often guessed, not imagined and guessing pleased him. He guessed of a natural kingdom and this implied a qualitative past and not a resplendent future. Blotting out the unpleasant never crossed his mind but like everyone else he suffered from minor imbalances now and again. 'It isn't my concern', he thought as he read of contemporary shifts of power, and in the same way he subjected himself to stained glass or the careful avoidance of the environmentalist's nightmare. Dogs should be kept in their proper place. Slowly he became attracted to space exploration, seeing in it a guide to the past, wondering if on previous occasions of exploration what was found to be of worth. He documented the packaging of fast food, the designs of postage stamps, the fashionable young and the expanse of caravans. Buildings to him were the sum of their buoyed up materials. He longed to be able to study the details of their interiors, the fixtures and fittings. In the same vein he noted that material is deposited from some behind or past in various forms and for no doubt various reasons, usually in haste and retreat from somewhere and someone (tangible if in the microcosm in the form of a lover, a sweetheart or sexual companion). When these notions became interstellar then one is stuck with them for more than, and different to what could ever be described as a day. Are you ever the same person? Thus he especially came to view particular colours in a certain light. He was attracted by them and likewise one can see in them his attraction to them: peppermint pink, orchid, gold apricot, sky blue, pale peach, pomegranate, iridescent salmon and olive green. They are all warmly mediterranean and attached to something other than a room or what is offered to a room in silk gloss or matt emulsion. These interiors are what attract him so

much, the fact that most of them will remain unknown to him.
These buildings crop up everywhere, the ones one wants to enter
and cannot. Here time hinders accomplishment and ticks away in a
small photograph or snapshot he keeps in his wallet. Like many of
us he does not have to look at the picture to know what it looks
like. It comes to mind adjacent at various homes. He can go into a
room in any building and find a bureau drawer which contains
mementoes of his past. Each encountered building provides
thoughts of heady dematerialization, self transportation and
passing moments.

Cattle

from this range it all goes out with becoming
naming the objects as they occur
especially if they are black and white the colour of cattle
but it's all packed meat and goodbye

hello to what's inside this outside and vice versa
mincing the chicken with pork, adding cream,
cloves, mace and plenty of seasoning
skipping to you in a blue dress

'I can read your mind' he said
somewhere in Cambridgeshire potted in the earth like
treasure trove lies our future
when they mean theirs

now eat your meat like a good thing
before hairs turn on my palm or I wither on
some cliff face like a whale I've turned up on some beach
plutonium the colour and texture of a pork terrine

Birds

sparrows pitch at the wooden walls
there are trays of these things for us on
shelves and behind refrigerated doors
chocolate, malt, apples, beer, yams

I wouldn't think there was any questioin of choice
as they smack up against the glass
I watch the feathers fly
it's all pennies from your pocket

being told to drink this you'll look good
for a packet of Kellog's this is quite remarkable
just like peering over a pan at the meat
add white wine, lemon zest and later cream

in a bed of down of goose and duck
but I'd rather be here over my boiled egg listening
to the sulphuric rain hit the lakes of Sweden
or the fact that government policies *are* working

that's circa July 1980
no I am not undernourished neither am I wired to
the elements but rather to these abstractions which
fill the house with running water, light

and heat, I watch parts of me fall apart with
the years coming to terms with myself only because of
the others and the others are going out to sea of a weekend
cars pulling yachts trailing people in rubber suits

the well mannered affluence of it all I find ironic

Imperfect Air

through the imperfect glass of windows
warm air and clouds
the rushings of hungry birds
the mumblings and calls of neighbours

and in the world beyond or contained by this
though never touchable
are the touchstones of a short life
in the world of power relations

the pettiness of it all
focusing its gaze upon 'excess'
meaning the behaviour of frustration
of coming down on petty offences and minor indecencies

undertaking to protect
separate and undoubtedly forewarn
signalling perils everywhere
awakening all of our attentions and/or fear

calling for stiffer action
piling up reports and statistics
arming themselves with the sophistications of and/or
water, gas, rubber, plastic

and yet tokens of wealth on the screen
and on the streets the acquisitions they are without
created by us, for us, wanting and longing
and in the long queue the flyleafs of poverty

a number of numbered papers in the hand
and through the letter-box formless
vast quantities of bargain goods
and on the news oppressed peoples everywhere

Primavera

1

that I loved them, & that meant
loving them forever a small window
that for me it would be an *eternal*
memory
lost a darkness utterly black
travel no visible record

2

so this is *image* poetry? he asked
no I said the voices faded in
afternoon air noise of traffic
early heat
I walked with my back to him
away into the crowd then turned
to face him he had already stopped filming

3

white chalk on a blackboard
blue chalk on a blackboard
green chalk on a blackboard
yellow chalk on a blackboard
white blue green yellow
chalk on the pavement

4
those children will take your hand
because unable to tell you
lead you away
they may kiss your mouth
to stop your commands
they will avoid your eyes then perhaps
stare fixedly into them
& then not look at your eyes again

5
light changing the features
right side of the face
I mean, scarcely visible in reproduction

6
the telephone the small window
table
no words
a gap at the heart of things
black space exactly next to
the light from the window

7
'looking into' someone's face
then hearing their words over the telephone
table centre of the room
diffused light of the afternoon

8

walking in the woods for miles
then coming into my room
beyond allegory beyond dreams
pavement the only guide
the figure stopped put her head to the window
looking out
her eyes pensive

9

two figures (one my friend) their backs
both of them facing
that wall
the Wailing Wall
a death

10

a wood a forest my own youth
city material images of high contrast
footsteps through a doorway to follow the differences
in how we walked
between some fragments O light of spring

■ **GERALDINE MONK**

**Poem for August –
or for my birthday**

August comes
deep challenging
poised on shipwreck:
undulating landscape
              hot loops of calligraphy
scrolling metal
       razor sh /
              fade /
                  mirage
black-eyed coins – belladonna / weep

and chink chink of acrimony

energy
      insinuates

this belligerent month
spread-eagled
with sheer gravity
thunder-sard-
onyx like waspish
on the frequency of brown
plain brown

disrepair

below immensity   I
struck zero
        AVULSION

Beneath the Radar –
for the RAF and all low flying aircraft

If you die you lose with rambling
                              words to stroke and recoil
to mix the lot with trouble kick
                              you sorrowing love
this idea   this notion   the caution of the crest
and the firing range subjects
                                   not rifles   rifles   fol de diddle
trifles and sweet obscenities
                    but pure move raiders
along the spine zone
                    loving curse and mouth grit
spit firing back a
                    shadow chill – peroxide
Its a spin off
              a toss of heads or tails
                                   shattering fine mosaic of chance
to confuse and intimidate
                    the fleshy targets
                                   surrounded with wall charts
                                        freckled hunters
                                   bird legged children cry
                                        MISTLE THRUSH

■

his hands old edging out of time
         hanging heavy
coated in cellophane
                    wizened stumps from a slender past
    mottled with unconscious gestures
creped with nicotine burning
                         stains with split
         nails to the half moons quick
rap rap and tap and tap and tap and

unpack all your cares and woe
              there they go flying low
bye bye black birds
                         air runners   rigor gunners

skimming lives
with just ten feet to shoot your load
        us below
                watch your slow
                                cock a doodle grin of triumph
a near miss shudder rolling long into night hatred
and anaemic afterthoughts
                        providing a spot of ivory
very neat   sugar sweet
                    coated in friction
we wait with baited lives
                   the hat trick black TORNADO.

Spring Bank

(I
my (self)-per-por-trait-(or)
roller coaster seaside
                  besides
my undercurrent
remains sub-
and slightly bilious)

the Alfa Romeo swoops downhill moor on hamlets
inhail of stereo blastsmooth and
swerves thick smoke/ash flying (from cradle to rocka rocka bye bye
                    white   ashen fall
and accents dry   calcification)
for ale and whiskey

hung over
through noon to Kildale
watching climbers
a voice drifts with volcano fall-out and
moon blue mix with fluoresce of Rape and rock moss
in shadow and sunsting/whilst
high on Roxby the fox ghost silhouetting
four remarkable empty bottles of guinness –
                          Aeolian sounds of execution

tight warren of tunnels and doors
designed for lost souls in states of embarrassing
                                        emergencies

(The Fox is heavy)

Night and tiny fingers on butterfly brooch mother
'o pearl wings and nails press then flutter
'Where's the cuckoo'
(a short measure this)
'Where's the cuckoo'

a drunk sings high from Loftus to full and cloud split moon

Make-Up

ran cranberry over logan
Japanese ginger orchid
spice glow mandarines
                        frost light clearly

stacked moonsmoke robe on aubergine
                        snow
peppered sweet on two metallic
                        lupins
frost laid oon aub mois   Tang rang
                                    ruby
                                        apple

mixed snow fizz pink shantung
laid ginger rum on maple
got fizz tung rum ba plum
                        or was it victoria

Lottery & Requiem
for Basil Bunting : 1900–1985

    pot lilac,
        pet thorn
          flick
            nest

back,

BLUE BLACK BLUE BLACK BLUE BLACK BLUE
                             BLACKED

            Night bloods
        putted rowdy roundeth liver

           laund

           The Amber
        bidden belly amidst
           cry
           dustling,

                    peril/pebble
                  endless
           reed, the day w/persimmon

                        Flex
raw, woollen hungering.

           Broke Paper.
           Larch Warblage.
           ladder & ladder
      Conifer, come caistor, crowle, winter
           in creases

           the bound paw.

Busk, Pierce

Injure Tinglit

fusen deam stroboscope deam skidder
_____

TLOKETS
mourn, leaden

belenders
lie & blister——
fetched silvers, these
NECRO
gutteral gardenias——————

screed
sneak tintering

Grief Entry.

Lick O,
badgered Rioja, carving

vulned butchery,
face
impaling wing
each buckle
quilted flute

lemoning
catched
ICY florist,

X/tinct-
ure

w/Sea,

dead violet.

Jagged Pebble Song.
Unlawful
Cliffs
Will, where no Cliffs be.

woundlark.
moochpennybreeze.

O

how the filthy

Keepsakes

Truckle Back Tripling

Ash.

Ink, launjer, red on leash,

BLOOD.

Crooked Swatch (ish.yellow)————

Fling Flaunden

Sheenies

Quick Poppy Tie of Axe————

Drumcut strip strung twists

brooch

&

pen Funerary tabletter, armistice,

Drown!

Keep
Geographies.

1	2		4			7	
	2	3	4		6		8
1			4	5		7	8
1	2			5		7	
		3	4		6		8

canker tap, olive ashake, Tranced
AXLE,
candy, the bridle————
fever, the train————

helted *INDIGO*

HAWK
Bloods Bleam

STRIKED
Purple,

tree
BLURTING

choux crab, ryed hare,
Soot Squeeze————
Clouted Triksty Gutter ran————
to Stone.
Crimson. Cockerel Cream. Tinker Tub.
Dolly Puke, Doily flak, Pinnie Gullet——
KISS MY ARSE———

rebellion
backwards.

FROWN RAVENS
Peak Nerve

NUMB w/ripened give————

                    the SKULL'S

        own
    stark

            jurried

                    storm
                cracks Gleed————

        inadequate coal

        ————Glaud
                    gutted w/Jet————

    fraudened harriers Punch
                &
            Beat
        fowled moorage,
                one cerise woken skin,
                    one bone of that

    zigzag, plateau, zigzag
            GRIEVED, GROUND,

        knarls move/Expulsions Deal/Galliards
                Brung,
            FLAME & WILDERNESS.

Watching Women With Children

1

Wood (and all else) by the sink.
Frozen winter clothes
moss on the path outside,
her veined life.
'Will you know me tomorrow like this?'
lines on her chapped hands
the storm of yesterday.

2

The day
she woke early
bright sharp dawn.
Eyes that broke the floor
with anger spilled at the child the night before.
'The prism of mere life is unbearable,
plants and animals in their secular change,
eaten up with will power.

3

The faun of winter has attended with sorrow
concrete and iron steps from the basement
– you could fall so easily –
she thought watching the child totter and smile as she
held out her hand.

4

His quick tears
swift as a balanced balloonist.
He cried bitterly – heard their shout
and anguish from between the banisters.
Ajax on the flannel and all over the
bathroom floor.
Life, it is known of love

so roughly tested and beaten across
the table.

5

Woke to find him stirring beside her,
his slight warm body had crept
in early light.
He who turns to look at moon and
name it space beyond all other value
to draw back the curtains and smile at
the stellar desire so gently regarded
as time.

6

Often walking across
the green square
she would pull the Oak towards her
and they would feed the Ducks,
wander home by the library
intent as the hospital steps where
she first heard him cry.

7

Cleaning the offices
her stern legs
and tired arms   men stand around
in their shoes
watching tightly guilty.
She met him from school
by the wire mesh gate.
He ran out, the last child.
'I wet my pants' he cried so hard.
Picked him up, the cold air and his wounds
whipping her heart.

8

They are laughing together at the back
of an old distant photograph.
A key at the door, he is home,
anxiously worn,

snapping at her for some small mistake.
Shipwrecked we are on so faint a seizure
of reality.

9
He caught her hand.
The weather, time of year, youth
and its ready soul
– how her Mother had laughed when
later she told him she would not see
him again as he'd almost a limp he'd
received as a boy in the Blitz.

10
'Seed Propagation' – the teacher told him
to underline it and read aloud from the book.
'Birds are responsible for a great many seeds, they
carry them in their beaks and feathers and drop
them as they pass.' He ran into the playground. –
kicking at a tennis ball.
'Come in right now' the teacher called from the
window 'come along quickly' he ran, his heart
sinking, she had found the torn book.
'It's your Mother' she said 'she's not very well.
Now I'll take you home to your Dad.'
He was not certain of tears, put his coat on and
the teacher did not mention the absence of his cap.

11
'As if pulled and gripped by pliers
the spine is severed and tortured, the
blood comes and the womb is drained.'
We're going to save your baby – the nurse had said.
But she knew it was helpless,
felt the warm pulse slide between her legs.

12
Maternal scream
spirit of Eithia damned into salt
unable shadow of trees.

Dreary the belly of cold sheep
scream of even air.
Death whips us from each other
long before we are ready.
Hot iced sleep.

13

Cut grass, creosote, tar and urine
in the phone box. She called him.
'I am barren, sterile, empty. My heart has
broken like a Robins egg. This wreck and
all unborn reach the horizon of all finite tears.'

14

'What are you doing?'
'I am listening to the moist cave where all
things begin.'

15

Along the High Street a woman slaps
her child. Livid at sound.
The lonely assault struck her ribs with clay;
heart broken as a Robins egg.

16

Leap, don't jump.
They caught her by the coat.
dangling
moth
like
eighteen storeys up, clothes
limply between the legs.
Shopping list falling from a pocket.

17

'Hello Mum, I'm home.'
he ran into the house.
'Yes, I can see that' she said leaning
away as he tried to kiss her.
'You haven't a cold have you, we don't want

anything spreading.'
He ran out into the garden as far
as the lawn would allow.

18
'The fate of the world today depends
on the common understanding by the
whole human race of what a human being
really is and on enlarging the common notion of man.'

Fyllr

leaning into the hill
she drew him
through green skirt, red knickers

a passage guarded
in modest bud

fear the rays of fire
sixty times a raging child

knitted the several parts
bone blood & limb

Garland
for Alan Halsey

Was out on the street, the word
that made us come across
and get a piece of that life,
so it's no longer a safety-valve
pushed into another time
or confined to holy days.

To speak in Saxon, do make it
a common storehouse for all:
do away with tithes & tolls,
the whole damn lot o' them.

Got into that rotation, doing smoke –
an emission from the devil's forge,
hah, those hot letters in the hands
of the composer, got it out real quick.

Simple and mean things
to confound the mighty and strong,
like you'd trust a thief
more than a priest or lawyer.

Dig and level, to let every one
quietly have earth to manure,
working the forests & wastes,
eating bread together.

Thinking it out and playing the parts:
planted carrots, parsnips, beans
to keep the cattle alive through winter
and so fertilize the land.

The earth our birthright,
being in her, flowers round the pole,
her voice of calm encouragement
a blast of joy in spring again.

Christ a corn of wheat
buried under the clods
for a time
to rise on this.

Adam before our eyes
walking up & down the street:
the land of tipsy topsy-turvydom
knit into a oneness. Maydays – overnight
Took: a futurists' drum.

■

Watching the night sky
with her in my arms,
April grasses underfoot

Berenice's hair clustered loose:
a thousand strands
in token of safe return

Arcturus light orange
from the curve
of the Great Bear's tail

Regulus white –
the dot of a question mark
or sickle-grip

Draco winding its way,
a faint trail
from the Pointers to Vega

a recognizable darkness,
her fire rings
the hint of tomorrow's countenance

Paris 1912

We spend our lives trying to construct sentences,
then ache to undo them when action will not fit
the mood. I told her things I did not mean,
she said a doll, dismantled to the tune of a tango:
nine to five, driving at seventy in the middle lane,
cramming more hours into the day. I saw her
pear-chopped beneath the girdered sky,
a bunch of bananas in the square, sprouting
from beside her torso. I wanted to say,
I meant to say, I always said, there is this wish,
egg, pipe, ball, rod, emblems of play
in a sailor's barracks. You come as a shadow
beneath the tower, the arches,
a muse with harlequin boxes & cylinders.
I have my canvas, framed. There is the smoke
of a train leaving, puffs as fish
in the living room. The scholar waits,
a balloon beckons. I take the words apart,
in imitation of the dream.

Exit on Feedback

Gunned down in New York City
for ink on an album sleeve,
he walked above girders & cables
screaming blood-red clouds.

It's all showbiz, you said,
from a military tunic to guru beams.
Police skids through the Mersey night,
a bar-room rather than a majestic sound,
Come on, straight into Boadicea,
I've done mine. She doesn't inhibit her throat,
she's not forcing each verse for dolby-heads.
Shave off all imagery – sing northern-blunt
with a rhyme and backbeat.

Standing there in blue denim & steel lantern specs,
hands working clean with instruments,
a sound pared down from orange blossom
letting the eighties in.

I never play things backwards/primaling
with bells slowed down. I wrote about me
when I could, not third-person songs
about people in concrete flats.
No smooth talk but some of the best ballads
were yours – four parts of the same person
walking apart, playing with a limited palette.
The piano does it for you –
your mind can do the rest;
songs just came out of me,
making the guitar speak:

Dropped-down drunk in art-school,
pills & drink from a waiter in Hamburg.
Satyricon on tour, touched & pawed,
knees bent in needle time,
jokes in pavement holes and pallor.
Everybody heads towards the centre,
crawling out of a whorehouse in Amsterdam,
you can't fill the sack with groupies.

Back to heartbeat in a scrapbook madness –
the blues is not a concept, it's a chair
in a barrelhouse. Just surviving
is what it's about.

Don't give me that brother, brother –
as if I owed them something.

Azimuth
for Norma Winstone

This I know to be my way,
plotted first by the wind-rose & the stars,
then by arcs of declination intersected:

a water space for the meshing of man & woman,
where one goes out to the innards of a lullaby,
its strains half remembered, moved
to another order. The trumpet cleaving
keyboard waves, a synthesized hover,
the voice stretching things out
as words are abandoned.
You thrash and wind
so you don't copy yourself –
it's not got from books.

In harbour dives, in the ocean ballroom
I saw her, raised to be agreeable,
with no white lace dress or velvet bow,
making glasses on the table sing.
And another, smiling in a strapless dress,
the red spotlight on her big diamond ring,
who paraded with flaming nostrils
for a group of guilt-ridden men.

Between pulses, a fluegelhorn
entering the darkness
speaks

I see you as a blonde,
the agent said,
but she got into the tempo
on her own terms,
a bellwether on the blowing track.

Her throat moist & loose,
arms reaching out for danger,
she slips through night foam
with a wipe and a slow dissolve.

ROBERT SHEPPARD

from Letter from the Blackstock Road

Robin once lunched with Herbert Read at his club.
Fawkes is the palace intruder, fresh from the Otway
Tomb. Robin goes round the 106 bus route pasting up
posters of 'the only man ever to enter Parliament
with honest intentions', then flits back to Highgate.
Robin performs miracles in his leafdom, squeezing
worms from old ladies' buttocks. George is a native
North England bird, arrives drunk at Highbury Vale
for the Big Match, yells impeccable Anglo-Saxon, a
terrace scop. Man kills crowing glory of inner-city
conservation area. Procrustean means literally to
have your feet cut off because you've lost your
bed-socks. Fawkes prints his claw-marks with the
blood-pad throats of the dead of Dussindale. Bob
bobbed. Roger rogered. The man in the ill-fitting
brown suit shows you his leg, asks for money, shuffling
the Blackstock Road in his slippers. George writes
a Proclamation in which each full stop is a dead
bat disappearing into a luxury swimming pool; dressed
as Errol Flynn, he reads it on Mousehold Heath, but
he's in the wrong story again, as the heroes storm
Bishop Bridge. A halal axe falls on anaemic chickens.
Police in vans, waiting, and ready, for the Finsbury
Park Riots. Low clouds move speedily over the city.
Although it is he who suggests it, Pearl's husband
is always shocked to see the sperm shooting on to her
face. Black men doing nothing purposefully on the
corner of the Blackstock and Seven Sisters Roads.
Robin Hood lifts his flaming wings; one minute he's
a wind-borne bird, the next he's a sentimental socialist
from between the wars. The Jewish children freeze
when the pavement is blocked by the neighbourhood
rough, while other children beg with Barnardo faces
in the Blackstock Road during their half-term holidays.
Hood and George print leaflets on petrol bombing,

poster Tottenham, but they're not to be seen when
the shit hits the fan. A mad black girl, swigging
cider, too drunk to sell herself, wears an ankle-
bracelet under 'flesh' stockings. When Fawkes is
arrested he is given bail, so long as he resides
at a friend's, in Hampstead. 'Have you got ten pennies?'
asks a plaintive monopede. Hood and Fawkes get George
off the rap. A lazy supermarket cockroach comes out
to die. Robin mugs old ladies in Stoke Newington.
An inferno lights up the quadrangle in high wind:
paraffin paroxysms flare the height of a tree and
we can feel the heat indoors. Exit Pearl. Hood is
remanded. The anger of politics subverts the tenderness
of love. Vice versa. Hood and Fawkes smash up the
house, make the rich young couple fuck, whimpering,
in front of them. Flirting with her image, injuries
watch outside them. The lama in old curtains chants
in front of the Evolution Mural, chuckles, can become
any of the animals he wishes. There was a feeble
bonfire burning by the lagoon. She stood where she
could see herself: to do what a painter does, she
was *given* a scene for the first time in her life.
The horror of the bed-sits going up in flames, while
the fire brigade takes photographs of itself for the
archive. It cost a bluey. Police vans shoot through
traffic, avoiding collision by inches. Picture postcard
phrases because it uses language, covering mirrors,
pulling curtains. Slurry as it began to flow. 'It'll
be the death of me,' Robyn said, realizing as she
did so that she'd condemned herself to death. Paratactic
tactics. Miles Davis to Dave Holland: 'Don't play
what you think you want to play; play something else.'
He snaps his fingers in a futile attempt to constitute
his vanished totality. Mother entered me for a poetry
competition under the name Conrad Sheppard. There is
a certain tenderness and pathos in the men playing
cards at the back of the kebab house that does no
business. Hands, strangely alien, were moving. She
turned away, embarrassed, only at the expense of a
forgetting of origins, an aged hologram from her

own film. Today's going boozy. One frame at a time,
the giant prisms zoomed. She writes to 'titillate'
herself with the ambivalence of masculine perception,
suddenly finds herself in a scene from a snuff-movie.
Factory farm chicken-flesh. Guy hangs about The
Blackstock – inside and out – drinking from a lager
can, organizing the men for Robyn, who stands shivering
on the corner in a short skirt, her slim black legs
catching the headlights. A complicated game of 3-D
chess in the cloudless skies of a dream-world, back
in the mind, where metaphor and concepts, rather than
'images' and percepts, stir. Use of certain words makes
certain philosophy. An inscape of Ket's head after
death haunts the re-tiented stills.

November 1985

The Materialization of Soap 1947

Suspicion in the capital: the ecstacy
Of austerity rationing the uniforms.
It must be like air, free and natural,
But there's a shortage of nature in this
Land of torrents and the surrounding seas.
What is happening? He used to *prefer* words!
Feed me a well-trimmed cut of news.
We couldn't find any wheels, but we're happy,
A well-dressed pair: even on the wireless
You've got to keep up appearances.
But we yearn for the parks and the azure skies
Of the tottering economies . . . Pearl
Opened her palm over the sink to reveal
A lump of fresh soap. She smelt it; her favourite
Scent. She turned the hissing tap, and
The slippery unthought-of object lathered
Her chapped Cinderella hands. All she needed
Was her hero silk-parachuting into
Her perversely dissatisfied embrace. I

Prefer to talk to the dead, well-fed
On scraps that cannot be sold.
They died from Manchuria to Manchester.
I did not want to report this but I did.
The news is that another man has been held.
That much is reliable. Beyond that,
The monochrome world flickers
At the emotive edge of our fake memories:
Two frying morsels on the gas stove.

■

Every metaphor sounds the same
in its sepia, dry blood melancholy

but if you cry, it drips blood
onto the quarry tiles

so you hasten for the authentic
rasp of the next & the next

leaving behind you dying homunculae

■

Clay when the wire slackens, sheds its velvet light
self-contained. No secret gleams out of the cleft
You take off an outside, make something of it. Take
the next outside, turn it too for the light's vessel

All the gang of your dreams rises out of the crease
you've lit, fanning with fruit beside the escalier
loaded with green pods of flesh. Your scooped shells
lie scattered & whitening, lime for the tree-roots

Your griefs will have worked the beautiful trellises
that fig has scaled; & a swag of fruit, the alien
pelf will be plumped in intimate gifts at your feet
Clay pods, they swell in your dreams' commissariat

bulging out like a thumb; or in civic statuary made
lush as the poor transfigured lives are fed to the
moloch of sleepy entanglement. Time they shall stick
for any respite, from time that knackers the flesh

splitting off over the dunes, in the cupped light
they quaff & by which they pay homage. Their figtree
staggers with leaden fruit, & the almond chokes up
floss. Outside are these witnesses to your fashion

■

We'd launch out, but a spiral failure binds so close
our dwindling inner city. Moths form their tiny scrip
with charred wings, flock the arena though we twist
a loop from their royal flight; fatty it too coils

scarred indelibly now drops through lipid space; what
vertical links, agents, forwarding or poste restante
can ever again grip the headstalk! With every reason
moths subdue the heart, reinforce its white bulwark

swift as a bat to sound our ugly orphans, to flush
the always-dear. They screw the head for kaleidoscope
how our dreams squawk! No choice but stand to reason
soon as look at a festered heart there's no two ways

but pitfall in a dead-stick-loop, but the backfire
from tongues which churn our spectra, which speculate
our sightedness; no, such canutes flesh the dry flesh
like a can of figs. Past help, & all saving. Reason

shuts the window tight & grouts the wall with cilia
mapping our neural paths; that moon we stir to launch
will only sail as transom for a moss-scented flush
of white peaks, rooftops, leaching the stooped pylon

■

He smears
fresh shit on his hands

he holds
them up with his arms

O fleece them
with blonde hair

thick as trowel, honky
ice

◼

Doors open to the metal crash of insects, & outside
the first stain of lichen bulks on blotting-paper
Capercailzie shriek. A buzz-saw coughs. Men pull
off, in hoof-prints they leave behind them. Hounds

chew their hide loops & totter about the shithouse:
All pain is deliberate, or it will be if it isn't
tractable to daddy's smirch, watch it in the mirror
Self-absorbed we might be, yet cruelly given over

to those micro-organisms swimming through our eyes
My face is what I see. You grind me for a choice
of if to grind me. You should, you might have done
within your rights. But the musculature degenerates

cells disperse to every joint & reach the brain
The outside world convulses like a coseismic web
It's 'non-organ-specific'. Rivers start to appear
& elms to creak. Kine appear to fall at their knees

■ THE POETS

JOHN AGARD was born in Guyana in 1949 and came to England in 1977. He works as a touring lecturer for the Commonwealth Institute. His publications include *Shoot Me With Flowers* (1973), *Limbo Dancer In Dark Glasses* (1983), *Man To Pan*, which won the Cuban Casa de las Americas poetry prize, and *Mangoes & Bullets* (Pluto, 1985). He has also written for children.

GILLIAN ALLNUTT was born in London in 1949. She is the author of *Spitting The Pips Out* (Sheba, 1981) and *Beginning The Avocado* (Virago, 1987). She is Poetry Editor of *City Limits* magazine.

Born in Lucknow, **IFTIKHAR ARIF** has worked with Radio Pakistan External Services and Pakistan Television as Senior Producer and Script Editor. He is presently working with the Third World Foundation and the Asian unit of BBC Television as presenter and interviewer. His first collection of Urdu poems, *Mehr-a-Do-Neem*, was published in 1983. In 1984 he received the Pakistani Writers' Guild Award for the best book of the year. His poems have been widely published in various Urdu magazines and translated into various languages. The poems included here have been translated by Professor Ralph Russell.

TONY BAKER was born on J. S. Bach's birthday in 1954, in Merton, South London. He makes his living playing the piano. His most recent collection of poems is *A Bit Brink Green Quartz-Like* (Pig Press, 1983); another is forthcoming in 1988. He has recently completed a prose work on mushrooms.

SOPHIE BEHRENS was born in London in 1959. She was educated at Dartington and the University of East Anglia. Her short stories have appeared in *Atlas Anthology, Bananas, Desire* and *Jennings Magazine*, and a poem in the 1980 Arvon Anthology. In 1981 she gave a poetry reading at Middlesex Polytechnic. She was working on a novel at the time of her premature death in late 1985.

ASA BENVENISTE was born in New York in 1925. He left the United States after World War Two and, after editing the magazine *Zero* from Tangiers, settled in England in the early 1950s. His skills as editor, book-designer, typographer and printer made his Trigram Press one of the most influential small publishing houses of the 1960s and 1970s. He now lives in West Yorkshire. His books include: *Poems of the Month* (Trigram, 1968), *Loose Use* (Pig Press, 1977), *Throw Out the Life Line, Lay Out the Corse: Poems 1965–83* (Anvil Press, 1983) and *Pommes Poems* (Arc Publications, 1988).

JAMES BERRY is a West Indian writer, resident in England for over thirty years. A frequent contributor to black and mainstream literary and cultural activities, he has a special interest in multicultural education. He has toured overseas for the British Council in Sweden, Germany and Poland, and has written and presented radio and television programmes on poetry. He edited two influential anthologies: *Bluefoot Traveller* (New Beacon) and *News for Babylon* (Chatto, 1984). Three books of his own poetry are currently in print, including *Lucy's Letters and Loving* (New Beacon) and *Chain of Days* (OUP). His book of short stories, *A Thief in the Village* won the 1987 Grand Prix Prize for children's fiction. He was awarded the National Poetry Prize in 1981.

VALERIE BLOOM was born in Clarendon, Jamaica, where she trained as a teacher and worked as a librarian. In England she has taught in schools on folk traditions in dance, song and poetry. She studied at the University of Kent. Her first collection of poems was *Touch Mi, Tell Mi* (Bogle-L'Ouverture, 1983).

EAVAN BOLAND was born in Dublin in 1944. Her volumes of poetry are *New Territory* (1967), *The War Horse* (1975), *In Her Own Image* (1980), *Night Feed* (Marion Boyars, 1982) and *The Journey* (Carcanet, 1987). She is married and lives in Dublin with two young daughters.

JEAN BINTA BREEZE, actress and first woman dub poet, was born in 1957 in Jamaica. She lives and works in Brixton. She believes in live poetry and is a recording artist. Her first collection, *Riddym Ravings*, is published by Race Today Publications. She teaches at Brixton College.

PAUL BROWN has published *Meetings & Pursuits* (Skyline, 1978) and *Masker* (Galloping Dog, 1982). A third, *A Cabin in the Mountains*, awaits publication. He runs Actual Size Press and the Collected Works bookshop in East Dulwich, London.

RICHARD CADDEL runs Pig Press in Durham. The poems reprinted here come from his collection *Sweet Cicely: New & Selected Poems* (Taxus, 1983).

B. CATLING was born in 1948 in London, where he still lives. His books include: *The First Electron Heresy, Vorticegarden, Pleiades in Nine* (all Albion Village Press), *Tulpa Index* (St George's Press) and *Boschlog* (A Few Goats Press, New York, 1987). He is a sculptor and performance artist whose most recent show was *Lair*, an installation at Matt's Gallery, Hackney, London. He teaches at Brighton Polytechnic and at the Royal College of Art, London.

FAUSTIN CHARLES was born in Trinidad and educated there. He came to England in 1962. He is also a novelist, short story writer and critic. He has worked as a visiting lecturer for the Commonwealth Institute in London and is a part-time tutor for the ILEA. He has published three collections of poetry: *Crab Track, The Expatriate* and *Days and Nights in the Magic Forest* (Bogle-L'Ouverture).

CRIS CHEEK has worked since 1972 as printer, poet, dancer, musician, teacher and gardener. As well as writing he makes graphic works, soundtracks for various dance performances, short super 8 films and video fictions. Travels and performance work throughout Europe, North America and Canada, and recent wanderings in Egypt, Tanzania, Kenya and Madagascar. Amongst his books are: *First Body of Work* (Bluff Books, 1978), *Antirrhinum* (Lobby Press, 1978), *A5 Momenta, 3, 7, 8* (Bluff Books, 1978), *A Present* (Bluff Books, 1980) and *m u d* (Spanner/Open Field, 1984).

THOMAS A. CLARK was born in Greenock, Scotland, in 1944. He now lives in Nailsworth, Gloucestershire where, with his wife Laurie, he runs Moschatel Press and Cairn Gallery, a centre for contemporary art. His books include: *A Still Life* (The Jargon Society, 1977), *Madder Lake* (Coach House Press, 1981), *Sixteen Sonnets* (Moschatel

Press, 1981), *The Hollow Way* (Moschatel Press, 1983) and *Out Of The Wind* (Moschatel Press, 1984).

BOB COBBING has performed at almost all the International Sound Poetry Festivals in Europe and America. He has been a member of many vocal and improvising vocal and instrumental groups and his thirteen volumes of Collected Poems are published by thirteen small presses in Britain, Canada and the USA. Amongst the more recent are *Vowels and Consequences* (Galloping Dog, 1985), *Lame, Limping, Mangled, Marred & Mutilated* (David Barton, 1986), *Processual* (New River Project, 1987) and *Entitled: Entitled* (Micro Brigade, 1987).

MERLE COLLINS is Grenadian. In Granada she has worked as a teacher and during the period 1979 to 1983, as a Research Officer on Latin American Affairs. Her work has been published in two previous anthologies: *Callaloo*, which featured four writers from Grenada, and *Words Unchained*, a publication on Language and Revolution in Grenada, edited by Chris Searle. A profoundly oral poet, inheritor of the African tradition of performance poetry, her work has received much critical acclaim. She is a member of *African Dawn*, a group whose work incorporates use of the traditional art forms of poetry, music and mime. Her poetry is collected in *Because The Dawn Breaks*. *Angel*, her first novel, was published by the Women's Press in 1987.

KELVIN CORCORAN was born in 1956 and lives in Cheltenham. His work has appeared in magazines and in: *Robin Hood in the Dark Ages* (Permanent Press, 1985), *The Red and Yellow Book* (Textures, 1986) and *Qiryat Sepher* (Galloping Dog, 1988).

JENI COUZYN was born in South Africa and lived there until she was twenty-three. Her first book of poems was published in 1970, and since then she has published six collections, the most recent of which is *Life by Drowning* (Bloodaxe). In recent years she has also been writing for children.

ANDREW CROZIER was born in 1943. He founded the Ferry Press, and was co-editor with Tim Longville of the anthology *A Various Art* (Carcanet, 1987). He has published numerous books since

1967, including *Pleats* (Great Works Editions, 1976) which won the Alice Hunt Bartlett Award. His poems are collected in *All Where Each Is* (Allardyce Barnett, 1985).

DAVID DABYDEEN was born in Guyana in 1957. His first book of poems, *Slave Song* (Dangaroo Press, 1984) was awarded the 1984 Commonwealth Poetry Prize. His second collection *Coolie Odyssey* (Hansib/Dangaroo Press) appeared in spring 1988. He teaches at the University of Warwick.

CAROL ANN DUFFY was born in Glasgow in 1955. Her poetry publications include *Standing Female Nude* (Anvil Press, 1985), *Selling Manhattan* (Anvil Press, 1987). Carol Ann is a poetry editor for *Ambit* magazine.

ANDREW DUNCAN was born in Leeds in 1956 to a Scottish Presbyterian family and brought up in Leicestershire. He began writing poetry in the collective excitement of punk rock and has worked since 1978 as an industrial planner in North London. His firm has shed 15,000 jobs in the past two years: 'Capitalism is spitting blood' G. Stead. Portions of his long work *Threads of Iron* have appeared in various magazines. He has spent the last five years writing a book about propaganda, to be entitled *Spectres* or *False Memories*. He is interested in Formalism, Daoism and organization design.

KEN EDWARDS, born in Gibraltar in 1950 is a London-based writer and editor of *Reality Studios*. His publications include *Drumming & Poems* (Galloping Dog, 1982), *Intensive Care* (Pig Press, 1986) and *A4 Landscape* (Reality Studios, 1988).

PAUL EVANS' books include *Sweet Lucy* (Pig Press, 1983) and *The Sofa Book* (Arc Publications, 1987)

ALISON FELL was born in Dumfries, Scotland and trained as a sculptor in Edinburgh. In 1970 she moved to London to work with the Women's Street Theatre Group and on underground and left-wing magazines. She was a member of *Spare Rib* collective for several years and edited its anthology of fiction, *Hard Feelings*. Her poetry has been published in anthologies and in *Kisses for*

Mayakovsky (Virago), which won the Alice Hunt Bartlett prize for poetry in 1984. In 1981 her children's novel *The Grey Dancer* was published, followed by two adult novels *Every Move You Make* and *The Bad Box* (Virago, 1984 and 1987).

PETER FINCH was born in Cardiff in 1947, where he still lives. He is married with three children and works for the Welsh Arts Council as manager of their Oriel Bookshop. He edited the influential magazine *second aeon* during the late sixties and early seventies. He works in both poetry and fiction. Many of his short stories have been broadcast by the BBC and are collected in *Between 35 and 42* (Alun Books). He has published many volumes of poetry, most recently *Selected Poems* (Poetry Wales Press).

ALLEN FISHER was born in 1944 and has been writing poetry since 1967. A printer, painter, publisher and editor, he has produced over eighty chapbooks and books of poetry, graphics and art documentation. He currently edits *Spanner* and is a visiting lecturer at Goldsmiths' College, painting and reading. He has exhibited paintings in many shows and examples of his work are in the Tate Gallery collection. Amongst his books are: *Bavuska* (1969), *Before Ideas, Ideas* (1971), *Place* (various books 1974–81), *The Apocalyptic Sonnets* (1978), *Poetry For Schools* (1980), *Blood Bone Brain* (1982), *Unpolished Mirrors* (1985), *Brixton Fractals* (1985) and *Buzzards and Bees* (1987).

ROY FISHER was born in Birmingham in 1930. For many years, as Edward Lucie-Smith noted, he had an international reputation without having a national one, his books appearing under the imprint of small presses. Finally his *Poems 1955–1980* were published by Oxford University Press in 1981. Since then, OUP have published *A Furnace* (1986) and Oasis Shearsman have re-published *The Cut Pages* (1986), a work from 1971 not included in the OUP collection.

ERROL FRANCIS was born in Oracabessa, in the parish of St Mary, Jamaica, in 1956. He lives and works in Brixton, South London. Apart from writing poetry Errol Francis is co-ordinator of a community psychiatric project and is currently engaged in research on the history of psychological theories of race.

ULLI FREER was born in 1947 in Luneburg, Germany. A writer, publisher, performer and painter, he has published under the names McCarthy, Lane, Flamme and Lox. His tape work includes *Pressed Curtains 2/3* (Hebden Bridge, 1978), *Trunk Calls & T Chest* (Balsam Flex, 1980). His most recent book is *Stepping Space* (Spectacular Diseases, 1988). He lives and works in London with much support and inspiration from Sue and Annie Freer.

GABRIEL GBADAMOSI was born in 1961 in London of Irish and Nigerian parents. He attended state schools in South London and Churchill College, Cambridge. His poems have appeared in *Coffee Incognito* (Suburban Press, 1980) and *West Africa* magazine. His plays *No Blacks, No Irish, A Broadside Murder* and *Shango's People* (a Yoruba version of Garcia-Lorca's *Bodas de Sangre*) have been performed in London at Riverside Studios and Young Vic Studios. He is a founder member of the Irish Irregulars Theatre Company.

GLENDA GEORGE was born in Maidstone, Kent in 1951. She has been writing for as long as she can recall and professionally since she was eighteen. She is currently working on her first novel.

ANGIE GILLIGAN was born in Leeds in 1950. She is an intermittent writer. Her work has been published in various small magazines over the past ten years. She now lives in Shepperton, Surrey.

BILL GRIFFITHS was born in 1948 in Middlesex, where he has mostly lived since. In the 1960s his main interest was in playing and writing for the piano, but around 1970 he switched to poetry, in a turbulent and exciting time, when a more direct means of communication seemed necessary. He remains happy with the wide scope of words, working also with translation (especially of Old English), short drama texts, sound poetry (performing with Bob Cobbing and Paula Claire) and melodrama (spoken word with music). His work has been published in numerous magazines and through his own Pirate Press. Amongst his books are: *War With Windsor* (Pirate Press, 1973), *A Tract Against The Giants: Poems and Texts* (Coach House Press, 1984), *The Bournemouth* (Writers Forum and Pirate Press, 1987) and *A Book of Drama* (Writers Forum and Pirate Press, 1987).

CAROLINE HALLIDAY was born in 1947 in London. Her work has appeared in the following anthologies: *One Foot on the Mountain* (1979), *Hard Words and Why Lesbians Have to Say Them* (1982), *Dancing the Tightrope* (1987), *Naming the Waves* (1988) and in her own collection, *Some Truth, Some Change* (1983). She writes novels as well as poetry and has co-produced a children's book *Everybody's Different* (with Ingrid Pollard). Her daughter has two co-mothers and lives with her for half the week.

LEE HARWOOD was born in Leicester in 1939 and grew up in Chertsey, Surrey. He has travelled extensively in Europe and lived in the USA, and he now lives in Brighton where he works for the Post Office. He started editing poetry magazines in 1963 and Fulcrum Press has published his books *The White Room* (1968) and *The Sinking Colony* (1970). *Monster Masks* (Pig Press, 1985) is a collection of his works written between 1977 and 1983. His translations of Tristan Tzara have recently been re-published by Coach House/Underwhich (1987). Paladin is publishing his selected poems, *Crossing The Frozen River* (1988).

RALPH HAWKINS lives in Brightlingsea, Essex. His books are: *English Literature* (The Many Press, 1978), *Well, you could do* (Curiously Strong, 1979), *The Word from the One* (Galloping Dog, 1980), and *Tell Me No More And Tell Me* (Grosseteste, 1981).

DAVID HAYNES was born in Castries, St Lucia, in 1957. He lives in Brixton, south London and is studying for a BA degree in History at Birkbeck College, University of London.

A. L. HENDRIKS was born in Jamaica in 1922. He has had a successful career in broadcasting in the Caribbean and internationally. In addition to seven books of poetry he has published children's stories, short stories and essays, and contributes frequently to the *Gleaner* newspapers in Jamaica.

SELIMA HILL was born in London in 1945. Both her parents were painters. She started to read philosophy at Cambridge, left early, travelled, married a painter (which she vowed she'd never do) and now has three children. Her first collection, *Saying Hello At The*

Station (Chatto, 1984) won the Cholmondeley Award in 1986. Her second book, *My Darling Camel* (Chatto), was published this year.

A respected broadcaster and performer of poetry, **FRANCES HOROVITZ** published four collections of her own poems, including *Water Over Stone* (Enitharmon Press, 1980) and *Snow Light, Water Light* (Bloodaxe Books, 1983). She died in 1983, aged 45.

LIBBY HOUSTON began writing and giving readings when the influence of the American Beat Poets was sweeping through Britain, and poets from all kinds of backgrounds (though relatively few of them women) took to the road; and continued. She has published three collections: *A Stained Glass Raree Show*, *Plain Clothes* and, most recently, *At the Mercy*. Since 1973 she has also written a body of work for children, commissioned by the BBC. An autobiographical piece was included in Michelene Wandor's *On Gender and Writing* (1983).

MAHMOOD JAMAL was born in Lucknow, India in 1948 and came to Britain in 1967. Co-ordinated readings at the Troubador Coffee House, 1972–75 and participated in 'Black Voices', a forum for Third World writers. His work was first published with that of three other poets in *Coins for Charon* (Courtfield Press, 1976) and later in *Silence Inside A Gun's Mouth* (Kala Press, 1984). He is also a translator and edited the *Penguin Book of Modern Urdu Poetry* (1986).

JOHN JAMES was born in Cardiff in 1939. Since leaving in 1957 he has lived mostly in Bristol, London and Cambridge. He edited *R* magazine and books 1963–69. Amongst his books are: *mmm . . . ah yes* (London, 1967), *The Welsh Poems* (Lincoln, 1967), *Trägheit* (Cambridge, 1968), *The Small Henderson Room* (London, 1969), *Letters From Sarah* (Cambridge, 1973), *Striking the Pavilion of Zero* (London, 1975), *A Theory of Poetry* (Cambridge, 1977), *War* (London, 1978), *Berlin Return* (Liverpool London Matlock, 1983), *In One Side & Out The Other*, with Andrew Crozier and Tom Phillips (London, 1970) and *Bruce McLean: Berlin/London*, with Dirk Buwalda and Bruce McLean (London and Berlin, 1983).

MARIA JASTRZEBSKA was born in Warsaw, Poland. She came to England as a child and grew up here. She writes in English, drawing inspiration from Polish, her first language. Her poems and translations have appeared in a number of magazines, including *Spare Rib*, *The Literary Review* and *Argo*. In 1986 she published *Six and a half poems* in conjunction with the Polish Women's Forum. She has been involved in women's writing groups and publishing projects for many years and also teaches women's self-defence.

AMRYL JOHNSON was born in Trinidad. Lived in England since age 11. Studied at the University of Kent. Her work is collected in *Long Road to Nowhere* (Virago, 1985). She does readings and works as a visiting writer in schools. Her Caribbean travel-book, *Sequins on a Ragged Hem*, is published by Virago.

LINTON KWESI JOHNSON was born in Jamaica in 1952 and came to England in 1961. He read sociology at Goldsmiths' College and has published three collections of poetry, *Voices of the Living and the Dead* (Race Today, 1974), *Dread Beat An' Blood* (Bogle L'Ouverture, 1975) and *Inglan is a Bitch* (Race Today, 1980) all of which have gone into several editions. He has also recorded four albums with Virgin records, the latest of which is *Making History* (Virgin, 1984). He is a member of the Race Today Collective, a former arts editor for the periodical *Race Today* and a fellow of Warwick University.

JACKIE KAY was born in Edinburgh in 1961 and brought up in Glasgow. Her poems have been published in *A Dangerous Knowing: Four Black Women Poets* (Sheba, 1983) and her short stories in *Everyday Matters 2* (1984) and *Stepping Out* (1986). Her first play, *Chairoscuro*, was performed by the Theatre of Black Women in 1986 and is published by Methuen. These poems form part of a long sequence entitled *The Adoption Papers*.

TOM LEONARD was born in 1944 in Glasgow. The dialect poems can all be found in *Intimate Voices* (Galloping Dog Press, Newcastle, 1984). Galloping Dog also published *Situations Theoretical and Contemporary* in 1986. 'On Knowing the Difference' was published in *Edinburgh Review* 76, February 1987.

LIZ LOCHHEAD was born in 1947 in Motherwell, Lanarkshire, and apart from a couple of years in Canada and the States, she has lived most of her adult life in Glasgow. Her *Dreaming Frankenstein and Collected Poems* (Polygon, 1982) contains all previous volumes. She has also published *True Confessions and New Cliches*, a set of monologues and theatre pieces and a Scots rhyming *Tartuffe*, both from the same publisher.

JOHN C. M. LYONS was born in Port-Of-Spain, Trinidad. He left in 1959 to study art at Goldsmith's College, London. He has been writing poetry for twenty-seven years, but the last six years have seen him emerge as a committed poet with numerous readings of his work. He has worked as an art teacher in secondary schools and currently lectures in Art and Design at South Trafford College, Manchester. In 1987 he won the Peterloo Poets Afro-Caribbean/Asian poetry prize. John Lyons is also a practising painter who has exhibited in Holland, Paris and widely in England.

BARRY MACSWEENEY was born in Newcastle upon Tyne in 1948. Since leaving school at sixteen, he has worked on various provincial English newspapers as investigative reporter, industrial correspondent and news editor. He is deputy editor of the *Shields Gazette*, South Tyneside's evening newspaper. His books include: *The Boy from the Green Cabaret Tells of his Mother* (Hutchinson, 1968), *Odes* (Trigram, 1978), *Black Torch* (New London Pride, 1978) and *Ranter* (Slow Dancer, 1985).

E. A. MARKHAM, former editor of *Artrage* magazine, was born in Montserrat in the West Indies and has lived mainly in Britain/Europe since the mid-fifties. His books of poetry are *Human Rites*, *Living in Disguise* and *Lambchops in Papua New Guinea*.

SUE MAY was born in London in 1955 and went to Woodberry Down School and Bristol Polytechnic, obtaining a degree in Social Sciences. She has been a member of several writers' workshops, including the Hackney Writers' Workshop, and taken part in numerous poetry readings. Some of her poems and short stories have appeared in anthologies including *B flat bebop scat* (Quartet) and *Dancing the Tightrope* (Women's Press).

DAVID MILLER was born in Melbourne, Australia and has lived in England since 1972. He is a writer of poetry, fiction and criticism. His publications include: *The Caryatids* (Enitharmon Press, London, 1975); *South London Mix* (Gaberbocchus Press, London, 1975); *Malcolm Lowry and the Voyage that Never Ends* (Enitharmon, 1976); *Appearance & Event* (Hawk Press, Paraparaumu, New Zealand, 1977); *Primavera* (Burning Deck Press, Providence, Rhode Island, 1979); *Unity* (Singing Horse Press, Blue Bell, Pennsylvania, 1981); *Orientation* (Bran's Head Books, Frome, Somerset, 1982); *There and Here* (Bran's Head, 1982); *Out of This World* (Spectacular Diseases Press, 1984); *The Claim* (Northern Lights, 1984); *Losing to Compassion* (Origin Press, 1985); *Three Poems* (hardPressed Poetry, 1986); (with others:) *Jennifer Durrant* (Serpentine Gallery/Arts Council of Great Britain, 1987).

LOTTE MOOS's volume of poems *Time to be Bold* was published in 1981. Several of the poems have been included in anthologies and cabarets. She is also a writer of short stories and a playwright. She feels that she has always had to work against pressure from urgent, everyday demands. Now she lives because she writes.

GERALDINE MONK was born in Blackburn, Lancashire in 1952 and is now based in Sheffield, Yorkshire. Her work has appeared in a wide selection of magazines and anthologies in the UK, USA and France. Her publications include: *Spreading the Cards* (Siren Press, 1980), *Tiger Lilies* (Rivelin Press, 1982), *La Quinta del Sordo* (Writers Forum, 1980), *Herein Lie Tales of Two Inner Cities* (Writers Forum, 1986), *Sky Scrapers* (Galloping Dog, 1986).

ERIC MOTTRAM is Professor of American Literature at the University of London. His books of poetry include *Elegies* (Galloping Dog Press), *A Book of Herne* (Arrowspire Press), *Interrogation Rooms* (Spanner) among many others, and his critical studies include *William Burroughs: The Algebra of Need*, published by Marion Boyars. He has lectured extensively in the USA, India, South-East Asia and elsewhere.

WENDY MULFORD grew up in Wales and lives in Cambridge. She ran the small press Street Editions (founded in 1972) and now works as a freelance writer. Her books include *Bravo to Girls and Heroes*

(Street Editions, 1977), *Reactions to Sunsets* (Ferry Press, 1980), *The Light Sleepers* (Mammon, 1980), *No Fee* (with Denise Riley) (CMR Press, 1982), *River Whose Eyes* (Avocadotoavocado, 1982), *Late Spring Next Year: Poems 1979–1985 (Loxwood Stoneleigh, 1987)* and *This Narrow Place: Sylvia Townsend Warner and Valentine Ackland* (Pandora Press, 1988).

GRACE NICHOLS was born in Guyana in 1950. She took a Diploma in Communications from the University of Guyana and worked as a reporter and freelance journalist. She came to Britain in 1977 and since then has had published a number of children's books and two collections of poetry; *I is a Long Memoried Woman* (winner of the 1983 Commonwealth Prize) and *Fat Black Woman's Poems* (1984). Her first adult novel, *Whole of a Morning Sky* was published in 1986.

JEFF NUTTALL is a painter, novelist, playwright, actor, musician and poet whose books include *Bomb Culture* (McGibbon & Kee, 1968/Paladin, 1970), *Poems 1962–69* (Fulcrum Press, 1970), *Performance Art Vols 1 & 2* (Calder, 1979), *Objects* (Trigram, 1976) among many others. His most recent poetry is in *Mad With Music* and *Scenes and Dubs* (both published by Writers Forum/Pirate Press, 1987).

DOUGLAS OLIVER was born in Southampton, England in 1937. He spent several years as a journalist before going to Essex University as a mature student, and where he later lectured in literature. He was also a tutor for Open University, a freelance writer and a lecturer at the British University in Paris. He now lives in New York. Apart from magazine publication, he has read and broadcast his work widely in England, Europe and America, acted as visiting poet in English schools, toured with music groups and has been awarded an Arts Council grant and bursary. His publications include: *Oppo Hectic* (Ferry Press, 1969), *In the Cave of Suicession* (Street Editions, 1974), *The Diagram Poems* (Ferry Press, 1979), *The Infant and the Pearl* (Silver Hounds for Ferry Press, 1985), *Kind, collected poems 1967–87* (Allardyce Barnett, 1987) and a novel, *The Harmless Building* (Ferry and Grosseteste Press, 1987).

ALBIE OLLIVIERRE was born in South London in 1961. He worked in an Art Studio before training as a dancer. He started choreographing in 1982 and has worked for a number of dance companies including the London Youth Dance Company, the Black Meridian Dance Company (which he co-founded), Artlink Dance Company and is currently a member of the Irie Dance Company. He began writing at an early age and has recently been working on a book of poems, *Tribes*.

MAGGIE O'SULLIVAN was born in 1951, of southern Irish parents. She is a London-based poet and visual artist and runs Magenta Press. Her seventh and most recent poetic work, *States of Emergency* was published by ICPA, Oxford in 1987.

EVANGELINE PATERSON was born in Limavady, Co. Londonderry. She grew up in Dublin and married an Englishman. She now lives in Leicester, where she edits *Other Poetry*. What she responds to in poetry, and what she tries to achieve, is a devastating simplicity, as Mark Halperin wrote, 'The kind of poetry I like is scalpel-like; you don't feel it cutting, then, all of a sudden, blood.'

TOM PICKARD was born in Newcastle upon Tyne in 1946, left school at 14 and started the Morden Tower poetry readings in 1964. He was published by Fulcrum Press in 1967 and 1971. His autobiographical novel *Guttersnipe* was published by City Lights, San Francisco, in 1971. More recently, Allison & Busby have published his poetry in *Hero Dust* and *Custom & Exile*, as well as his history *Jarrow March*, co-written with his wife, the Polish artist Joanna Voit.

ELAINE RANDELL was born in London in 1951. She lives in Kent in rural isolation with sheep, geese, dogs, cats, children. She works as a social worker in child care matters and other contentious issues. She edited *Amazing Grace* magazine in the 1960s. Her work is collected in: *Beyond All Other* (Pig Press, 1986).

TOM RAWORTH: Publications include: *The Relation Ship* (Goliard, 1969), *The Big Green Day* (Trigram, 1968), *A Serial Biography* (Fulcrum, 1969/Turtle Island, 1977), *Lion Lion* (Trigram, 1970), *Moving* (Cape Goliard: Grossman, London and New York, 1971), *Act* (Trigram Press, 1973), *Ace* (Goliard, London, 1974/The Figures, Berkeley, 1977), *The Mask* (Poltroon Press, Berkeley, 1976), *Logbook* (Poltroon Press, Berkeley, 1977), *Sky Tails* (Lobby Press, 1978), *Writing* (The Figures, 1982), *Tottering State, New and Selected Poems*

(The Figures, 1984/Paladin, 1988), *Lazy Left Hand* (Actual Size, 1986). Recordings: *Little Trace Remains of Emmet Miller* (Stream Records, London 1969), *Thirty Four Minutes* ('V'.Cassettes, Switzerland, 1987).

DENISE RILEY was born in Carlisle in 1948. She now lives in London. Her publications include: *Marxism for Infants* (Street Editions, 1977), *No Fee* (with Wendy Mulford) (Street Editions, 1978), *Dry Air* (Virago, 1985), *War in the Nursery: theories of the child and mother* (Virago, 1983), *Am I That Name? Feminism and the Category of 'Women' in History* (Macmillan, 1988).

PETER RILEY: Publications include: *Love-Strife Machine* (Ferry Press, 1969), *The Whole Band* (Sesheta Press, 1972), *The Linear Journal* (Grosseteste Press, 1973), *The Musician The Instruments* (Many Press, 1978), *Preparations* (Curiously Strong, 1979), *Lines on the Liver (*Ferry Press, 1981), *Tracks and Mineshafts* (Grosseteste Press, 1983), *Two Essays* (Grosseteste Press, 1983), *Ospita* (Poetical Histories, 1987).

MICHÈLE ROBERTS was born in 1949. She lives and works in London. She has co-authored four collections of poetry, her first solo collection being *The Mirror of the Mother* (Methuen, 1986), and two collections of short stories. Her publications also include four novels, the latest being *The Book of Mrs Noah* (Methuen, 1987). She has also published essays and children's stories. She regularly reads her work at a wide variety of venues around the country.

GAVIN SELERIE was born in London in 1949. He is a tutor at the Extra-Mural Department of London University and Editor of *The Riverside Interviews*. His publications include: *Playground for the Working Line* (1981), *Hymenaei* (1981), *Amergin* (1982), *Azimuth* (1984), *Strip Signals* (1986), *Puzzle Canon* (1986). Other works include studies of Charles Olson and Tom McGrath.

ROBERT SHEPPARD was born in 1955. His books include *The Frightened Summer* (Pig Press, 1981) and *Returns* (Textures, 1985). He ran Rock Drill magazine with Penelope Bailey.

COLIN SIMMS' writings on ornithology, herpatology and motorcycles have an international reputation. His own selection of over 20 years' poetry is published by Pig Press under the title *Eyes Own Ideas*.

IAIN SINCLAIR is a bookdealer. He has lived for 20 years in East London, from where he has published eleven books of poetry, including *The Birth Rug* (1973), *Lud Heat* (1975) and *Suicide Bridge* (1979). His first novel, *White Chappell Scarlet Tracings* (Goldmark, 1987), is published in paperback by Paladin and his selected poems, *Flesh Eggs & Scalp Metal* is forthcoming.

LEMN SISSAY was born in the Midlands in 1967. He is a popular performer of his poetry. His first collection is due from Bogle L'Ouverture in autumn 1988.

KEN SMITH, born in Yorkshire, has published numerous books and pamphlets of poetry in Britain and America since his first, *The Pity* (1967). His selected poems 1962–80, *The Poet Reclining*, was published in 1982 by Bloodaxe Books.

JANET SUTHERLAND was born in Salisbury in 1957. She now lives in Tower Hamlets, London. She studied at University College Cardiff and the University of Essex. She works on jobshare for the London Borough of Hackney, in Housing Benefits. Her poems have been included in various books and magazines, including *Angels of Fire* (Chatto, 1986) and *Dancing the Tightrope* (Women's Press, 1987).

LEVI TAFARI was born in Liverpool in 1960 to Jamaican parents. He works regularly in schools and has performed his poetry nationwide. He won a ACER Penmanship Award in 1982.

GAEL TURNBULL was born in Edinburgh in 1928. He grew up in the north of England and in Winnipeg. He returned to England to study Natural Science at Cambridge, and qualified in medicine at the University of Pennsylvania in 1951. He has lived and worked as a general practitioner in Northern Ontario, California, London and Worcestershire. He founded Migrant Press in 1957. Anvil published *A Gathering of Poems 1950–1980* in 1983 and since then there has been *A Winter Journey* (Pig Press, 1987).

MICHELENE WANDOR was Poetry Editor of *Time Out* from 1971–1982. Her poetry publications include *Upbeat* (Journeyman Press), *Gardens of Eden* (Journeyman Press) and *Touch Papers* (with Judith Kazantzis and Michèle Roberts), (Allison & Busby). She has written extensively for radio, stage and television. Her stage plays are published in *Five Plays* (Journeyman Press), and she has edited four volumes of *Plays by Women* (Methuen). Her writing on theatre includes *Carry On Understudies* (Routledge) and *Look Back in Gender* (Methuen). Her dramatization of Eugene Sue's *The Wandering Jew* was produced at the National Theatre in 1987. Her short stories are published in *Guests in the Body* (Virago).

JOHN WILKINSON was born in London in 1953. He is a Registered Mental Nurse, working for Social Services in Walsall and practising group analytic psychotherapy in Birmingham. His publications include: *Useful Reforms* (1976), *The Central Line* (1976), *Tracts of the Country* (1977), *Clinical Notes* (1980) and *Proud Flesh* (1986).

Literature in Paladin Books

Fear and Loathing in Las Vegas   £2.95 ☐
Hunter S. Thompson
As knights of old sought the Holy Grail so Hunter Thomson entered
Las Vegas armed with a veritable magus's arsenal of 'heinous
chemicals' in his search for the American Dream. 'The whole book
boils down to a kind of mad, corrosive poetry that picks up where
Norman Mailer's *An American Dream* left off and explores what Tom
Wolfe left out.' *New York Times.*

The Stranger in Shakespeare   £2.50 ☐
Leslie A. Fiedler
A complete radical analysis of Shakespeare's work which illuminates
the sub-surface psychological tensions.

Confessions of a Knife   £1.95 ☐
Richard Selzer
In this riveting book Richard Selzer seeks meaning in the ritual of
surgery, a ritual 'at once murderous, painful, healing, and full of
love'. In the careening, passionate language of a poet he speaks of
mortality and medicine, of flesh and fever, and reveals something of
the surgeon's thoughts and fears as he delves into the secret linings of
our bodies. 'I was awed and strangely exalted,' Bernard Crick, *The
Guardian*.

Notes from Overground   £2.50 ☐
'Tiresias'
Man is born free, and is everywhere in trains. More than a com-
muter's lament, *Notes from Overground* is a witty, wide-ranging
meditation on a horribly familiar form of travel.

To order direct from the publisher just tick the titles you want
and fill in the order form.

Fiction in Paladin

The Businessman: A Tale of Terror   £2.95   ☐
Thomas M. Disch
'Each of the sixty short chapters of THE BUSINESSMAN is a *tour de force* of polished, distanced, sly narrative art . . . always the vision of America stays with us: melancholic, subversive and perfectly put . . . In this vision lies the terror of THE BUSINESSMAN'
Times Literary Supplement

'An entertaining nightmare out of Thomas Berger and Stephen King'
Time

Filthy English   £2.95   ☐
Jonathan Meades
'Incest and lily-boys, loose livers and ruched red anal compulsives, rape, murder and literary looting . . . Meades tosses off quips, cracks and crossword clues, stirs up the smut and stuffs in the erudition, pokes you in the ribs and prods you in the kidneys (as in Renal, home of Irene and Albert) . . . a delicious treat (full of fruit and nuts) for the vile and filthy mind to savour'
Time Out

Dancing with Mermaids   £2.95   ☐
Miles Gibson
'An excellent, imaginative comic tale . . . an original and wholly entertaining fiction . . . extremely funny and curiously touching'
Cosmopolitan

'The impact of the early Ian McEwan or Martin Amis, electrifying, a dazzler'
Financial Times

'It is as if Milk Wood had burst forth with those obscene-looking blossoms one finds in sweaty tropical palm houses . . . murder and mayhem decked out in fantastic and erotic prose'
The Times

To order direct from the publisher just tick the titles you want and fill in the order form.

Original Fiction in Paladin

Paper Thin   £2.95   ☐
Philip First
From the author of THE GREAT PERVADER: a wonderfully original
collection of stories about madness, love, passion, violence, sex and
humour.

Don Quixote   £2.95   ☐
Kathy Acker
From the author of BLOOD AND GUTS IN HIGH SCHOOL: a
visionary collage–novel in which Don Quixote is a woman on an
intractable quest; a late twentieth-century LEVIATHAN; a stingingly
powerful and definitely unique novel.

To order direct from the publisher just tick the titles you want
and fill in the order form.

All these books are available at your local bookshop or newsagent, or can be ordered direct from the publisher.

To order direct from the publishers just tick the titles you want and fill in the form below.

Name _____

Address _____

_____

Send to:
Paladin Cash Sales
PO Box 11, Falmouth, Cornwall TR10 9EN.

Please enclose remittance to the value of the cover price plus:

UK 60p for the first book, 25p for the second book plus 15p per copy for each additional book ordered to a maximum charge of £1.90.

BFPO 60p for the first book, 25p for the second book plus 15p per copy for the next 7 books, thereafter 9p per book.

Overseas including Eire £1.25 for the first book, 75p for second book and 28p for each additional book.

Paladin Books reserve the right to show new retail prices on covers, which may differ from those previously advertised in the text or elsewhere.

It is 1988 and I no longer feel I know what 'feminist' means. It is a word which, like 'hippy', has been part of common parlance in this country for the past twenty years – though, of course, 'feminist' has a longer, if intermittent, history. It is a word whose status has changed with the rapidly changing values of these twenty years. In some circles it has always been a dirty word: it is now one which I use with circumspection in circles – broadly speaking, left-wing or avant-garde circles – where I once used it, of myself, with confidence.

When it comes to 'feminist poetry', I suspect that, in the minds of most publishers' editors, the phrase is still synonymous with mere propaganda: only the marketing managers have realized that 'feminist' is a label that sells all kinds of books, including poetry.

In my own mind 'feminist poetry' is a phrase that has never sat comfortably. To put any sociologically descriptive tag – be it black, working-class, gay, lesbian or feminist – in front of poetry, is to limit its possibilities. To me, poetry must be one of the few areas of language use where it is acceptable, indeed obligatory, to try and break up the boxes we ordinarily think in and, in an increasingly computer-prone culture which values information and cognitive meaning above all, to reclaim the power of words to affect us emotionally and physically.

It was therefore with mixed feelings that I took on the task of compiling sixty or so pages of 'feminist poetry' for this anthology. From an initial list of fifty I chose the nineteen poets whose work is represented here by two or three poems apiece. I chose poets whose work I like and respect; I chose poems, some of which I have known and loved for a long time, some of which were new to me. In my own mind I let 'feminist' slide into 'woman', concentrating on the quality of the poetry, relying, for guidance, on my agreement with Adrienne Rich's resounding declaration that 'the daughter of the fathers is a literary hack'. My own definition of a successful feminist poem is one that is written by a woman with respect not only for her own 'truth', her own way of seeing and feeling the world, but also for the language – 'man-made' but not, given a little loving attention, unmalleable – which she uses to express that 'truth'.

I confronted my fear of the assumed need to be objective and representative in making choices. 'Objective' and 'representative' are, to me, man-made words or illusory concepts. Imagine an established body of published work commonly agreed to constitute 'feminist poetry and accompanying lit. crit. of the past twenty years': there would then be something to 'represent' here, something in relation to which my choice of poets and poems could be seen to be more or less 'objective'. But something like that is still in the making (and that's optimistic); something like this anthology has to contribute to its making.

In making my choices I employed a motley assortment of criteria or boxes-for-thinking-in, so that I would not end up with sixty pages of poems written by white English middle-class heterosexual women born since the war on the theme of nuclear power. There are no black women here – I 'gave away' the black and the 'experimental' poets I would have included to other sections in the book, because I wanted the anthology to have as many women poets in it as possible. The poets in this section represent, to my knowledge, six different 'countries of origin' and at least two social classes. Sexual orientation varies, and among the poets included are those who feel that their choice of lesbianism or heterosexuality is a significant component of self-definition and those who do not. Our 'themes' are multifarious: they encompass the recognizably feminist (abortion, sexism in husbands, the reshaping of Greek goddesses and the women of the Old Testament); the traditionally womanly (birth, childcare, the untrivially domestic); and the neutral ground of love, death, war, international politics, music, dolphins – and how *do* you classify *Crossing the Desert in a Pram*?

My conception of the feminist poetry of the past twenty years is ahistorical or non-chronological. In her poem *The Message* Jeni Couzyn writes: 'The message of the men is linear.' The message of the women has never in the history of Western literature been permitted to grow into and out of itself in a coherent way. The 'line' has been broken again and again. In the last twenty years the women's movement in America and Britain has led to the establishment of women's publishing houses which have made available feminist writings from the past that previously were not only unavailable but, often, had 'never been heard of'. It is now